William Selby
2432 Portland Ave
Louisville Kentucky

Bruce G. Irby
2422 Bank St,
Louisville K.

Miss Anna Roberts
333 N. 26th St

H. W. (Tuesday)
What I saw at the Fair.

Eng 1 C
name
Date
Subject

READINGS
FROM LITERATURE

EDITED BY

REUBEN POST HALLECK, M.A., LL.D.

AUTHOR OF "HISTORY OF AMERICAN LITERATURE"
"HALLECK'S NEW ENGLISH LITERATURE"

AND

ELIZABETH GRAEME BARBOUR, B.A.

HEAD OF ENGLISH DEPARTMENT
GIRLS HIGH SCHOOL, LOUISVILLE, KY.

AMERICAN BOOK COMPANY

NEW YORK   CINCINNATI   CHICAGO

PREFACE

THE editors of this volume have tried to choose from both English and American prose writers and poets such entire selections or complete units as will interest pupils. Modern experience shows increasingly the difficulty of developing a love for literature through what is disliked. If the experience of the editors with their own classes is any basis for prediction, these selections will make pupils wish to read more from the same authors and from others that resemble them.

Enjoyment of literature is a progressive art, gradually developed like other arts, hence these selections are not arranged in chronological order. They begin with a simple, humorous prose story and end with Milton's poetry.

The taste for poetry is often an acquired one, but experience has taught the editors that by starting with the right selections a lasting love of poetry can be developed. Teachers should encourage pupils to memorize at least parts of the poems in this volume and to read all of them aloud. Former pupils have often taken the trouble to say to the editors that memorizing and reading aloud certain poems resulted in an increased liking for poetry. Matthew Arnold has truly said that we ought "to have always in mind lines and expressions from the great masters and apply them as a touchstone to other poetry." Such touchstones from the masters will be found in this volume.

An endeavor is made to stress the social side of English, — the side that appeals to everyday human needs and interests. Social discussion ought to be as natural as breathing, after the class have read Kipling's *The Law of the Jungle*, O. Henry's *The Chaparral Prince*, Thomas Hardy's *The Three Strangers*, Lincoln's *Letter to General Joseph Hooker*, Huxley's *The Game of Life*, or any of the other selections, whether prose or poetry. The "Study Hints" of the several groups of lyrics, for instance, are given so as to make them a social exercise. It is hoped that both teacher and pupil will take pleasure in entertaining the entire class with oral reproduction or expressive reading of some of the books indicated in the "Suggested Readings" which follow each selection or group. Oral English is commonly social English, and this entire book calls for a social interchange of opinion on every author read. (See pages 6, 7.)

These *Readings* are also planned to supplement the work in composition and rhetoric, since they present the four principles of discourse and suggest definite practice in those forms of expression necessary in actual life. The "Oral and Written English" is based on the accompanying prose selections. The literature and composition courses may, however, be separated if so desired.

While the great classic English authors are well represented in these selections, the new tendency not to neglect modern writers is recognized. Permission has accordingly been secured to use copyright material from such writers as Rudyard Kipling, O. Henry, Alfred Noyes, John Masefield, William Butler Yeats, James Whitcomb Riley, Joel Chandler Harris, Helen Keller, and from many others to whom acknowledgment is made in a footnote on the first page of their selections.

R. P. H.
E. G. B.

PRACTICE IN ORAL AND WRITTEN
ENGLISH

PUPILS should be required to practice the use of oral English every day. They should relate definitely something that they have seen, heard, or read. The walk to or from school, each ride in a street car, every conversation with a friend, all recitations in school, the news of the day, every page read in a book or a magazine, every subject that needs brief argument or longer debate, all experience with work or play, will furnish enough material for a number of connected oral sentences. The business of life, as a rule, requires not lengthy oral or written compositions but readiness and definiteness in dealing briefly with the matter in hand.

Oral English requires a readier vocabulary than written English. A vocabulary never drops down like manna from heaven. Words and their meanings must be learned. Careful reading of the selections in this book and rigorous use of the dictionary for every word not intimately known will add materially to the vocabulary of the pupil.

Words entirely unused have little value. The pupil must have daily practice in employing the words that he has learned. Their oral use affords the readiest practice. Every pupil should keep a notebook in which he may write words with which he is not well acquainted. He should frequently consult this list to see if he remembers having actually used them. The teacher should have the pupil use intelligently the words in the vocabulary under "Study Hints."

All persons have an active and a semi-passive vocabulary. Words actually used in speaking and writing constitute the

5

active vocabulary. The semi-passive vocabulary includes the larger number comprehended only when we interpret the speech of others or the matter that we read. The everyday working life of the world requires that our English training shall be such as to fit us for two different reactions: (1) to understand what others say and write, (2) to make others understand our speech and writing. The same kind of practice will not make one proficient in both fields.

A good working rule for every student is:

Be ever on the watch to add to your vocabulary. Have sufficient practice in oral and written English to make your semi-passive vocabulary coincide more nearly with your active vocabulary.

Language is an imitative art. We bewail the fact that children learn slang and incorrect expressions through imitation. Good English is just as contagious as bad English. The only trouble is that we have not been giving pupils sufficient of the best models. Teachers will find that the careful reading of the selections in this book will improve the pupil's spoken and written English. If Macaulay had not read widely in his youth, he could never have acquired such grasp of vigorous language. Much of this mastery came to him unconsciously as a result of the deep interest that he took in what he read and of his practice in spoken English. He was a speaker as well as a writer. The teacher should remember that oral English functions naturally and easily with everyday life.

An interested, suggestive teacher can make every one of the following selections serve for practice in oral English. Fortunately pupils are anxious to tell a good story. They may also be easily encouraged to give a brief, vigorous statement of what appeals to them in matter that is not in narrative form, and to compare various selections with each other. Sometimes oral discussion will be found more interesting and more social than narration. For instance, the teacher will find that the class will enjoy discussing the question whether they would be tempted by a reward to help officers of the law catch the "Prince,' in O. Henry's *The Chaparral Prince* (p. 201), and what sort of verdict they would feel like returning if they happened to be on the jury that tried him. Many questions for discussion will naturally suggest themselves in the other selections, *e.g.* in Hardy's *The Three Strangers* (p. 269), where pupils will talk sensibly on such questions as: "Would you be willing to eat only bread for a week, if you could thereby enable the condemned man to escape? Would it be right for you to aid him in avoiding the penalty of the law? Suppose a member of your class were to aid in catching him, what standing in the class would that member have? What do you think about this English law that considered property more sacred than persons?"

Not a few of the subjects given after the selections under the heading "Suggestions for Oral and Written English" may be used interchangeably for oral or written composition. The "Study Hints" also furnish numerous suggestions for practice in oral English. The "Suggestions for Additional Readings" will also serve the same purpose. The teacher should constantly use the leverage of social stimulus in connection with this volume and should encourage the student to tell his family and friends what he has read. A genuine desire to interest them will cause him to master the subject matter so that he can present it in a vigorous way and with no hesitation. The same motive may be used to cause him to profit by the "Suggestions for Additional Readings," and to search for matter that his classmates or other associates will enjoy hearing him read.

CONTENTS

		PAGE
ZENOBIA'S INFIDELITY	*Henry Cuyler Bunner*	13
THE LAW OF THE JUNGLE	*Rudyard Kipling*	29
(From *The Second Jungle Book*)		
GULLIVER'S FIRST DINNER AT BROBDINGNAG	*Jonathan Swift*	33
(From *Gulliver's Travels*)		
GARDENING	*Charles Dudley Warner*	38
(From *My Summer in a Garden*)		
THE RESCUE OF THE SHEEP	*Richard D. Blackmore*	42
(From *Lorna Doone*)		
THE ANGEL AND THE CHILD	*Margaret Steele Anderson*	48
HEREWARD'S ADVENTURE WITH THE WHITE BEAR	*Charles Kingsley*	50
(From *Hereward the Wake*)		
THE PARTING OF MARMION AND DOUGLAS	*Sir Walter Scott*	59
(From *Marmion*)		
THE ESCAPE FROM THE TOWER	*Charles Reade*	63
(From *The Cloister and the Hearth*)		
THE HIGHWAYMAN	*Alfred Noyes*	69
WEE WILLIE WINKIE	*Rudyard Kipling*	76
A GROUP OF NATURE LYRICS:		91
The Wind	*Robert Louis Stevenson*	91
The Grass	*Emily Dickinson*	92
The Brook	*John B. Tabb*	93
Written in March	*William Wordsworth*	93
Song from *Pippa Passes*	*Robert Browning*	94

9

		PAGE
How Mr. Rabbit was too Sharp for Mr Fox .	*Joel Chandler Harris* .	. 97
(From *Uncle Remus, His Songs and His Sayings*)		
Christian and Hopeful in the Dungeon . .	*John Bunyan* . .	. 102
(From *The Pilgrim's Progress*)		
Skipper Ireson's Ride .	*John Greenleaf Whittier*	. 107
The Two Matches . .	*Robert Louis Stevenson*	. 112
The Ballad of the Oyster-man	*Oliver Wendell Holmes*	. 115
Three Sea Pictures and a Moral . . .	*Samuel Taylor Coleridge*.	. 117
(From *The Ancient Mariner*)		
A Descent into the Mael-strom . . .	*Edgar Allan Poe* .	. 122
A Group of Bird Poems: .	. . . . .	. 141
The Skylark . . .	*Percy Bysshe Shelley* .	. 141
The First Mocking Bird in Spring	*Paul Hamilton Hayne*	. 142
Tampa Robins . .	*Sidney Lanier* . .	. 143
The Whippoorwill . .	*Madison Cawein* .	. 144
The First Bluebird . .	*James Whitcomb Riley* .	. 146
Captain Phips's Search for Sunken Treasure .	*Cotton Mather* . .	. 149
(From *Magnalia*)		
Speech on a Resolution to put Virginia into a State of Defense .	*Patrick Henry* . .	. 158
The Skeleton in Armor .	*Henry Wadsworth Longfellow*	164
The Pine-Tree Shillings .	*Nathaniel Hawthorne*.	. 171
(From *Grandfather's Chair*)		
Wouter Van Twiller .	*Washington Irving* .	. 177
(From *Knickerbocker's History of New York*)		

CONTENTS

		PAGE
A SECOND GROUP OF NATURE LYRICS:		182
Ariel's Song, from *The Tempest*	*William Shakespeare*	182
Daffodils	*William Wordsworth*	182
On the Grasshopper and Cricket	*John Keats*	183
Three Pictures from *The Palace of Art*	*Alfred Tennyson*	184
The Lake Isle of Innisfree	*William Butler Yeats*	185
LOVE IS STRONGER THAN HATE	*Charles Dickens*	188
(From *A Tale of Two Cities*)		
A DAY IN JUNE	*James Russell Lowell*	198
(From *The Vision of Sir Launfal*)		
THE CHAPARRAL PRINCE	*O. Henry*	201
THE OLD HUSBAND AND THE YOUNG WIFE	*Richard Brinsley Sheridan*	215
(From *The School for Scandal*)		
THE STORM AT SEA	*William Shakespeare*	221
(From *The Tempest*)		
PLAIN LANGUAGE FROM TRUTHFUL JAMES	*Bret Harte*	231
THE AMBITIOUS GUEST	*Nathaniel Hawthorne*	234
THE HUMBLEBEE	*Ralph Waldo Emerson*	246
AN EPITAPH ON SALATHIEL PAVY	*Ben Jonson*	250
TO A WATERFOWL	*William Cullen Bryant*	252
A GROUP OF LETTERS:		254
Letter to St. Nicholas	*Helen Keller*	254
Letter to Gertrude	*Lewis Carroll*	255
Letter to Mrs. James T. Fields	*Charles Dickens*	256

CONTENTS

			PAGE
Letter to General Joseph Hooker	*Abraham Lincoln*	.	258
ANNABEL LEE	*Edgar Allan Poe*	.	262
THE SEEING HAND	*Helen Keller*	.	264
(From *The World I Live In*)			
THE THREE STRANGERS	*Thomas Hardy*	.	269
LAUGH AND BE MERRY	*John Masefield*	.	298
THE LONDON VISITS OF A COUNTRY LORD IN THE TIME OF CHARLES II.	*Thomas Babington Macaulay*		300
(From *History of England*)			
HOW MANY WAYS	*Cale Young Rice*	.	304
THE CELESTIAL SURGEON	*Robert Louis Stevenson*	.	306
THE GAME OF LIFE	*Thomas Henry Huxley*	.	307
(From *A Liberal Education and Where to Find It*)			
A COUNTRY SUNDAY	*Joseph Addison*	.	310
(From *The Spectator*)			
AUTOBIOGRAPHY	*John Ruskin*	.	315
(From *Præterita*)			
SATAN	*John Milton*	.	318
(From *Paradise Lost*)			

READINGS FROM LITERATURE

ZENOBIA'S INFIDELITY [1]

HENRY CUYLER BUNNER

Henry Cuyler Bunner (1855–1896) was born in Oswego, New York. He was for many years editor of *Puck*, one of the most famous humorous magazines of the United States. He wrote three volumes of short stories, most of which show an unusual and delightful humor. See also:

National Cyclopedia of American Biography.
Warner's *World's Best Literature*, Vol. VII, 2731–2733.
Brander Matthews' *The Historical Novel and Other Essays.*

DR. TIBBITT stood on the porch of Mrs. Pennypepper's boarding house, and looked up and down the deserted Main Street of Sagawaug with a contented smile, the while he buttoned his driving gloves. The little doctor had good cause to be content with himself and with everything else — with his growing practice, with his comfortable boarding house, with his own good looks, with his neat attire, and with the world in general. He could not but be content with Sagawaug, for there never was a prettier country town. The doctor looked across the street and picked out the very house that he proposed to buy when the one remaining desire of his soul was gratified. It was a house with a hip roof and with a long garden running down to the river.

There was no one in the house to-day, but there was no one in any of the houses. Not even a pair of round bare arms was visible among the clothes that waved in the August breeze in every backyard. It was circus day in Sagawaug.

The doctor was climbing into his gig when a yell startled him. A freckled boy with saucer eyes dashed around the corner.

"Doctor!" he gasped, "come quick! The circus got afire an' the trick elephant's most roasted!"

"Don't be silly, Johnny," said the doctor, reprovingly.

"Hope to die — Honest Injun — cross my breast!" said the boy. The doctor knew the sacredness of this juvenile oath.

"Get in here with me," he said, "and if I find you're trying to be funny, I'll drop you in the river."

As they drove toward the outskirts of the town, Johnny told his tale.

"Now," he began, "the foiks was all out of the tent after the show was over, and one of the circus men, he went to the oil barrel in the green wagon with Dan'l in the Lion's Den onto the outside of it, an' he took in a candle an' left it there, and fust thing the barrel busted, an' he wasn't hurted a bit, but the trick elephant she was burned awful, an' the ring-tailed baboon, he was so scared he had a fit. Say, did you know baboons had fits?"

When they reached the circus grounds, they found a crowd around a small side-show tent. A strong odor of burnt leather confirmed Johnny's story. Dr. Tibbitt pushed his way through the throng, and gazed upon the huge beast, lying on her side on the grass, her broad shoulder charred and quivering. Her bulk expanded and contracted with spasms of agony, and from time to time she uttered a moaning sound. On her head was a structure of red cloth, about the size of a bushel basket, apparently intended to look like a British soldier's forage cap. This was secured by a strap that went under her chin — if an elephant has a chin. This scarlet cheese box every now and then slipped down over her eye, and the faithful animal patiently, in all her anguish, adjusted it with her prehensile trunk.

By her side stood her keeper and the proprietor of the show, a large man with a dyed mustache, a wrinkled face, and hair oiled and frizzed. These two bewailed their loss alternately.

"The boss elephant in the business!" cried the showman. "Barnum never had no trick elephant like Zenobia. And them lynes and Dan'l was painted in new before I took the road this season. Oh, there's been a hoodoo on me since I showed ag'inst the Sunday-school picnic!"

"That there elephant's been like my own child," groaned the keeper, "or my own wife, I may say."

The doctor had been carefully examining his patient.

"If there is any analogy —" he began.

"Neuralogy!" snorted the indignant showman; "'t ain't neuralogy, you jay pill box, she's *cooked!*"

"If there is any analogy," repeated Dr. Tibbitt, flushing a little, "between her case and that of a human being, I think I can save your elephant. Get me a barrel of linseed oil, and drive these people away."

The doctor's orders were obeyed with eager submission. He took off his coat and went to work. He had never doctored an elephant, and the job interested him. At the end of an hour, Zenobia's sufferings were somewhat alleviated. She lay on her side, chained tightly to the ground, and swaddled in bandages. Her groans had ceased.

"I'll call to-morrow at noon," said the doctor — "good gracious, what's that?" Zenobia's trunk was playing around his waistband.

"She wants to shake hands with you," her keeper explained. "She's a lady, she is, and she knows you done her good."

"I'd rather not have anything of the sort," said the doctor, decisively.

When Dr. Tibbitt called at twelve on the morrow, he found Zenobia's tent neatly roped in, an amphitheater of circus benches constructed around her, and this amphitheater packed with people.

"Got a quarter apiece from them jays," whispered the showman, "jest to see you dress them wownds." Subsequently the showman relieved his mind to a casual acquaintance. "He's got a heart like a gunflint, that doctor," he said, "made me turn out every one of them jays and give 'em their money back before he'd lay a hand to Zenobia."

But if the doctor suppressed the clinic, neither he nor the showman suffered. From dawn till dusk people came from miles around to stare a quarter's worth at the burnt elephant. Once in a while, as a rare treat, the keeper lifted a corner of her bandages, and revealed the seared flesh. The show went off in a day or two, leaving Zenobia to recover at leisure; and as it wandered westward, it did an increased business simply because it had had a burnt trick elephant. Such, dear friends, is the human mind.

The doctor fared even better. The fame of his new case spread far and wide. People seemed to think that if he could cure an elephant he could cure anything. He was called into consultation in neighboring towns. Women in robust health imagined ailments, so as to send for him and ask him shuddering questions about "that *wretched* animal." The trustees of the orphan asylum made him staff physician — in this case the doctor thought he could trace a connection of ideas, in which children and a circus were naturally associated. And the local newspaper called him a *savant*.

He called every day upon Zenobia, who greeted him with trumpetings of joyful welcome. She also desired to shake hands with him, and her keeper had to sit on her head and hold her trunk to repress the familiarity. In two weeks she was cured, except for extensive and permanent scars, and she waited only for a favorable opportunity to rejoin the circus.

The doctor had got his fee in advance.

Upon a sunny afternoon in the last of August, Dr. Tibbitt jogged slowly toward Sagawaug in his neat little gig. He had been to Pelion, the next town, to call upon Miss Minetta Bunker, the young lady whom he desired to install in the house with the garden running down to the river. He had found her starting out for a drive in Tom Matson's dogcart. Now, the doctor feared no foe, in medicine or in love; but when a young woman is inscrutable as to the state of her affections, when the richest young man in the county is devoting himself to her, and when the young lady's mother is backing the rich man, a young country doctor may well feel perplexed and anxious over his chance of the prize.

The doctor was so troubled, indeed, that he paid no heed to a heavy, repeated thud behind him, on the macadamized road. His gentle little mare heard it, though, and began to curvet and prance. The doctor was pulling her in, and calming her with a "soo — soo — down, girl, down!" when he interrupted himself to shout,

"Great Cæsar! get off me!"

Something like a yard of rubber hose had come in through the side of the buggy, and was rubbing itself against his face.

He looked around, and the cold sweat stood out on him as he saw Zenobia, her chain dragging from her hind foot, her red cap a-cock on her head, trotting along by the side of his vehicle, snorting with joy, and evidently bent on lavishing her pliant, serpentine, but leathery caresses upon his person.

His fear vanished in a moment. The animal's intentions were certainly pacific, to put it mildly. He reflected that if he could keep his horse ahead of her, he could toll her around the block and back toward her tent. He had hardly guessed, as yet, the depth of the impression which he had made upon Zenobia's heart, which must have been a large organ, if the size of her ears was any indication — according to the popular theory.

The doctor tolled his elephant around the block without further misadventure, and they started up the road toward Zenobia's tent, Zenobia caressing her benefactor while shudders of antipathy ran over his frame. In a few minutes the keeper hove in sight. Zenobia saw him first, blew a shrill blast on her trumpet, close to the doctor's ear, bolted through a snake fence, lumbered across a turnip field, and disappeared in a patch of woods, leaving the doctor to quiet his excited horse and to face the keeper, who advanced with rage in his eye.

"What do you mean, you cuss," he began, "weaning a man's elephant's affections away from him? You ain't got no more morals than a Turk, you ain't. That elephant an' me has been side-partners for fourteen years, an' here you come between us."

"I don't want your confounded elephant," roared the doctor. "Why don't you keep it chained up?"

"She busted her chain to git after you," replied the keeper. "Oh, I seen you two lally-gaggin' all along the road. I knowed you wa'n't no good the first time I set eyes on yer, a-sayin' hoodoo words over the poor dumb beast."

The doctor resolved to banish "analogy" from his vocabulary.

. . . . . .

The next morning, about four o'clock, Dr. Tibbitt awoke with a troubled mind. He had driven home after midnight from a late call, and he had had an uneasy fancy that he saw a great shadowy bulk ambling along in the mist-hid fields by the roadside. He jumped out of bed and went to the window. Below him, completely covering Mrs. Pennypepper's nasturtium bed, her prehensile trunk ravaging the early chrysanthemums, stood Zenobia, swaying to and fro, the dew glistening on her seamed sides beneath the early morning sunlight. The doctor hastily dressed himself and slipped downstairs and out, to meet this Frankenstein's-monster of affection.

There was but one thing to do. Zenobia would follow him

wherever he went — she rushed madly through Mrs. Pennypepper's roses to greet him — and his only course was to lead
her out of the town before people began to get up, and to
detain her in some remote meadow until he could get her
keeper to come for her and secure her by force or stratagem.
He set off by the least frequented streets, and he experienced
a pang of horror as he remembered that his way led him past
the house of his one professional rival in Sagawaug. Suppose Dr. Pettengill should be coming home or going out as he
passed !

The doctor found a secluded pasture, near the woods that
encircled the town, and there he sat him down, in the corner of
a snake fence, to wait until some farmer or market gardener
should pass by, to carry his message to the keeper. He had
another message to send, too. He had several cases that
must be attended to at once. Unless he could get away
from his pachydermatous familiar, Dr. Pettengill must care
for his cases that morning. It was hard — but what was he
to do?

Zenobia stood by his side, dividing her attention between
the caresses she bestowed on him and the care she was obliged
to take of her red cap, which was not tightly strapped on,
and slipped in various directions at every movement of her
gigantic head. She was unmistakably happy. From time
to time she trumpeted cheerily. She plucked up tufts of
grass, and offered them to the doctor. He refused them, and
she ate them herself. Once he took a daisy from her, absent-
mindedly, and she was so greatly pleased that she smashed
his hat in her endeavors to pet him. The doctor was a kind-
hearted man. He had to admit that Zenobia meant well.
He patted her trunk, and made matters worse. Her elephan-
tine ecstasy came near being the death of him.

Still the farmer came not, nor the market gardener. Dr.

Tibbitt began to believe that he had chosen a meadow that was *too* secluded. At last two boys appeared. After they had stared at him and at Zenobia for half an hour, one of them agreed to produce Dr. Pettengill and Zenobia's keeper for fifty cents. Dr. Pettengill was the first to arrive. He refused to come nearer than the farthest limit of the pasture.

"Hello, doctor," he called out, "hear you've been seeing elephants. Want me to take your cases? Guess I can. Got a half hour free. Brought some bromide down for you, if you'd like to try it."

To judge from his face, Zenobia was invisible. But his presence alarmed that sensitive animal. She crowded up close to the fence, and every time she flicked her skin to shake off the flies she endangered the equilibrium of the doctor, who was sitting on the top rail, for dignity's sake. He shouted his directions to his colleague, who shouted back professional criticisms.

"Salicylate of soda for that old woman? What's the matter with salicylate of cinchonidia? Don't want to kill her before you get out of this swamp, do you?"

Dr. Tibbitt was not a profane man, but at this moment he could not restrain himself.

"*D—— you!*" he said, with such vigor that the elephant gave a convulsive start. The doctor felt his seat depart from under him — he was going — going into space for a brief moment, and then he scrambled up out of the soft mud of the cow-wallow back of the fence on which he had been sitting. Zenobia had backed against the fence.

The keeper arrived soon after. He had only reached the meadow when Zenobia lifted her trunk in the air, emitted a mirthful toot, and struck out for the woods with the picturesque and cumbersome gallop of a mastodon pup.

"Dern *you*," said the keeper to Dr. Tibbitt, who was try-

ing to fasten his collar, which had broken loose in his fall;
"if the boys was here, and I hollered 'Hey, Rube!' — there
wouldn't be enough left of yer to spread a plaster fer a baby's
bile!"

The doctor made himself look as decent as the situation
allowed, and then he marched toward the town with the light
of a firm resolve illuminating his face. The literature of
his childhood had come to his aid. He remembered the
unkind tailor who pricked the elephant's trunk. It seemed
to him that the tailor was a rather good fellow.

"If that elephant's disease is gratitude," thought the doctor, "I'll give her an antidote."

He went to the drug store, and, as he went, he pulled out
a blank pad and wrote down a prescription, from mere force
of habit. It read thus:

 ### PESSELS & MORTON,

DRUGGISTS,

Commercial Block, Main Street, Sagawaug.

☞ PRESCRIPTIONS CAREFULLY COMPOUNDED. ☜

℞   Calcium sul   ℨ ij

      Calcis chl   ℨ xvj

      Capsicum pulv   ℨ i

M et ft. Bol.

Sig. Take at once.

                       Tibbitt

When the druggist looked at it, he was taken short of
breath.

"What's this?" he asked — "a bombshell?"

"Put it up," said the doctor, "and don't talk so much."
He lingered nervously on the druggist's steps, looking up and
down the street. He had sent a boy to order the stableman
to harness his gig. By and by, the druggist put his head out
of the door.

"I've got some asafetida pills," he said, "that are kind o'
tired, and half a pound of whale-oil soap that's higher 'n
Haman —"

"Put 'em in!" said the doctor, grimly, as he saw Zenobia
coming in sight far down the street.

She came up while the doctor was waiting for the bolus.
Twenty-three boys were watching them, although it was only
seven o'clock in the morning.

"Down, Zenobia!" said the doctor, thoughtlessly, as he
might have addressed a dog. He was talking with the druggist, and Zenobia was patting
his ear with her trunk. Zenobia
sank to her knees. The doctor
did not notice her. She folded
her trunk about him, lifted him
to her back, rose with a heave
and a sway to her feet, and
started up the road. The boys
cheered. The doctor got off on
the end of an elm-branch. His
descent was watched from nineteen second-story windows.

His gig came to meet him at last, and he entered it and
drove rapidly out of town, with Zenobia trotting contentedly
behind him. As soon as he had passed Deacon Burgee's
house, he drew rein, and Zenobia approached, while his
perspiring mare stood on her hind legs.

"Zenobia — pill!" said the doctor.

As she had often done in her late illness, Zenobia opened her

mouth at the word of command, and swallowed the infernal
bolus. Then they started up again, and the doctor headed
for Zenobia's tent.

But Zenobia's pace was sluggish. She had been dodging
about the woods for two nights, and she was tired. When
the doctor whipped up, she seized the buggy by any convenient projection, and held it back. This damaged the
buggy and frightened the horse; but it accomplished Zenobia's end. It was eleven o'clock before Jake Bumgardner's
"Half-Way-House" loomed up white, afar down the dusty
road, and the doctor knew that his round-about way had at
length brought him near to the field where the circus tent
had been pitched. He drove on with a lighter heart in his
bosom. He had not heard Zenobia behind him for some
time. He did not know what had become of her, or what
she was doing, but he learned later.

The doctor had compounded a pill well calculated to upset
Zenobia's stomach. That it would likewise give her a con-

suming thirst he
had not considered.
But chemistry was
doing its duty with-
out regard to him.
A thirst like a fur-
nace burned within
Zenobia. Capsicum
and chloride of lime
were doing their
work. She gasped and groaned. She searched for water.
She filled her trunk at a wayside trough and poured the
contents into her mouth. Then she sucked up a puddle
or two. Then she came to Bumgardner's, where a dozen
kegs of lager beer and a keg of what passed at Bumgardner's for gin stood on the sidewalk. Zenobia's circus

experience had taught her what a water barrel meant. She applied her knowledge. With her forefoot she deftly staved in the head of one keg after another, and with her trunk she drew up the beer and the gin, and delivered them to her stomach. If you think her taste at fault, remember the bolus.

Bumgardner rushed out and assailed her with a bung-starter. She turned upon him and squirted lager beer over him until he was covered with an iridescent lather of foam from head to foot. Then she finished the kegs and went on her way to overtake the doctor.

The doctor was speeding his mare merrily along, grateful for even a momentary relief from Zenobia's attentions, when, at one and the same time, he heard a heavy, uncertain thumping on the road behind him, and the quick patter of a trotter's hoofs on the road ahead of him. He glanced behind him first, and saw Zenobia. She swayed from side to side, more than was her wont. Her red cap was far down over her left eye. Her aspect was rakish, and her gait was unsteady. The doctor did not know it, but Zenobia was drunk.

Zenobia was sick, but intoxication dominated her sickness. Even sulphide of calcium withdrew courteously before the might of beer and gin. Rocking from side to side, reeling across the road and back, trumpeting in imbecile inexpressive tones, Zenobia advanced.

The doctor looked forward. Tom Matson sat in his dog-cart, with Miss Bunker by his side. His horse had caught sight of Zenobia, and he was rearing high in air, and whinnying in terror. Before Tom could pull him down, he made a sudden break, overturned the dogcart, and flung Tom and Miss Minetta Bunker on a bank by the side of the road. It was a soft bank, well-grown with mint and stinging nettles, just above a creek. Tom had scarce landed before he was up and off, running hard across the fields

Miss Minetta rose and looked at him with fire in her eyes. "Well!" she said aloud, "I'd like mother to see you *now!*"

The doctor had jumped out of his gig and let his little mare go galloping up the road. He had his arm about Miss Minetta's waist when he turned to face his familiar demon — which may have accounted for the pluck in his face.

But Zenobia was a hundred yards down the road, and she was utterly incapable of getting any farther. She trumpeted once or twice, then she wavered like a reed in the wind; her legs weakened under her, and she sank on her side. Her red cap had slipped down, and she picked it up with her trunk, broke its band in a reckless swing that resembled the wave of jovial farewell, gave one titanic hiccup, and fell asleep by the roadside.

An hour later, Dr. Tibbitt was driving toward Pelion, with Miss Bunker by his side. His horse had been stopped at the tollgate. He was driving with one hand. Perhaps he needed the other to show how they could have a summer-house in the garden that ran down to the river.

But it was evening when Zenobia awoke to find her keeper sitting on her head. He jabbed a cotton hook firmly and decisively into her ear, and led her homeward down the road lit by the golden sunset. That was the end of Zenobia's infidelity.

STUDY HINTS

Study the spelling and meaning of these words:

structure	alleviate	nasturtium
adjust	bondage	endeavor
submission	extension	gigantic
incapable	perplexed	courteous

Describe Sagawaug. At what point does the story begin to interest you? Is the boy natural when he brings the message? How does Zenobia show her gratitude at first? Later? Do you think her keeper was kind? Why do you think so? Was the doctor kind? Do you like the way the story ends? What makes the reader have a certain affection for Zenobia?

SUGGESTIONS FOR STUDYING AND WRITING A SHORT STORY

(A) A story may begin in one of the following ways: with a description of the scene, *i.e.* the setting; with a description of the chief characters; with an incident; with a conversation *between* or *about* the chief characters; with a statement of the reason for the author's writing the story; with a statement of the central idea of the story. Which method is used here?

(B) Every story is told from the point of view of one of three people: an onlooker; the person to whom the story happens; some one who holds the place, so to speak, of Providence, *i.e.* who knows *everything* about the story and the characters. Which point of view is used here?

Begin a story entitled "My First Circus," with a short description of the appearance of the town on "circus day." Then give a brief conversation between yourself and some friend about going to the circus. Be sure to write *only* what *you* could see and know. Perhaps your chum was with you that day. If so, get him to write of your visit as he saw it, *i.e.* as an onlooker.

SUGGESTIONS FOR ORAL AND WRITTEN ENGLISH
THEME SUBJECTS

Tell a friend orally in a vigorous way without hesitation the story of *Zenobia's Infidelity*. Remember that success in the use of oral or written English depends on your being interested yourself. Keep the fixed determination to interest those who listen to you.

Read Kipling's *Toomai of the Elephants* and tell the story.

Tell the most interesting story you know of an elephant or of some other animal.

Give the autobiography of a cat or a dog for twenty-four hours.

The Gratitude of Animals.	The Most Faithful Animal.
My Favorite Animal.	What My Pet Taught Me.
A Ride on an Elephant.	Can Animals Reason?

SUGGESTIONS FOR ADDITIONAL READINGS

Smith's Love Letters (from *Short Sixes*).   Henry Cuyler Bunner.

The Tenor (from *Short Sixes*).   Henry Cuyler Bunner.

The Pitcher of Mignonette (*Verse*).   Henry Cuyler Bunner.

A Passion in the Desert (from *Scenes of Military Life*).   Honoré de Balzac.

Moti Guj — Mutineer (from *Life's Handicap*).   Rudard Kipling.

Toomai of the Elephants (from *Jungle Book*, I).   Rudyard Kipling.

The Cat: The Doctor's Horse (from *Understudies*).   M. E. Wilkins-Freeman.

The Call of the Wild.   Jack London.

White Fang.   Jack London.

Johnny Bear (in *Lives of the Hunted*).   Ernest Thompson Seton.

Lobo, the King of Currumpaw (in *Wild Animals I Have Known*).   Ernest Thompson Seton.

The Trail of the Sand Hill Stag.   Ernest Thompson Seton.

The Kindred of the Wild.   Charles G. D. Roberts.

The Training of Wild Animals.   Frank Bostock.

The Wilderness Hunter.   Theodore Roosevelt.

Hunting the Elephant in Africa.   C. H. Stigand.

THE LAW OF THE JUNGLE [1]

RUDYARD KIPLING

Rudyard Kipling (1865–   ), one of the most brilliant writers of the nineteenth century, was born in India. He began writing stories and poems when quite young for the *Military Gazette* in India. His stories of life in India, his *Jungle Books*, and his poem the *Recessional* have won for him world-wide reputation. See also:

Halleck's *New English Literature*, pp. 568–576, 586.

Knowles's *Kipling Primer*.

Canby's *The Short Story in English*.

JUST to give you an idea of the immense variety of the Jungle Law, I have translated into verse (Baloo [2] always recited them in a sort of singsong) a few of the laws that apply to the wolves. There are, of course, hundreds and hundreds more, but these will do for specimens of the simpler rulings.

Now this is the Law of the Jungle — as old and as true as the sky;
And the Wolf that shall keep it may prosper, but the Wolf that shall break it must die.

---

[1] From *The Second Jungle Book*. Used by special arrangement with Rudyard Kipling and the Century Company.

[2] The brown bear who taught the wolf cubs the Law of the Jungle.

As the creeper that girdles the tree trunk the Law runneth
    forward and back —
For the strength of the Pack is the Wolf, and the strength of
    the Wolf is the Pack.

Wash daily from nose tip to tail tip; drink deeply, but never
    too deep;
And remember the night is for hunting, and forget not the day
    is for sleep.

The Jackal may follow the Tiger, but, Cub, when thy whiskers
    are grown,
Remember the Wolf is a hunter — go forth and get food of
    thine own.

Keep peace with the Lords of the Jungle — the Tiger, the
    Panther, the Bear;
And trouble not Hathi [1] the Silent, and mock not the Boar
    in his lair.

When Pack meets with Pack in the Jungle, and neither will
    go from the trail,
Lie down till the leaders have spoken — it may be fair words
    shall prevail.

When ye fight with a Wolf of the Pack, ye must fight him
    alone and afar,
Lest others take part in the quarrel, and the Pack be dimin-
    ished by war.

The Lair of the Wolf is his refuge, and where he has made him
    his home,
Not even the Head Wolf may enter, not even the Council
    may come.

[1] The wild elephant.

The Lair of the Wolf is his refuge, but where he has digged it
too plain,
The Council shall send him a message, and so he shall change
it again.

If ye kill before midnight, be silent, and wake not the woods
with your bay,
Lest ye frighten the deer from the crops, and the brothers
go empty away.

Ye may kill for yourselves, and your mates, and your cubs
as they need, and ye can;
But kill not for pleasure of killing, and *seven times never kill
Man.*

If ye plunder his Kill from a weaker, devour not all in thy
pride;
Pack-Right is the right of the meanest; so leave him the head
and the hide.

The Kill of the Pack is the meat of the Pack. Ye must eat
where it lies;
And no one may carry away of that meat to his lair, or he
dies.

The Kill of the Wolf is the meat of the Wolf. He may do
what he will,
But, till he has given permission, the Pack may not eat of
that Kill.

Cub-Right is the right of the Yearling. From all of his Pack
he may claim
Full-gorge when the killer has eaten; and none may refuse
him the same.

Lair-Right is the right of the Mother.   From all of her year
    she may claim
One haunch of each kill for her litter, and none may deny her
    the same.

Cave-Right is the right of the Father — to hunt by himself
    for his own :
He is freed of all calls to the Pack ; he is judged by the Council
    alone.

Because of his age and his cunning, because of his grip and
    his paw,
In all that the Law leaveth open, the word of the Head Wolf
    is Law.

Now these are the Laws of the Jungle, and many and mighty are
    they;
But the head and the hoof of the Law and the haunch and the
    hump is — Obey!

STUDY HINTS

What constitutes good citizenship among wolves?   Among men?
What are the individual rights of the wolf?   The pack rights?   How
does the pack protect its young?   Does this affect its own existence?
Upon what foundation do the laws of the jungle rest?   The laws of
man?

SUGGESTIONS FOR ADDITIONAL READINGS

Gunga Din.   Rudyard Kipling.
Oonts!   Rudyard Kipling.
The Overland Mail.   Rudyard Kipling.
Tommy.   Rudyard Kipling.
The Ballad of East and West.   Rudyard Kipling.
Recessional.   Rudyard Kipling.
The Jungle Books.   Rudyard Kipling.

GULLIVER'S FIRST DINNER AT BROBDINGNAG

Jonathan Swift

Jonathan Swift (1667–1745), a clergyman and great eighteenth-century prose writer, was born of English parents in Dublin. *Gulliver's Travels* (1726), his best-known book, is interesting to young and old, for the hero has remarkable experiences, especially in Lilliput, where the men are six inches tall, and in Brobdingnag, where they grow to a height of sixty feet. See also:

Halleck's *New English Literature*, pp. 276–284, 302.
Leslie Stephen's *Swift*.
Thackeray's *English Humorists* (Swift).

IT was about twelve at noon, and a servant brought in dinner. It was only one substantial dish of meat (fit for the plain condition of an husbandman) in a dish of about four and twenty feet diameter. The company were the farmer and his wife, three children, and an old grandmother : when they were sat down, the farmer placed me at some distance from him on the table, which was thirty feet high from the floor. I was in a terrible fright, and kept as far as I could from the edge for fear of falling. The wife minced a bit of meat, then crumbled some bread on a trencher, and placed it before me.  I made her a low bow, took out my knife and fork, and fell to eat, which gave them exceeding delight. The mistress sent her maid for a small dram-cup, which held about two gallons, and filled it with drink; I took up the vessel with much difficulty in both hands, and in a most respectful manner drank her ladyship's health, expressing the words as loud as I could in English, which made the company laugh so heartily, that I was almost deafened with the noise. This liquor tasted like a small cider, and was not unpleasant. Then the master made me a sign to come to his trencher-side; but as I walked on the table, being in great surprise all the time, as the indulgent reader will easily conceive and excuse, I happened to stumble against a crust, and fell flat on my face, but received no hurt. I got up immediately, and observing the good people to be in much concern, I took my hat (which I held under my arm out of good manners) and, waving it over my head, made three hurrahs, to show I had got no mischief by my fall. But advancing forwards toward my master (as I shall henceforth call him) his youngest son who sat next him, an arch boy of about ten years old, took me up by the legs, and held me so high in the air, that I trembled in every limb; but his father snatched me from him, and at the same time gave him such a box on the left ear, as would have felled an European troop of horses to the earth, ordering him to be taken from the table. But being afraid the boy might owe me a spite, and well remembering how mischievous all children among us naturally are to sparrows, rabbits, young kittens, and puppy dogs, I fell on my knees, and pointing to the boy made my master to understand, as well as I could, that I desired his son might be pardoned. The father complied, and the lad took his seat again; whereupon I went to him and kissed his hand, which my master took, and made him stroke me gently with it.

In the midst of dinner, my mistress's favorite cat leaped into her lap. I heard a noise behind me like that of a dozen stocking weavers at work; and, turning my head, I found it proceeded from the purring of that animal, who seemed to be three times larger than an ox, as I computed by the view of her head and one of her paws, while her mistress was feeding and stroking her. The fierceness of this creature's countenance altogether discomposed me; though I stood at the farther end of the table, above fifty feet off; and although my mistress held her fast, for fear she might give a spring, and seize me in her talons. But it happened there was no danger; for the cat took not the least notice of me, when my master placed me within three yards of her. And as I have been always told, and found true by experience in my travels, that flying or discovering fear before a fierce animal is a certain way to make it pursue or attack you, so I resolved in this dangerous juncture to show no manner of concern. I walked with intrepidity five or six times before the very head of the cat, and came within half a yard of her; whereupon she drew herself back, as if she were more afraid of me.

I had less apprehension concerning the dogs, whereof three or four came into the room, as it is usual in farmers' houses; one of which was a mastiff equal in bulk to four elephants, and a greyhound somewhat taller than the mastiff, but not so large.

When dinner was almost done, the nurse came in with a child of a year old in her arms, who immediately spied me, and began a squall, that you might have heard from London-Bridge to Chelsea, after the awful oratory of infants to get me for a plaything. The mother out of pure indulgence took me up, and put me toward the child, who presently seized me by the middle, and got my head into his mouth, where I roared so loud that the urchin was frightened, and let me drop, and I should infallibly have broken my neck, if the mother had not held her apron under me.

STUDY HINTS

Study the spelling and meaning of these words:

substantial	mischief	countenance
indulgent	mischievous	intrepidity
diameter	urchin	mastiff
experience	break, broke, broken	proceed

How does the account of Gulliver begin? (See *A, B*, p. 27.) How did Gulliver conceal his terror? Try to imagine how immense everything seemed to him. How did he appear to the family? Why did they laugh when he drank to the lady's health? Was he wise to ask the father to pardon the boy? In what ways did he show his courage? His politeness? Did the baby act as babies usually act? Does the conclusion deepen your realization of the size of Gulliver as compared with the Brobdingnagians?

SUGGESTIONS FOR ORAL AND WRITTEN ENGLISH
THEME SUBJECTS

Note the suggestions given in (*A, B*) on page 27 and write a story as if you were the Brobdingnagian small boy telling a boy friend your experience with Gulliver. Relate an imaginary account of yourself as a man of normal size traveling among people six inches high. Have a dwarf tell the same story from his own point of view.

Use one of the following topics for a theme:

Gulliver's First Dinner at Brobdingnag.
An Experience with a Giant.
The Adventures of Hercules.
The Experience of Ulysses with the Cyclops.
Adventures in Search of the Golden Fleece.
An Adventure of a Knight at King Arthur's Court.
The Story of Jack the Giant Killer.
The Story of Red Riding Hood.

SUGGESTIONS FOR ADDITIONAL READINGS

A Voyage to Lilliput (from *Gulliver's Travels*, first four chapters). Jonathan Swift.

A Voyage to Brobdingnag (from *Gulliver's Travels*, first three chapters).   Jonathan Swift.

Arabian Nights' Entertainments: History of Aladdin, or The Wonderful Lamp; History of Sinbad, the Sailor; History of Ali Baba and the Forty Robbers; History of the Enchanted Horse.

Legends Every Child Should Know.   Hamilton W. Mabie.

Robinson Crusoe.   Daniel Defoe.

Greek Heroes.   Charles Kingsley.

The Odyssey (particularly Ulysses's adventure with the Cyclops). George Herbert Palmer (translation).

GARDENING [1]

CHARLES DUDLEY WARNER

Charles Dudley Warner (1829–1900) was born in Plainfield, Massachusetts. He was at one time editor of *Harper's Magazine*, also the author of many delightful essays and books of travel. See also:

Mrs. James T. Fields's *Charles Dudley Warner*.

Vedder's *American Writers of To-day* (Warner).

I BELIEVE in the intellectual, if not the moral, qualities of vegetables, and especially weeds. There was a worthless vine that (or who) started up about midway between a grape trellis and a row of bean poles, some three feet from each, but a little nearer the trellis. When it came out of the ground, it looked around to see what it should do. The trellis was already occupied. The bean pole was empty. There was evidently a little the best chance of light, air, and sole proprietorship on the pole. And the vine started for the pole, and began to climb it with determination. Here was as distinct an act of choice, of reason, as a boy exercises when he goes into a forest, and, looking about, decides which tree he will climb. And, besides, how did the vine know enough to travel in exactly the right direction, three feet, to find what it wanted? This is intellect. The weeds, on the other hand, have hateful moral qualities. To cut down a weed is, therefore, to do a moral action. I feel as if I were destroying sin. My hoe becomes an instrument of retributive justice. I am an apostle of Nature. This view of the matter lends a dig-

[1] From *My Summer in a Garden*, copyright 1870 and 1885, by Houghton Mifflin Company. This selection is used by permission of, and by arrangement with, Houghton Mifflin Company, authorized publishers of his works.

38

nity to the art of hoeing which nothing else does, and lifts it into the region of ethics. Hoeing becomes, not a pastime, but a duty. And you get to regard it so, as the days and the weeds lengthen.

Observation. — Nevertheless, what a man needs in gardening is a cast-iron back, with a hinge in it. The hoe is an ingenious instrument, calculated to call out a great deal of strength at a great disadvantage.

The striped bug has come, the saddest of the year. He is a moral double-ender, ironclad at that. He is unpleasant in two ways. He burrows in the ground so that you cannot find him, and he flies away so that you cannot catch him. He is rather handsome, as bugs go, but utterly dastardly, in that he gnaws the stem of the plant close to the ground, and ruins it without any apparent advantage to himself. I find him on the hills of cucumbers (perhaps it will be a cholera-year, and we shall not want any), the squashes (small loss), and melons (which never ripen). The best way to deal with the striped bug is to sit down by the hills, and patiently watch for him. If you are spry, you can annoy him. This, however, takes time. It takes all day and part of the night. For he flieth in darkness, and wasteth at noonday. If you get up before the dew is off the plants, — it goes off very early, — you can sprinkle soot on the plant (soot is my panacea; if I can get the disease of a plant reduced to the necessity of soot, I am all right); and soot is unpleasant to the bug. But the best thing to do is to set a toad to catch the bugs. The toad at once establishes the most intimate relations with the bug. It is a pleasure to see such unity among the lower animals. The difficulty is to make the toad stay and watch the hill. If you know your toad it is all right. If you do not, you must build a tight fence round the plants, which the toad cannot jump over. This, however, introduces a new element. I find that I have a zoölogical garden on my hands. . . .

There is another subject which is forced upon my notice. I like neighbors, and I like chickens; but I do not think they ought to be united near a garden. Neighbors' hens in your garden are an annoyance. Even if they did not scratch up the corn, and peck the strawberries, and eat the tomatoes, it is not pleasant to see them straddling about in their jerky, high-stepping, speculative manner, picking inquisitively here and there. It is of no use to tell the neighbor that his hens eat your tomatoes: it makes no impression on him, for the tomatoes are not his. The best way is to casually remark to him that he has a fine lot of chickens, pretty well grown, and that you like spring chickens broiled. He will take them away at once.

The neighbors' small children are also out of place in your garden, in strawberry and currant time. I hope I appreciate the value of children. We should soon come to nothing without them, though the Shakers have the best gardens in the world. Without them the common school would languish. But the problem is, what to do with them in a garden. For they are not good to eat, and there is a law against making away with them. The law is not very well enforced, it is true; for people do thin them out with constant dosing, paregoric and soothing sirups, and scanty clothing. But I, for one, feel that it would not be right, aside from the law, to take the life even of the smallest child, for the sake of a little fruit, more or less, in the garden. I may be wrong; but these are my sentiments, and I am not ashamed of them. My plan would be to put them into Sunday schools more thoroughly, and to give the Sunday schools an agricultural turn; teaching the children the sacredness of neighbors' vegetables. I think that our Sunday schools do not sufficiently impress upon children the danger, from snakes and otherwise, of going into the neighbors' gardens.

STUDY HINTS

Study the spelling and meaning of these words:

proprietor	panacea	enforced
annoyance	agricultural	dosing
inquisitively	disadvantage	pastime

When, according to the author, does hoeing become the greatest duty? How does he console himself for the ravages of the striped bug? When he says you can "annoy" the bug, what does he imply? Is the description of the chickens natural? Does he say much about gardening as one usually thinks of the term? What is the most noticeable quality in this selection? Is it interesting? Is it lively? Is it amusing? Find several illustrations of the most noticeable quality. Is it more marked or less so as the selection draws to a close? Do you not feel that Warner has been talking to you? Has he any surprising turns in his thought?

SUGGESTIONS FOR ORAL AND WRITTEN ENGLISH
THEME SUBJECTS

Tell in the same informal way some experience like those suggested below, jotting down your points and following Warner's plan.

How to Plant Potatoes.
Making a Garden.
Our Neighbor's Chickens.
A Window Box.
The Perversity of Weeds.
The Biography of a Toad.
Some of Burbank's Experiments.

How to Make an Unsightly Lot Attractive.
Human Traits in Chickens.
The Change in the Garden after a Rain.
The Joys and Troubles of a Flower Garden.

SUGGESTIONS FOR ADDITIONAL READINGS

Being a Boy. Charles Dudley Warner.
A-Hunting of the Deer. Charles Dudley Warner.
Mary's Garden and How It Grew. Frances Duncan.
A Self-Supporting Home. Kate V. St. Maur.
The Green Things Growing (verse). Dinah Mulock Craik.
The Story of a Bad Boy. Thomas Bailey Aldrich.
Penrod. Booth Tarkington.

For the teacher to read to the class:
Selections from Warner's *My Summer in a Garden*, and *Backlog Studies; Adventures in Contentment*, by David Grayson; Markham's *The Man with the Hoe;* Dobson's *A Garden Song.*

THE RESCUE OF THE SHEEP[1]

RICHARD D. BLACKMORE

Richard D. Blackmore (1825–1900) was of English birth. He has celebrated the beautiful Devonshire country of England in many stories, of which his masterpiece is *Lorna Doone*. John Ridd, who is represented as telling this story, really lived in the seventeenth century. He was so famous for his great size and power that stories of his feats of strength are told in Devonshire to-day. See also:

Frederick J. Snells's *The Blackmore Country.*

It must have snowed most wonderfully to have made that depth of covering in about eight hours. For one of Master Stickles's men, who had been out all night, said that no snow began to fall until nearly midnight. And here it was, blocking up the doors, stopping the ways and the watercourses, and making it very much worse to walk than in a saw pit newly used. However, we trudged along in a line; I first, and the other men after me; trying to keep my track, but finding legs and strength not up to it. Most of all, John Fry was groaning; certain that his time was come, and sending messages to his wife, and blessings to his children. For all this time it was snowing harder than it ever had snowed before, so far as a man might guess at it; and the leaden depth of the sky came down, like a mine turned upside down on us. Not that the flakes were so very large; for I have seen much larger flakes in a shower of March, while sowing peas; but that there was no room between them, neither any relaxing, nor any change of direction.

Watch, like a good and faithful dog, followed us very cheer-

[1] From *Lorna Doone* (1869).

42

fully, leaping out of the depth, which took him over his back and ears already, even in the level places; while in the drifts he might have sunk to any distance out of sight, and never found his way up again. However, we helped him now and then, especially through the gaps and gateways; and so after a deal of floundering, some laughter, and a little swearing, we came all safe to the lower meadows, where most of our flock was hurdled.

But behold, there was no flock at all! None, I mean, to be seen anywhere; only at one corner of the field, by the eastern end, where the snow drove in, a great white billow, as high as a barn and as broad as a house. This great drift was rolling and curling beneath the violent blast, tufting and combing with rustling swirls, and carved (as in patterns of cornice) where the grooving chisel of the wind swept round. Ever and again, the tempest snatched little whiffs from the channeled edges, twirled them round, and made them dance over the chine of the monster pile, then let them lie like herring bones, or the seams of sand where the tide had been. And all the while from the smothering sky, more and more fiercely at every blast, came the pelting pitiless arrows, winged with murky white, and pointed with the barbs of frost.

But although, for people who had no sheep, the sight was a very fine one (so far at least as the weather permitted any sight at all); yet for us, with our flock beneath it, this great mount had but little charm. Watch began to scratch at once, and to howl along the sides of it; he knew that his charge was buried there, and his business taken from him. But we four men set to in earnest, digging with all our might and main, shoveling away at the great white pile, and fetching it into the meadow. Each man made for himself a cave, scooping at the soft cold flux, which slid upon him at every stroke, and throwing it out behind him, in piles of castled fancy. At last we drove our tunnels in (for we worked indeed for the lives of us), and all converging towards the middle, held our tools and listened.

The other men heard nothing at all; or declared that they heard nothing, being anxious now to abandon the matter, because of the chill in their feet and knees. But I said, "Go, if you choose, all of you. I will work it out by myself, you pie crusts": and upon that they gripped their shovels, being more or less of Englishmen; and the least drop of English blood is worth the best of any other, when it comes to lasting out.

But before we began again, I laid my head well into the chamber; and there I heard a faint "ma-a-ah," coming through some ells of snow, like a plaintive buried hope, or a last appeal. I shouted aloud to cheer him up, for I knew what sheep it was, to wit the most valiant of all the wethers, who had met me when I came home from London, and been so glad to see me. And then we all fell to again; and very soon we hauled him out. Watch took charge of him at once, with an air of the noblest patronage, lying on his frozen fleece, and licking all his face and feet, to restore his warmth to him. Then fighting Tom jumped up at once, and made a little butt at Watch, as if nothing had ever ailed him, and then set off to a shallow place, and looked for something to nibble at.

Farther in, and close under the bank, where they had huddled themselves for warmth, we found all the rest of the poor sheep packed as closely as if they were in a great pie. It was strange to observe how their vapor, and breath, and the moisture exuding from their wool had scooped, as it were, a coved room for them, lined with a ribbing of deep yellow snow. Also the churned snow beneath their feet was as yellow as gamboge. Two or three of the weaklier hoggets were dead, from want of air, and from pressure; but more

than threescore were as lively as ever; though cramped and
stiff for a little while.

"However shall us get 'em home?" John Fry asked in
great dismay, when we had cleared about a dozen of them;
which we were forced to do very carefully, so as not to fetch
the roof down. "No manner of maning to draive 'un, drough
all they girt driftnesses."

"You see to this place, John," I replied, as we leaned on
our shovels a moment, and the sheep came rubbing round
us. "Let no more of them out for the present; they are
better where they be. Watch, here boy, keep them!"

Watch came, with his little scut of a tail cocked as sharp
as duty; and I set him at the narrow mouth of the great snow
antre. All the sheep sidled away, and got closer, that the
other sheep might be bitten first, as the foolish things imagine:
whereas no good sheep dog
even so much as lips a
sheep to turn it.

Then of the outer sheep
(all now snowed and frizzled
like a lawyer's wig) I took
the two finest and heaviest,
and with one beneath my
right arm, and the other
beneath my left, I went
straight home to the upper
sheppy, and set them in-
side, and fastened them.
Sixty and six I took home
in that way, two at a time

on each journey; and the work grew harder and harder
each time, as the drifts of the snow were deepening. No
other man should meddle with them: I was resolved to
try my strength against the strength of the elements; and

try it I did, ay and proved it. A certain fierce delight burned in me, as the struggle grew harder; but rather would I die than yield; and at last I finished it. People talk of it to this day: but none can tell what the labor was, who have not felt that snow and wind.

Of the sheep upon the mountain, and the sheep upon the western farm, and the cattle on the upper burrows, scarcely one in ten was saved; do what we would for them. And this was not through any neglect (now that our wits were sharpened), but from the pure impossibility of finding them at all. That great snow never ceased a moment for three days and nights.

STUDY HINTS

Study the spelling and meaning of these words:

floundering	tunnel	yield
chisel	plaintive	impossibility
pitiless	patronage	elements
neglect	shovel	pressure

This account is given by John Ridd, the hero of the book. When he describes the snow, does he begin with its appearance, or its effect? At what point does the storm seem fiercest? Did John Ridd see any beauty in the mound of snow? What plan did he and his companions follow to reach the sheep? Why does he call the other men "pie crusts"? How do you know that Watch was intelligent? Do you understand what John Ridd meant by "a certain fierce delight" burning in him? Did John Fry feel it? Did he work for the same reason as John Ridd? Note the language of John Fry. Why does the writer devote so much space to describing the snow?

SUGGESTIONS FOR ORAL AND WRITTEN ENGLISH
THEME SUBJECTS

Do you feel anxious about the sheep? Do you wonder where they are? Whether they are alive? How, if found, they can be taken to a safe place? This feeling of interest, expectation, sometimes of excitement, is called suspense. The point of greatest suspense is called the climax. Short stories usually end very quickly after the climax is reached. Where is the climax of this story? You have finally conquered some difficult task or met with some adventure. Describe the different stages of your experience. Try to make each difficulty a little greater, a little more interesting than the preceding one. Which of the following subjects would make the best title for your account?

Caught in a Storm.   A Snow Fort.
How to Make a Sand Fort.   How We Made a Snow Man.
How Streets are Cleaned.   A Remarkable Feat.
After a Snow Storm.   My First Hay Ride.
My First Sleigh Ride.   How I Finally Succeeded.
What Causes the Snow.

Describe the snow to some one who has never seen it, (a) its appearance, (b) its effect.

SUGGESTIONS FOR ADDITIONAL READINGS

Lorna Doone. Richard D. Blackmore.
Bob, Son of Battle. Alfred Ollivant.
Stickeen: The Story of My Dog. John Muir.
Grayfriars Bobby. Eleanor Atkinson.
Rab and his Friends. Dr. John Brown.
A Boy I Knew and Four Dogs. Laurence Hutton.
A Dog of Flanders. De la Ramée.
A Dog's Tale. S. L. Clemens.
The Bar Sinister. Richard Harding Davis.
Goliath (from *Two Bites at a Cherry*). Thomas Bailey Aldrich.
To Flush, My Dog (verse). Elizabeth Barrett Browning.
The Little Shepherd of Kingdom Come. John Fox, Jr.
The Animal Story Book. Andrew Lang.

THE ANGEL AND THE CHILD [1]

MARGARET STEELE ANDERSON

Margaret Steele Anderson lives in her birthplace, Louisville, Kentucky. She is a lecturer on art, a writer of books on that subject, a literary critic, and the author of a volume of exquisite verse entitled *The Flame in the Wind* (1913). See also:
Townsend's *Kentucky in American Letters*, pp. 318–320.

"OH, was it on that awful road,
  The way of death, you came?" [2]
"It was a little road," he said,
  "I never knew its name."

"Is it not rough along that road?"
  "I cannot tell," said he,
"Up to your gate, in her two arms,
  My mother carried me.

"And will you show me Christ?" he said,
  "And must we seek Him far?"
"That is our Lord, with children round,
  Where little bluebells are."

"Why, so my mother sits at night,
  When all the lights are dim!
Oh, would He mind — would it be right —
  If I should sit by Him?"

[1] Copyright, 1913, by Margaret Steele Anderson. This poem is used by special arrangement with the author.
[2] In the first two lines, the angel addresses the child, asking if he came to heaven by "that awful road" of death. Then follows the reply of the child, referred to as "he."

STUDY HINTS

What beautiful thought runs through the entire poem?   Why did the child feel so much at home?

SUGGESTIONS FOR ADDITIONAL READINGS

We are Seven.   William Wordsworth.
Little Lamb.   William Blake.
I remember, I remember.   Thomas Hood.

For the teacher to read to the class:
The Fighting Weak, Habit, The Trees from *The Flame in the Wind*, by Margaret Steele Anderson; *The Night, The Chimney-Sweeper, On Another's Sorrow, The Land of Dreams*, by William Blake; and parts of Dante Gabriel Rossetti's *The Blessed Damozel.*

HEREWARD'S ADVENTURE WITH THE WHITE BEAR [1]

Charles Kingsley

Charles Kingsley (1819–1875), born in Devonshire, England, was both clergyman and teacher. He held many responsible positions, among them that of teacher of English literature at Queen's College, London, and later of history at Oxford. One of his best-known books is *Westward Ho!* which is, like *Hereward the Wake*, an historical novel. Perhaps his most widely read books to-day are *Water Babies* and *Greek Heroes*. He gives very vivid pictures of English history and customs. See also: *Letters and Memories of his Life*, edited by his wife.

GILBERT of Ghent, who owned many a fair manor in Lincolnshire, heard that Hereward [2] was outlawed, and sent for him, having, it would seem, some connection with his father. And there they lived, doubtless happily enough, fighting Celts and hunting deer, so that as yet the pains and penalties of exile did not press very hardly upon him. The handsome, petulant, good-humored lad had become in a few weeks the darling of Gilbert's ladies, and the envy of all his knights and gentlemen.

Hereward the singer, harp player, dancer, Hereward the rider and hunter, was in all mouths: but he himself was discontented as having as yet fallen in with no adventure worthy of a man; and he looked curiously and longingly at the menagerie of wild beasts enclosed in strong wooden cages, which Gilbert kept in one corner of the great courtyard, not for any scientific purposes, but to try with them, at Christ-

[1] From *Hereward the Wake* (1866).
[2] Hereward was an English hero living in the eleventh century.

mas, Easter, and Whitsuntide, the mettle of the young gentlemen who were candidates for the honor of knighthood. But after looking over the bulls and stags, wolves and bears, Hereward settled it in his mind that there was none worthy of his steel, save one huge white bear, whom no man had yet dared to face, and whom Hereward, indeed, had never seen, hidden as he was all day in the old oven-shaped Pict's house of stone, which had been turned into his den. There was a mystery about the uncanny brute which charmed Hereward. He was said to be half human, perhaps wholly human; to be a son of the Fairy Bear, near kinsman, if not brother, uncle or cousin, of Siward Digre himself. He had, like his fairy father, iron claws; he had human intellect, and understood human speech, and the arts of war, — at least so all in the palace believed, and not as absurdly as at first sight seems.

For the brown bear, and much more the white, was, among the Northern nations, in himself a creature magical and superhuman. "He is God's dog," whispered the Lapp, and called him "the old man in the fur cloak," afraid to use his right name, even inside the tent, for fear of his overhearing and avenging the insult. "He has twelve men's strength, and eleven men's wit," sang the Norseman, and prided himself accordingly, like a true Norseman, on outwitting and slaying an enchanted monster.

Terrible was the brown bear; but more terrible "the white sea-deer," as the Saxons called him; "the whale's bane," "the seal's dread," "the rider of the iceberg," "the sailor of the floe," who ranged for his prey under the six months' night. To slay him was a feat worthy of Beowulf's [1] self; and the greatest wonder, perhaps, among all the wealth of Crowland, was the twelve white bearskins which lay before

---

[1] An English hero living probably in the eighth century. His character and exploits have been celebrated in the greatest Anglo-Saxon poem, *Beowulf*. It is one of the great epics of the world.

the altars, the gift of the great Canute. How Gilbert had obtained his white bear, and why he kept him there in durance vile, was a mystery over which men shook their heads. Again and again Hereward asked his host to let him try his strength against the monster of the North. Again and again the shrieks of the ladies, and Gilbert's own pity for the stripling youth, brought a refusal. But Hereward settled it in his heart, nevertheless, that somehow or other, when Christmas time came round, he would extract from Gilbert, drunk or sober, leave to fight that bear; and then either make himself a name, or die like a man.

Meanwhile Hereward made a friend. Among all the ladies of Gilbert's household, however kind they were inclined to be to him, he took a fancy only to one — a little girl of ten years old. Alftruda was her name. He liked to amuse himself with this child, without as he fancied any danger of falling in love; for already his dreams of love were of the highest and most fantastic; and an Emir's [1] daughter, or a princess of Constantinople, was the very lowest game at which he meant to fly. Alftruda was beautiful, too, exceedingly, and precocious, and it may be, vain enough to repay his attentions in good earnest. Moreover she was English, as he was, and royal likewise. Between the English lad then and the English maiden grew up in a few weeks an innocent friendship, which had almost become more than friendship, through the intervention of the Fairy Bear.

For as Hereward was coming in one afternoon from hunting, hawk on fist, with Martin Lightfoot trotting behind, crane and heron, duck and hare, slung over his shoulder, on reaching the courtyard gates he was aware of screams and shouts within, tumult and terror among man and beast. Hereward tried to force his horse in at the gate. The beast stopped and turned, snorting with fear; and no

[1] A ruling prince among the Arabs.

wonder; for in the midst of the courtyard stood the Fairy Bear; with his white mane bristled up till he seemed twice as big as any of the sober brown bears which Hereward yet had seen, his long snake neck and cruel visage wreathing about in search of prey. A dead horse, its back broken by a single blow of the paw, and two or three writhing dogs, showed that the beast had turned (like too many of his human kindred in those days) "Berserker." [1] The courtyard was utterly empty; but from the ladies' bower came shrieks and shouts, not only of women but of men; and knocking at the bower door, adding her screams to those inside, was a little white figure, which Hereward recognized as Alftruda's. They had barricaded themselves inside, leaving the child out; and now dared not open the door, as the bear swung and rolled towards it, looking savagely right and left for a fresh victim.

Hereward leaped from his horse, and drawing his sword, rushed forward with a shout which made the bear turn round.

He looked once back at the child; then round again at Hereward; and, making up his mind to take the largest morsel first, made straight at him with a growl which there was no mistaking.

He was within two paces; then he rose on his hind legs, a head and shoulders taller than Hereward, and lifted the iron talons high in the air. Hereward knew that there was but one spot at which to strike; and he struck true and strong, before the iron paw could fall, right on the muzzle of the monster.

He heard the dull crash of the steel; he felt the sword jammed tight. He shut his eyes for an instant, fearing lest, as in dreams, his blow had come to naught; lest his sword had turned aside, or melted like water in his hand, and the next

---

[1] At first a warrior who wore a bearskin shirt; later from his fierceness the term grew to represent a very fierce warrior of Scandinavia.

moment find him crushed to the earth, blinded and stunned. Something tugged at his sword. He opened his eyes and saw the huge carcass bend, reel, roll slowly over to one side, dead, tearing out of his hand the sword, which was firmly fixed into the skull.

Hereward stood awhile staring at the beast like a man astonished at what he himself had done. He had had his first adventure, and he had conquered. He was now a champion in his own right — a hero of the heroes — one who might take rank, if he went on, beside Beowulf or Harold Hardraade.[1] He had done this deed. What was there after this which he might not do? And he stood there in the fullness of his pride, defiant of earth and heaven, while in his heart arose the thought of that old Viking who cried, in the pride of his godlessness, "I never on earth met him whom I feared, and why should I fear him in heaven? If I met Odin [2] I would fight with Odin. If Odin were the stronger he would slay me; if I were the stronger I would slay him." There he stood staring, and dreaming over renown to come, a true pattern of the half-savage hero of those rough times, capable of all vices except cowardice, and capable too of all virtues save humility.

"Do you not see," said Martin Lightfoot's voice close by, "that there is a fair lady trying to thank you, while you are so rude or so proud that you will not vouchsafe her one look?"

It was true. Little Alftruda had been clinging to him for five minutes past. He took the child up in his arms and kissed her with pure kisses, which for the moment softened his hard heart; then, setting her down, he turned to Martin.

"I have done it, Martin."

[1] Harold Hardraade meant Harold the hard-headed, the stern. He was king of Nor way in the eleventh century.

[2] The chief Norse god.

"Yes, you have done it; I spied you. What will the old folks at home say to this?"

"What care I?"

Martin Lightfoot shook his head and drew out his knife.

"What is that for?" said Hereward.

"When the master kills the game, the knave can but skin it. We may sleep warm under this fur in many a cold night by the sea and moor."

"Nay," said Hereward laughing, "when the master kills the game, he must first carry it home. Let us take him and set him up against the bower door there, to astonish the brave knights inside." And stooping down he attempted to lift the huge carcass; but in vain. At last, with Martin's help, he got it fairly on his shoulders, and the two dragged their burden to the bower, and dashed it against the door, shouting with all their might to those within to open it.

Windows, it must be remembered, were in those days so few and far between, that the folks inside had remained quite unaware of what was going on without.

The door was opened cautiously enough; and out looked, to the shame of knighthood be it said, two or three knights who had taken shelter in the bower with the ladies.   Whatever they were going to say the ladies forestalled, for, rushing out across the prostrate bear, they overwhelmed Hereward with praises, thanks, and after the straightforward custom of those days, with substantial kisses.

"You must be knighted at once," cried they.   "You have knighted yourself by that single blow."

"A pity then," said one of the knights to the others, "that he had not given that accolade to himself, instead of the bear."

"Unless some means are found," said another, "of taking down this boy's conceit, life will soon be not worth while here."

"Either he must take ship," said a third, "and look for adventures elsewhere, or I must."

Martin Lightfoot heard those words; and knowing that envy and hatred, like all other vices in those rough-hewn times, were apt to take very startling unmistakable shapes, kept his eye accordingly on those three knights.

"He must be knighted—he shall be knighted, as soon as Sir Gilbert comes home," said all the ladies in chorus.

"I should be sorry to think," said Hereward, with the blundering mock humility of a conceited boy, "that I had done anything worthy of such an honor. I hope to win my spurs by greater feats than these."

A burst of laughter from the knights and gentlemen followed.

"How loud the young cockerel crows after his first scuffle!"

"Hark to him! What will he do next? Eat a dragon? Fly to the moon? Marry the Sophy of Egypt's daughter?"

This last touched Hereward to the quick, for it was just what he thought of doing; and his blood was heated enough already, as some one cried, with the evident intent of picking a quarrel:

"That was meant for us. If the man who killed the bear has not deserved knighthood, what must we have deserved, who have not killed him? You understand his meaning, gentlemen — do not forget it!"

Hereward looked down, and setting his foot on the bear's head, wrenched out of it the sword, which he had left till now, with pardonable pride, fast set in the skull.

Martin Lightfoot, for his part, drew stealthily from his bosom the little magic ax, keeping his eye on the brain-pan of the last speaker.

The lady of the house cried "Shame!" and ordered the knights away with haughty words and gestures, which, because they were so well deserved, only made the quarrel more deadly.

Then she commanded Hereward to sheathe his sword.

He did so; and turning to the knights, said with all courtesy, "You mistake me, sirs. You were where brave knights should be, within the beleaguered fortress, defending the ladies. Had you remained outside, and been eaten by the bear, what must have befallen them had he burst open the door? As for this little lass, whom you left outside, she is too young to requite knight's prowess by lady's love; and therefore beneath your attention, and only fit for the care of a boy like me." And taking up Alftruda in his arms, he carried her in and disappeared.

Who now but Hereward was in all men's mouths? The minstrels made ballads on him; the lasses sang his praises (says the chronicler) as they danced upon the green. Gilbert's lady would need give him the seat, and all the honors of a belted knight, though knight he was none. And daily and weekly the valiant lad grew and hardened into a valiant man, and a courteous one withal, giving no offense himself, and not over ready to take offense at other men.

STUDY HINTS

Study the spelling and meaning of these words:

innocent	unmistakable	ingratitude
deficient	blundering	treachery
champion	prowess	hospitality
minstrel	valiant	stealthily

Why did Hereward want to kill the white bear? How had the bear shown his strength before Hereward came? After he strikes the bear, how does he realize the animal's size? Criticize the action of the knights in regard to the boy's valiant deed. Is Kingsley's picture of a knight the usual one? How does the author secure suspense in this story? What is the climax? Outline each point leading to the climax.

SUGGESTIONS FOR ORAL AND WRITTEN ENGLISH
THEME SUBJECTS

Relate Hereward's adventure as if you had been present. Relate the adventure as if you were Hereward himself. Select one of the theme subjects suggested below. Decide what you consider the most exciting point, *i.e.* the climax, and try to "work up" your hearers' interest to that point. Write an incident and stop short of the climax, letting the class suggest what it shall be, and how it shall end.

A Rescue.

How I Tamed a Wild Animal.

When I was Most Terrified.

A Brave Deed.

How I Got my Nickname.

When the Bear Escaped.

How the Bear Fights.

The Best and Worst Way to "Get Even."

The Best Captain for a Football Team.

A Friend in Need.

SUGGESTIONS FOR ADDITIONAL READINGS

Hereward the Wake. Charles Kingsley.

Westward Ho! Charles Kingsley.

Alton Locke. Charles Kingsley.

Harold, the Last of the Saxons. Bulwer Lytton.

Ivanhoe. Sir Walter Scott.

The Merry Adventures of Robin Hood. Howard Pyle.

In the Days of William the Conqueror. Eva March Tappan.

THE PARTING OF MARMION AND DOUGLAS

SIR WALTER SCOTT

Sir Walter Scott (1771–1832) was born in Edinburgh. On account of lameness, he could not run and play with other boys; so gathering them about him, he recited stories from the Scottish ballads in Percy's *Reliques of Ancient English Poetry*. He was educated for the profession of law, but adopted that of letters. In addition to history and poetry, he wrote twenty-nine novels, all of which show the love of romance which had been fostered by his reading when a boy. At the age of fifty-four, when a publishing firm with which he was connected failed, he honorably set himself to work to pay the debts. He nearly achieved the heroic task, but died from the long strain of unremitting toil.

The poem *Marmion*, from which this selection was taken, was published in 1808. The *Lay of the Last Minstrel*, *The Lady of the Lake*, and *Marmion* form his best poetic works. See also:

Halleck's *New English Literature*, pp. 374–398, 444, 445.

Lockhart's *Life of Scott.*

[At the period of this story, the relations between England and Scotland were strained. Marmion has been sent by the king of England, Henry VIII, as envoy to the court of Scotland to complain of the depredations of the Scotch on the border between the two countries, and to warn James II not to interfere with Henry's continental affairs. Douglas at the command of his sovereign has been Marmion's host during his stay in Scotland. This particular incident begins with the departure of Marmion from Douglas's castle. The poem, *Marmion*, ends with the battle of Flodden Field (1513), one of the greatest disasters in Scotch history, for the English completely routed the Scotch, slaying their king and almost exterminating their nobility.]

THE train from out the castle drew,
But Marmion stopped to bid adieu:

"Though something I might plain," he said,
"Of cold respect to stranger guest,
Sent hither by your king's behest,
    While in Tantallon's towers I stayed;
Part we in friendship from your land,
And, noble earl, receive my hand."
But Douglas round him drew his cloak,
Folded his arms, and thus he spoke:
"My manors, halls, and bowers shall still
Be open, at my sovereign's will,
To each one whom he lists, howe'er
Unmeet to be the owner's peer.
My castles are my king's alone,
From turret to foundation stone —
The hand of Douglas is his own,
And never shall in friendly grasp
The hand of such as Marmion clasp."

Burned Marmion's swarthy cheek like fire,
And shook his very frame for ire,
    And — "This to me!" he said, —
"An 'twere not for thy hoary beard,
Such hand as Marmion's had not spared
    To cleave the Douglas head!
And, first, I tell thee, haughty peer,
He, who does England's message here,
Although the meanest in her state,
May well, proud Angus, be thy mate:
And, Douglas, more I tell thee here,
    Even in thy pitch of pride,
Here, in thy hold, thy vassals near
(Nay, never look upon your lord,
And lay your hands upon your sword), —
    I tell thee, thou'rt defied!

And if thou said'st, I am not peer
To any lord in Scotland here,
Lowland or Highland, far or near,
   Lord Angus, thou hast lied!" —

On the earl's cheek the flush of rage
O'ercame the ashen hue of age:
Fierce he broke forth, — "And dar'st thou then
To beard the lion in his den,
   The Douglas in his hall?
And hop'st thou hence unscathed to go? —
No, by Saint Bride of Bothwell, no! —
Up drawbridge, grooms — what, warder, ho!
   Let the portcullis fall."
Lord Marmion turned, — well was his need, —
And dashed the rowels in his steed,
Like arrow through the archway sprung,
The ponderous grate behind him rung:
To pass there was such scanty room,
The bars, descending, razed his plume.

The steed along the drawbridge flies,
Just as it trembled on the rise;
Not lighter does the swallow skim
Along the smooth lake's level brim:
And when Lord Marmion reached his band,
He halts, and turns with clinchèd hand,
And shout of loud defiance pours,
And shook his gauntlet at the towers.
"Horse! horse!" the Douglas cried, "and chase!"
But soon he reined his fury's pace;
"A royal messenger he came,
Though most unworthy of the name. — . . .
Saint Mary mend my fiery mood!

Old age ne'er cools the Douglas blood,
I thought to slay him where he stood.
'Tis pity of him, too," he cried,
"Bold can he speak, and fairly ride,
I warrant him a warrior tried."
With this his mandate he recalls,
And slowly seeks his castle halls.

STUDY HINTS

What are the most noticeable qualities of this selection? Note how not one unnecessary word is used to give a graphic idea of the quarrel. What kind of host has Douglas shown himself? Do you think Marmion acted nobly in offering his hand to Douglas? Marmion's indignation at Douglas's refusal was for two reasons. What are they? What thought makes Douglas calm down? Suppose a deaf man had been present at this interview, how would he have known it was a quarrel? What words show this? Which man shows to better advantage in this quarrel? Memorize at least one stanza.

SUGGESTIONS FOR ADDITIONAL READINGS

The Lady of the Lake, Canto I, "The Chase." Sir Walter Scott.
Gathering Song of Donald Dhu. Sir Walter Scott.
Lullaby of an Infant Chief. Sir Walter Scott.
Bruce to his Men at Bannockburn. Robert Burns.
The Ballad of Chevy Chase (*Reliques*). Thomas Percy.
Robin Hood and Allan-a-Dale. Thomas Percy.
The Pipes at Lucknow. John G. Whittier.
The Battle of Blenheim. Robert Southey.

THE ESCAPE FROM THE TOWER

Charles Reade

Charles Reade (1814–1884), the English novelist, was born in Oxford-shire. He wrote several novels of which the best was *The Cloister and the Hearth* (1861), from which this episode is taken. This novel is a careful and fascinating study of fifteenth-century life. See also:

Charles Reade, Dramatist, Novelist, Journalist, by Charles L. Reade and the Reverend Compton Reade.

———

[Gerard is the son of a Tergouw (a town twelve miles from Rotterdam) merchant, who intends him to become a priest. He falls in love, however, with Margaret Brandt, the daughter of a poor scholar, and gives up his church career. This so enrages his father that he thrusts Gerard into prison. His faithful friend Martin, and Margaret Brandt, devise a plan to rescue him.]

———

GERARD was taken up several flights of stairs and thrust into a small room lighted only by a narrow window with a vertical iron bar. The whole furniture was a huge oak chest. Imprisonment in that age was one of the highroads to death, for it implied cold, unbroken solitude, torture, starvation, and often poison. Gerard felt that he was in the hands of an enemy. And he kneeled down and commended his soul to God.

Presently he rose and sprang at the iron bar of the window, and clutched it. This enabled him to look out by pressing his knees against the wall. Falling back somewhat heavily, he wrenched the rusty iron bar, held only by rusty nails, away from the stonework just as Ghysbrecht Van Swieten,

63

the burgomaster,[1] opened the door stealthily behind him. He brought a brown loaf and a pitcher of water, and set them on the chest in solemn silence. Gerard's first impulse was to brain him with the iron bar, and fly downstairs; but the burgomaster, seeing something wicked in his eye, gave a little cough, and three stout fellows, armed, showed themselves directly at the door.

"My orders are to keep you until you shall bind yourself by an oath to leave Margaret Brandt, and return to the church to which you have belonged from your cradle."

"Death sooner."

"With all my heart." And the burgomaster retired.

As the sun declined, Gerard's heart too sank and sank; with the waning light even the embers of hope went out. He was faint, too, with hunger; for he was afraid to eat the food Ghysbrecht had brought him; and hunger alone cows men. He sat upon the chest, his arms and his head drooping before him, a picture of despondency. Suddenly something struck the wall beyond him very sharply, and then rattled on the floor at his feet. It was an arrow; he saw the white feather. A chill ran through him, — they meant to assassinate him from the outside. He crouched. No more missiles came. He crawled on all fours, and took up the arrow; there was no head to it. He uttered a cry of hope: had a friendly hand shot it?

He took it up and felt it over; he felt a soft substance attached to it. Then one of his eccentricities was of grand use to him. His tinder box enabled him to strike a light; it showed him two things that made his heart bound with delight. Attached to the arrow was a skein of silk, and on the arrow itself were words written. How his eyes devoured them, his heart panting the while!

"Well-beloved, make fast the silk to thy knife and lower

[1] A mayor, or other city official in Holland.

to us: but hold thine end fast: then count a hundred and draw up."

Gerard seized the oak chest, and with almost superhuman energy dragged it to the window. Standing on the chest and looking down he saw figures at the tower foot. They were so indistinct they looked like one huge form. He waved his bonnet [1] to them with trembling hand. Then he undid the silk rapidly but carefully, and made one end fast to his knife and lowered it till it ceased to draw.

Then he counted a hundred, then pulled the silk carefully up; it came up a little heavier. At last he came to a large knot, and by that knot a stout whipcord was attached to the silk. What could this mean? While he was puzzling himself, Margaret's voice came up to him, low but clear. "Draw up, Gerard, till you see liberty." At the word, Gerard drew the whipcord line up, and drew and drew until he came to another knot, and found a cord of some thickness take the place of the whipcord. He had no sooner begun to draw this up than he found that he now had a heavy weight to deal with. Then the truth suddenly flashed upon him, and he went to work and pulled and pulled till the perspiration rolled down him; the weight got heavier and heavier, and at last he was well-nigh exhausted; looking down he saw in the moonlight a sight that revived him: it was as it were a great snake coming up to him out of the deep shadow cast by the tower.

He gave a shout of joy, and a score more wild pulls, and lo! a stout new rope touched his hand: he hauled and hauled, and dragged the end into his prison, and instantly passed it through both handles of the chest in succession, and knotted it firmly; then sat for a moment to recover his breath and collect his courage. The first thing was to make sure that the chest was sound, and capable of resisting his weight

[1] A soft woolen cap.

poised in mid-air. He jumped with all force upon it. At the third jump the whole side burst open, and out scuttled the contents, a host of parchments.

This shook his confidence in the chest's powers of resistance; so he gave it an ally: he took the iron bar and fastened it with the small rope across the large rope, and across the window. He now mounted the chest, and from the chest put his foot through the window, and sat half in and half out, with one hand on that part of the rope which was inside. In the silent night he heard his own heart beat.

The free air breathed on his face, and gave him the courage to risk what we must all lose one day — for liberty. Many dangers awaited him, but the greatest was the first getting on the rope outside. Gerard reflected. Finally, he put himself in the attitude of a swimmer, his body to the waist, being in the prison, his legs outside. Then holding the inside rope with both hands, he felt anxiously with his feet for the outside rope, and, when he had got it, he worked it in between the soles of his feet, and kept it there tight; then he uttered a short prayer, and, all the calmer for it, put his left hand on the sill and gradually wriggled out.

Then he seized the iron bar, and for one fearful moment hung outside from it by his right hand, while his left hand felt for the rope down at his knees; it was too tight against the wall for his fingers to get round it higher up. The moment he had fairly grasped it, he left the bar, and swiftly seized the rope with his right hand too; but in this maneuver his body necessarily fell about a yard. A stifled cry came up from below. Gerard hung in mid-air. He clenched his teeth, and nipped the rope tight with his feet and gripped it with his hands, and went down slowly hand below hand.

He passed by one huge rough stone after another. He saw there was green moss on one. He looked up and he looked down. The moon shone into his prison window; it seemed very near. The fluttering figures below seemed an awful distance. It made him dizzy to look down; so he fixed his eyes steadily on the wall close to him, and went slowly down, down, down.

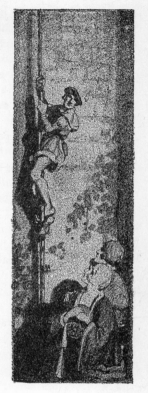

He passed a rusty, slimy streak on the wall: it was some ten feet long. The rope made his hands very hot. He stole another look up.

The prison window was a good way off now.

Down — down — down — down.

The rope made his hands sore.

He looked up. The window was so distant, he ventured now to turn his eyes downward again; and there, not more than thirty feet below him, were Margaret and Martin, their faithful hands up-stretched to catch him should he fall. He could see their eyes and their teeth shine in the moonlight.

For their mouths were open, and they were breathing hard.

"Take care, Gerard! O, take care! Look not down."

"Fear me not," cried Gerard, joyfully, and eyed the wall, but came down faster.

In another minute his feet were at their hands. They seized him ere he touched the ground, and all three clung together in one embrace.

STUDY HINTS

Study the spelling and meaning of these words :

furniture	impulse	maneuver
imprisonment	resistance	dizzy
torture	anxiously	cling, clung, clung

What do you learn from this incident about a fifteenth-century father's power over his child? What does Gerard fear? Follow carefully every stage in his escape. Is the description clear? What seems most vivid to you? How does the author give the impression of the great height of the tower? From whose viewpoint? What is the climax?

SUGGESTIONS FOR ORAL AND WRITTEN ENGLISH
THEME SUBJECTS

In *Hereward's Adventure with the White Bear*, you have made a list of the different points of suspense leading to the highest point, *i.e.* to the climax. In other words, you have outlined the plot. A plot is a series of incidents, each growing out of the preceding one, and increasing in interest until the climax is reached. After the climax, comes one or more points that relieve the suspense. The relief is called the *resolution* (*i.e. untying*) *of the plot*. Each point, or incident, in a well-constructed plot is a link in a chain, and can no more be left out than a link can. You can trace this in Gerard's actions from the moment he sees the arrow.

Outline one of the following theme subjects, imitating Reade's outline, and trying to make your account as vivid as his. Try to see each point with your imagination before writing about it.

A Lucky Escape.   An Adventure in a Fire.
How to Come Down a Rope.   A Steady Head.
How I was Imprisoned in a Medieval Castle and Escaped from It.

SUGGESTIONS FOR ADDITIONAL READINGS

The Cloister and the Hearth. Charles Reade.
Hugh Wynne. S. Weir Mitchell.
St. Ives. Robert Louis Stevenson.
David Balfour. Robert Louis Stevenson.
The Black Tulip. Alexander Dumas.
The Prisoner of Zenda. Anthony Hope (Hawkins).
The Splendid Spur. A. T. Quiller-Couch.
Wonderful Escapes by Americans. W. S. Booth.

THE HIGHWAYMAN [1]

ALFRED NOYES

Alfred Noyes (1880–   ) was born in England.   He is considered one of
the leading poets of the twentieth century.   He has traveled in America,
reading his poems and lecturing.   His poetry is full of vigor, as you will
see from *The Highwayman*.   See also:

Halleck's *New English Literature*, pp. 603–605, 623.
Hamilton W. Mabie's Introduction to *Poems* by Alfred Noyes (1906).
Who is Alfred Noyes?   *Catholic World*, Vol. 97, pp. 289–304.
(June, 1913.)

PART ONE

I

THE wind was a torrent of darkness among the gusty trees,
The moon was a ghostly galleon tossed upon cloudy seas,
The road was a ribbon of moonlight over the purple moor,
And the highwayman came riding —
    Riding — riding —
The highwayman came riding, up to the old inn door.

II

He'd a French cocked hat on his forehead, a bunch of lace
    at his chin,
A coat of the claret velvet, and breeches of brown doeskin;
They fitted with never a wrinkle: his boots were up to the
    thigh!

---

[1] From *Poems* by Alfred Noyes. Copyright, 1906, by The Macmillan Company.   Published in this volume by special arrangement with The Macmillan Company and Frederick
A. Stokes Company.

And he rode with a jeweled
    twinkle,
    His pistol butts a-twinkle,
His rapier hilt a-twinkle, under
    the jeweled sky.

III

Over the cobbles he clattered
    and clashed in the dark
    inn yard,
And he tapped with his whip
    on the shutters, but all
    was locked and barred;
He whistled a tune to the win-
    dow, and who should be
    waiting there
But the landlord's black-eyed daughter,
    Bess, the landlord's daughter,
Plaiting a dark red love knot into her long black hair.

IV

And dark in the dark old inn yard a stable-wicket creaked
Where Tim the ostler listened; his face was white and peaked;
His eyes were hollows of madness, his hair like moldy hay,
But he loved the landlord's daughter,
    The landlord's red-lipped daughter,
Dumb as a dog he listened, and he heard the robber say —

V

"One kiss, my bonny sweetheart, I'm after a prize to-night,
But I shall be back with the yellow gold before the morning
    light;
Yet, if they press me sharply, and harry me through the day,

Then look for me by moonlight,
  Watch for me by moonlight,
I'll come to thee by moonlight, though hell should bar the
    way."

VI

He rose upright in the stirrups; he scarce could reach her
    hand,
But she loosened her hair i' the casement! His face burned
    like a brand
As the black cascade of perfume came tumbling over his
    breast;
And he kissed its waves in the moonlight,
  (Oh, sweet black waves in the moonlight!)
Then he tugged at his rein in the moonlight, and galloped
    away to the West.

PART TWO

I

He did not come in the dawning; he did not come at noon;
And out o' the tawny sunset, before the rise o' the moon,
When the road was a gypsy's ribbon, looping the purple
    moor,
A redcoat troop came marching —
  Marching — marching —
King George's men came marching, up to the old inn door.

II

They said no word to the landlord, they drank his ale instead,
But they gagged his daughter and bound her to the foot of
    her narrow bed;
Two of them knelt at her casement, with muskets at their
    side!

There was death at every window;
   And hell at one dark window;
For Bess could see, through her casement, the road that *he*
   would ride.

III

They had tied her up to attention, with many a sniggering
   jest;
They had bound a musket beside her, with the barrel beneath
   her breast!
"Now keep good watch!" and they kissed her.
   She heard the dead man say [1]
Look for me by moonlight;
   Watch for me by moonlight;
I'll come to thee by moonlight, though hell should bar the way!

IV

She twisted her hands behind her; but all the knots held
   good!
She writhed her hands till her fingers were wet with sweat
   or blood!
They stretched and strained in the darkness, and the hours
   crawled by like years,
Till, now, on the stroke of midnight,
   Cold on the stroke of midnight,
The tip of one finger touched it! The trigger at least was
   hers!

V

The tip of one finger touched it; she strove no more for the
   rest!
Up, she stood up to attention, with the barrel beneath her
   breast,
She would not risk their hearing; she would not strive again;

[1] In her fear she already thought of her lover as dead.

For the road lay bare in the moonlight;
  Blank and bare in the moonlight;
And the blood of her veins in the moonlight throbbed to her
    love's refrain.

VI

Tlot-tlot; tlot-tlot! Had they heard it? The horse-hoofs
    ringing clear;
Tlot-tlot, tlot-tlot, in the distance! Were they deaf that they
    did not hear?
Down the ribbon of moonlight, over the brow of the hill,
The highwayman came riding,
  Riding, — riding!
The redcoats looked to their priming! She stood up, straight
    and still!

VII

Tlot-tlot, in the frosty silence! *Tlot-tlot,* in the echoing night!
Nearer he came and nearer! Her face was like a light!
Her eyes grew wide for a moment; she drew one last deep
    breath,
Then her finger moved in the moonlight,
  Her musket shattered the moonlight,
Shattered her breast in the moonlight and warned him —
    with her death.

VIII

He turned; he spurred to the Westward; he did not know
    who stood
Bowed, with her head o'er the musket, drenched with her
    own red blood!
Not till the dawn he heard it, and slowly blanched to hear
How Bess, the landlord's daughter,
  The landlord's black-eyed daughter,
Had watched for her love in the moonlight, and died in the
    darkness there.

IX

Back, he spurred like a madman, shrieking a curse to the sky,
With the white road smoking behind him, and his rapier
brandished high !
Blood-red were his spurs i' the golden noon ; wine-red was his
velvet coat ;
When they shot him down on the highway,
  Down like a dog on the highway,
And he lay in his blood on the highway, with the bunch of
lace at his throat.

    .   .   .   .   .

And still of a winter's night, they say, when the wind is in the
*   trees,*
When the moon is a ghostly galleon tossed upon cloudy seas,
When the road is a ribbon of moonlight over the purple moor,
A highwayman comes riding —
* Riding — riding —*
A highwayman comes riding, up to the old inn door.

XI

Over the cobbles he clatters and clangs in the dark inn yard;
And he taps with his whip on the shutters, but all is locked and
*   barred;*
He whistles a tune to the window, and who should be waiting
*   there*
But the landlord's black-eyed daughter,
* Bess, the landlord's daughter,*
Plaiting a dark red love knot into her long black hair.

STUDY HINTS

This spirited poem needs little comment. Try to see each picture
clearly. Read it aloud and note the splendid swing of the verse. What
is the climax? Was Bess as brave as her lover? After reading the poem,
tell it aloud to some one. Try to make him see the pictures as clearly
as you do.

SUGGESTIONS FOR ADDITIONAL READINGS

A Song of the Plow.   Alfred Noyes.
The Admiral's Ghost.   Alfred Noyes.
Hervé Riel.   Robert Browning.
How They Brought the Good News from Ghent to Aix.   Robert Browning.

For the teacher to read to the class:
Prelude to *The Flower of Old Japan.*   Alfred Noyes.
Selections from *Drake: An English Epic.*   Alfred Noyes.
Selections from *The Barrel Organ.*   Alfred Noyes.
Selections from *The Wine-press.*   Alfred Noyes.

WEE WILLIE WINKIE [1]

RUDYARD KIPLING

[For biographical sketch see page 29.]

"An officer and a gentleman."

His full name was Percival William Williams, but he picked up the other name in a nursery book, and that was the end of the christened titles.   His mother's *ayah* [2] called him Willie-*Baba*, but as he never paid the faintest attention to anything that the *ayah* said, her wisdom did not help matters.

His father was the colonel of the 195th, and as soon as Wee Willie Winkie was old enough to understand what military discipline meant, Colonel Williams put him under it.   There was no other way of managing the child.   When he was good for a week, he drew good-conduct pay ; and when he was bad, he was deprived of his good-conduct stripe. Generally he was bad, for India offers so many chances to little six-year-olds of going wrong.

Children resent familiarity from strangers, and Wee Willie Winkie was a very particular child.   Once he accepted an acquaintance, he was graciously pleased to thaw.   He accepted Brandis, a subaltern of the 195th, on sight.   Brandis was having tea at the colonel's, and Wee Willie Winkie entered strong in the possession of a good-conduct badge won for not chasing the hens round the compound.   He regarded Brandis with gravity for at least ten minutes, and then delivered himself of his opinion.

"I like you," said he slowly, getting off his chair and

[1] First published in 1888 in Allahabad, India.   [2] Maid.

coming over to Brandis. "I like you. I shall call you Coppy, because of your hair. Do you *mind* being called Coppy? It is because of ve hair, you know."

Here was one of the most embarrassing of Wee Willie Winkie's peculiarities. He would look at a stranger for some time, and then, without warning or explanation, would give him a name. And the name stuck. No regimental penalties could break Wee Willie Winkie of this habit. He lost his good-conduct badge for christening the commissioner's wife "Pobs"; but nothing that the colonel could do made the station forego the nickname, and Mrs. Collen remained Mrs. "Pobs" till the end of her stay. So Brandis was christened "Coppy," and rose, therefore, in the estimation of the regiment.

If Wee Willie Winkie took an interest in any one, the fortunate man was envied alike by the mess and the rank and file. And in their envy lay no suspicion of self-interest. "The colonel's son" was idolized on his own merits entirely. Yet Wee Willie Winkie was not lovely. His face was permanently freckled, as his legs were permanently scratched, and in spite of his mother's almost tearful remonstrances he had insisted upon having his long yellow locks cut short in the military fashion. "I want my hair like Sergeant Tummil's," said Wee Willie Winkie, and, his father abetting, the sacrifice was accomplished.

Three weeks after the bestowal of his youthful affections on Lieutenant Brandis — henceforward to be called "Coppy" for the sake of brevity — Wee Willie Winkie was destined to behold strange things and far beyond his comprehension.

Coppy returned his liking with interest. Coppy had let him wear for five rapturous minutes his own big sword — just as tall as Wee Willie Winkie. Coppy had promised him a terrier puppy; and Coppy had permitted him to witness the miraculous operation of shaving. Nay, more — Coppy had said that even he, Wee Willie Winkie, would rise in time to the ownership of a box of shiny knives, a silver soap box and a silver-handled "sputter-brush," as Wee Willie Winkie called it. Decidedly, there was no one except his father, who could give or take away good-conduct badges at pleasure, half so wise, strong, and valiant as Coppy with the Afghan and Egyptian medals on his breast. Why, then, should Coppy be guilty of the unmanly weakness of kissing — vehemently kissing — a "big girl," Miss Allardyce to wit? In the course of a morning ride, Wee Willie Winkie had seen Coppy so doing, and, like the gentleman he was, had promptly wheeled round and cantered back to his groom, lest the groom should also see.

Under ordinary circumstances he would have spoken to his father, but he felt instinctively that this was a matter on which Coppy ought first to be consulted.

"Coppy," shouted Wee Willie Winkie, reining up outside that subaltern's bungalow early one morning — "I want to see you, Coppy!"

"Come in, young 'un," returned Coppy, who was at early breakfast in the midst of his dogs. "What mischief have you been getting into now?"

Wee Willie Winkie had done nothing notoriously bad for three days, and so stood on a pinnacle of virtue.

"I've been doing nothing bad," said he, curling himself into a long chair with a studious affectation of the colonel's languor after a hot parade. He buried his freckled nose in a teacup and, with eyes staring roundly over the rim, asked: — "I say, Coppy, is it pwoper to kiss big girls?"

"By Jove! You're beginning early. Who do you want to kiss?"

"No one. My muvver's always kissing me if I don't stop her. If it isn't pwoper, how was you kissing Major Allardyce's big girl last morning, by ve canal?"

Coppy's brow wrinkled. He and Miss Allardyce had with great craft managed to keep their engagement secret for a fortnight. There were urgent and imperative reasons why Major Allardyce should not know how matters stood for at least another month, and this small marplot had discovered a great deal too much.

"I saw you," said Wee Willie Winkie, calmly. "But ve groom didn't see. I said, '*Hut jao.*'"

"Oh, you had that much sense, you young Rip," groaned poor Coppy, half amused and half angry. "And how many people may you have told about it?"

"Only me myself. You didn't tell when I twied to wide ve buffalo ven my pony was lame; and I fought you wouldn't like."

"Winkie," said Coppy enthusiastically, shaking the small hand, "you're the best of good fellows. Look here, you can't understand all these things. One of these days — hang it, how can I make you see it — I'm going to marry Miss Allardyce, and then she'll be Mrs. Coppy, as you say. If your young mind is so scandalized at the idea of kissing big girls, go and tell your father."

"What will happen?" said Wee Willie Winkie, who firmly believed that his father was omnipotent.

"I shall get into trouble," said Coppy, playing his trump card with an appealing look at the holder of the ace.

"Ven I won't," said Wee Willie Winkie briefly. "But my faver says it's un-man-ly to be always kissing, and I didn't fink *you'd* do vat, Coppy."

"I'm not always kissing, old chap. It's only now and then, and when you're bigger you'll do it too. Your father meant it's not good for little boys."

"Ah!" said Wee Willie Winkie, now fully enlightened. "It's like ve sputter-brush?"

"Exactly," said Coppy gravely.

"But I don't fink I'll ever want to kiss big girls, nor no one, 'cept my muvver.   And I *must* vat, you know."

There was a long pause, broken by Wee Willie Winkie.

"Are you fond of vis big girl, Coppy?"

"Awfully!" said Coppy.

"Fonder van you are of Bell or ve Butcha — or me?"

"It's in a different way," said Coppy.   "You see, one of these days Miss Allardyce will belong to me, but you'll grow up and command the regiment and — all sorts of things. It's quite different, you see."

"Very well," said Wee Willie Winkie, rising.   "If you're fond of ve big girl, I won't tell any one.   I must go now."

Coppy rose and escorted his small guest to the door, adding: "You're the best of little fellows, Winkie.   I tell you what.   In thirty days from now you can tell if you like — tell any one you like."

Thus the secret of the Brandis-Allardyce engagement was dependent on a little child's word.   Coppy, who knew Wee Willie Winkie's idea of truth, was at ease, for he felt that he would not break promises.   Wee Willie Winkie betrayed a special and unusual interest in Miss Allardyce, and, slowly revolving round that embarrassed young lady, was used to regard her gravely with unwinking eye.   He was trying to discover why Coppy should have kissed her.   She was not half so nice as his own mother.   On the other hand, she was Coppy's property, and would in time belong to him.   Therefore it behooved him to treat her with as much respect as Coppy's big sword or shiny pistol.

The idea that he had shared a great secret in common with Coppy kept Wee Willie Winkie unusually virtuous for three weeks.   Then the Old Adam broke out, and he made what he called a "camp fire" at the bottom of the garden.   How could he have foreseen that the flying sparks would have lighted the Colonel's little hayrick and consumed a week's

store for the horses? Sudden and swift was the punishment
— deprivation of the good-conduct badge, and, most sorrowful
of all, two days' confinement to barracks — the house and
veranda — coupled with the withdrawal of the light of his
father's countenance.

He took the sentence like the man he strove to be, drew
himself up with a quivering under-lip, saluted, and, once
clear of the room, ran to weep bitterly in his nursery — called
by him "my quarters." Coppy came in the afternoon and
attempted to console the culprit.

"I'm under awwest," said Wee Willie Winkie mourn-
fully, "and I didn't ought to speak to you."

Very early the next morning he climbed on to the roof of the
house — that was not forbidden — and beheld Miss Allardyce going for a ride.

"Where are you going?" cried Wee Willie Winkie.

"Across the river," she answered, and trotted forward.

Now the cantonment in which the 195th lay was bounded
on the north by a river — dry in the winter. From his earli-
est years, Wee Willie Winkie had been forbidden to go across
the river, and had noted that even Coppy — the almost
almighty Coppy — had never set foot beyond it. Wee
Willie Winkie had once been read to, out of a big blue book,
the history of the Princess and the Goblins — a most wonderful tale of a land where the Goblins were always warring with
the children of men until they were defeated by one Curdie.
Ever since that date it seemed to him that the bare black
and purple hills across the river were inhabited by Goblins,
and, in truth, every one had said that there lived the Bad
Men. Even in his own house the lower halves of the windows
were covered with green paper on account of the Bad Men
who might, if allowed clear view, fire into peaceful drawing
rooms and comfortable bedrooms. Certainly, beyond the
river, which was the end of all the earth, lived the Bad Men.

And here was Major Allardyce's big girl, Coppy's property, preparing to venture into their borders! What would Coppy say if anything happened to her? If the Goblins ran off with her as they did with Curdie's Princess? She must at all hazards be turned back.

The house was still. Wee Willie Winkie reflected for a moment on the very terrible wrath of his father; and then — broke his arrest! It was a crime unspeakable. The low sun threw his shadow, very large and very black, on the trim garden paths, as he went down to the stables and ordered his pony. It seemed to him in the hush of the dawn that all the big world had been bidden to stand still and look at Wee Willie Winkie guilty of mutiny. The drowsy groom handed him his mount, and, since the one great sin made all others insignificant, Wee Willie Winkie said that he was going to ride over to Coppy Sahib,[1] and went out at a foot pace, stepping on the soft mold of the flower-borders.

The devastating track of the pony's feet was the last misdeed that cut him off from all sympathy of humanity. He turned into the road, leaned forward, and rode as fast as the pony could put foot to the ground in the direction of the river.

But the liveliest of twelve-two ponies can do little against the long canter of a Waler.[2] Miss Allardyce was far ahead, had passed through the crops, beyond the police post, when all the guards were asleep, and her mount was scattering the pebbles of the river bed as Wee Willie Winkie left the cantonment and British India behind him. Bowed forward and still flogging, Wee Willie Winkie shot into Afghan territory, and could just see Miss Allardyce a black speck, flickering across the stony plain. The reason of her wandering was simple enough. Coppy, in a tone of too-hastily-assumed authority, had told her overnight that she must not ride out

---

[1] A term of respect, as master or mistress.   [2] A specially fine breed of cavalry horse.

by the river. And she had gone to prove her own spirit and teach Coppy a lesson.

Almost at the foot of the inhospitable hills, Wee Willie Winkie saw the Waler blunder and come down heavily. Miss Allardyce struggled clear, but her ankle had been severely twisted, and she could not stand. Having thus demonstrated her spirit, she wept copiously, and was surprised by the apparition of a white, wide-eyed child in khaki, on a nearly spent pony.

"Are you badly, badly hurted?" shouted Wee Willie Winkie, as soon as he was within range. "You didn't ought to be here."

"I don't know," said Miss Allardyce ruefully, ignoring the reproof. "Good gracious, child, what are *you* doing here?"

"You said you was going acwoss ve wiver," panted Wee Willie Winkie, throwing himself off his pony. "And nobody — not even Coppy — must go acwoss ve wiver, and I came after you ever so hard, but you wouldn't stop, and now you've hurted yourself, and Coppy will be angwy wiv me, and — I've bwoken my awwest! I've bwoken my awwest!"

The future colonel of the 195th sat down and sobbed. In spite of the pain in her ankle the girl was moved.

"Have you ridden all the way from cantonments, little man? What for?"

"You belonged to Coppy. Coppy told me so!" wailed Wee Willie Winkie disconsolately. "I saw him kissing you, and he said he was fonder of you van Bell or ve Butcha or me. And so I came. You must get up and come back. You didn't ought to be here. Vis is a bad place, and I've bwoken my awwest."

"I can't move, Winkie," said Miss Allardyce, with a groan. "I've hurt my foot. What shall I do?"

She showed a readiness to weep afresh, which steadied Wee Willie Winkie, who had been brought up to believe that tears were the depth of unmanliness. Still, when one is as great a sinner as Wee Willie Winkie, even a man may be permitted to break down.

"Winkie," said Miss Allardyce, "when you've rested a little, ride back and tell them to send out something to carry me back in. It hurts fearfully."

The child sat still for a little time and Miss Allardyce closed her eyes; the pain was nearly making her faint. She was roused by Wee Willie Winkie tying up the reins on his pony's neck and setting it free with a vicious cut of his whip that made it whicker. The little animal headed towards the cantonments.

"Oh, Winkie! What are you doing?"

"Hush!" said Wee Willie Winkie. "Vere's a man coming — one of ve Bad Men. I must stay wiv you. My faver says a man must *always* look after a girl. Jack will go home, and ven vey'll come and look for us. Vat's why I let him go."

Not one man, but two or three had appeared from behind the rocks of the hills, and the heart of Wee Willie Winkie sank within him, for just in this manner were the Goblins wont to steal out and vex Curdie's soul. Thus had they played in Curdie's garden, he had seen the picture, and thus had they frightened the Princess's nurse. He heard them talking to each other, and recognized with joy the bastard Pushto [1] that he had picked up from one of his father's grooms lately dismissed. People who spoke that tongue could not be the Bad Men. They were only natives after all.

They came up to the bowlders on which Miss Allardyce's horse had blundered.

Then rose from the rock Wee Willie Winkie, child of the dominant race, aged six and three quarters, and said briefly and emphatically "*Jao!*" [2] The pony had crossed the river bed.

[1] An Indian dialect.　　[2] *I.e.* halt!

The men laughed, and laughter from natives was the one thing Wee Willie Winkie could not tolerate. He asked them what they wanted and why they did not depart. Other men with most evil faces and crooked-stocked guns crept out of the shadows of the hills, till, soon, Wee Willie Winkie was face to face with an audience some twenty strong. Miss Allardyce screamed.

"Who are you?" said one of the men.

"I am the Colonel Sahib's son, and my order is that you go at once. You black men are frightening the Miss Sahib. One of you must run into cantonments and take the news that the Miss Sahib has hurt herself, and that the colonel's son is here with her."

"Put our feet into the trap!" was the laughing reply. "Hear this boy's speech!"

"Say that I sent you — I, the colonel's son. They will give you money."

"What is the use of this talk? Take up the child and the girl, and we can at least ask for the ransom. Ours are the villages on the heights," said a voice in the background.

These *were* the Bad Men — worse than Goblins — and it needed all Wee Willie Winkie's training to prevent him from bursting into tears. But he felt that to cry before a native, excepting only his mother's *ayah*, would be an infamy greater than any mutiny. Moreover, he, as future colonel of the 195th, had that grim regiment at his back.

"Are you going to carry us away?" said Wee Willie Winkie, very blanched and uncomfortable.

"Yes, my little *Sahib Bahadur*," [1] said the tallest of the men, "and eat you afterwards."

"That is child's talk," said Wee Willie Winkie. "Men do not eat men."

A yell of laughter interrupted him, but he went on firmly, — "And if you do carry us away, I tell you that all my regiment will come up in a day and kill you all without leaving one. Who will take my message to the Colonel Sahib?"

Speech in any vernacular — and Wee Willie Winkie had a colloquial acquaintance with three — was easy to the boy who could not yet manage his "r's" and "th's" aright.

Another man joined the conference, crying: "O foolish men! What this babe says is true. He is the heart's heart of those white troops. For the sake of peace let them go both, for if he be taken, the regiment will break loose and gut the valley. *Our* villages are in the valley, and we shall not escape. That regiment are devils. They broke Khoda Yar's breastbone with kicks when he tried to take the rifles; and if we touch this child they will fire and plunder for a month, till nothing remains. Better to send a man back to take the message and get a reward. I say that this child is their God, and that they will spare none of us, nor our women, if we harm him."

It was Din Mahommed, the dismissed groom of the colonel, who made the diversion, and an angry and heated discussion followed. Wee Willie Winkie, standing over Miss Allardyce, waited the upshot. Surely his "wegiment," his own "wegiment," would not desert him if they knew of his extremity.

. . . .

[1] A very formal term of respect, as *Your Excellency*. The man is of course making sport of the child.

The riderless pony brought the news to the 195th, though there had been consternation in the colonel's household for an hour before. The little beast came in through the parade ground in front of the main barracks, where the men were settling down to play spoil-five till the afternoon. Devlin, the color-sergeant of E Company, glanced at the empty saddle and tumbled through the barrack rooms, kicking up each room corporal as he passed. "Up, ye beggars! There's something happened to the colonel's son," he shouted.

"He couldn't fall off! S'elp me, 'e *couldn't* fall off," blubbered a drummer boy. "Go an' hunt acrost the river. He's over there if he's anywhere, an' maybe those Pathans have got 'im. For the love o' Gawd don't look for 'm in the nullahs![1] Let's go over the river."

"There's sense in Mott yet," said Devlin. "E Company, double out to the river — sharp!"

So E Company, in its shirt sleeves mainly, doubled for the dear life, and in the rear toiled the perspiring sergeant, adjuring it to double yet faster. The cantonment was alive with the men of the 195th hunting for Wee Willie Winkie, and the colonel finally overtook E Company, far too exhausted to swear, struggling in the pebbles of the river bed.

Up the hill under which Wee Willie Winkie's Bad Men were discussing the wisdom of carrying off the child and the girl, a lookout fired two shots.

"What have I said?" shouted Din Mahommed. "There is the warning! The *pulton*[2] are out already and are coming across the plain! Get away! Let us not be seen with the boy!"

The men waited for an instant, and then, as another shot was fired, withdrew into the hills, silently as they had appeared.

[1] *I.e.* ravines or gorges.

[2] *I.e.* regiment.

"The wegiment is coming," said Wee Willie Winkie confidently to Miss Allardyce, "and it's all wight.   Don't cwy!"

He needed the advice himself, for ten minutes later, when his father came up, he was weeping bitterly with his head in Miss Allardyce's lap.

And the men of the 195th carried him home with shouts and rejoicings; and Coppy, who had ridden a horse into a lather, met him, and, to his intense disgust, kissed him openly in the presence of the men.

But there was balm for his dignity.   His father assured him that not only would the breaking of arrest be condoned, but that the good-conduct badge would be restored as soon as his mother could sew it on his blouse sleeve.   Miss Allardyce had told the colonel a story that made him proud of his son.

"She belonged to you, Coppy," said Wee Willie Winkie, indicating Miss Allardyce with a grimy forefinger.   "I *knew* she didn't ought to go acwoss ve wiver, and I knew ve wegiment would come to me if I sent Jack home."

"You're a hero, Winkie," said Coppy — "a *pukka*[1] hero !"

"I don't know what vat means," said Wee Willie Winkie, "but you mustn't call me Winkie any no more.   I'm Percival Will'am Will'ams."

And in this manner did Wee Willie Winkie enter into his manhood.

STUDY HINTS

Study the spelling and meaning of these words :

christen	dependent	emphatically
nickname	hazard	blanched
urgent	bowlder	barracks
possession	dominant	badge

[1] Sure-enough.

How has respect for army discipline been trained in Wee Willie Winkie? What makes him promise Coppy that he will keep his secret? Can you explain why he feels so deeply breaking his arrest? What other circumstances made it hard for him to go to Miss Allardyce's aid? What fine quality for friendship does he show when he goes? The English race had for many generations treated the natives of India as their inferiors, which partly explains Wee Willie Winkie's commanding ways with them. What other explanation can you suggest? After reading the story, can you understand why he was idolized by the regiment? When do you think he "entered into manhood," when he assumed his full name or before?

SUGGESTIONS FOR ORAL AND WRITTEN ENGLISH
THEME SUBJECTS

There are two ways of showing the characters of people in stories. In one the writer tells what traits they have; in the other he makes them act so that we discover their traits from their actions. The last way is called the "dramatic method." Does the plot of *Wee Willie Winkie* interest you? Does the boy himself interest you? Look around you and see if you can find an incident that illustrates unselfishness. Make a study of some small boy for a day, without his knowledge, and write what you have observed. The next day make a note of a particular trait that you have seen, and find other illustrations of it through his actions. After carefully selecting the climax, tell a story in which a friend of yours is the central figure. Have the action in the story reveal his strongest trait. Do not state what it is, but allow the class to guess it.

A friend of yours has been accused of cheating on an examination. Defend his honor by the *dramatic method*.

A friend has been said to be selfish in her home. You know it is not true. Defend her reputation.

A Young Girl on the Train.
A Good Loser.
A Good Winner.
Learning to Ride.
How my Dog Knows I Love Him.
How We Knew His Team Won.
How I Know my Dog Loves Me.
What is Loyalty?

SUGGESTIONS FOR ADDITIONAL READINGS

Jungle Books I and II. Rudyard Kipling.
Just So Stories. Rudyard Kipling.
On Greenhow Hill (in *Life's Handicap*). Rudyard Kipling.
The Day's Work. Rudyard Kipling.
William the Conqueror. Rudyard Kipling.
.007. Rudyard Kipling.
The Ship that Found Herself. Rudyard Kipling.
The Brushwood Boy. Rudyard Kipling.
Baa, Baa, Black Sheep (in *Under the Deodars*). Rudyard Kipling.
Captains Courageous. Rudyard Kipling.
Puck of Pook's Hill. Rudyard Kipling.
Kim. Rudyard Kipling.
Story of Sonny Sahib. Sarah J. Duncan.

A GROUP OF NATURE LYRICS

THE brief expression of a single emotion in poetry is called a lyric. Lyrics may express joy, sorrow, love of nature, of one's country, or of human beings. These five lyrics have some aspect of nature for their chief subject.

THE WIND [1]

ROBERT LOUIS STEVENSON

[For biographical sketch see page 112.]

I SAW you toss the kites on high
And blow the birds about the sky;
And all around I heard you pass,
Like ladies' skirts across the grass —
    O wind, a-blowing all day long,
    O wind, that sings so loud a song!

I saw the different things you did,
But always you yourself you hid.
I felt you push, I heard you call,
I could not see yourself at all —
    O wind, a-blowing all day long,
    O wind, that sings so loud a song!

O you that are so strong and cold,
O blower, are you young or old?
Are you a beast of field and tree,
Or just a stronger child than me?
    O wind, a-blowing all day long,
    O wind, that sings so loud a song!

[1] From *A Child's Garden of Verse.*

91

THE GRASS [1]

EMILY DICKINSON

Emily Dickinson (1830–1886) was the daughter of a prominent lawyer in Amherst, Massachusetts. Of a very retiring nature, she rarely saw any one, and for many years did not even cross the threshold of her own home. Her work is most unusual, but she would permit only three or four of her poems to be published. After her death they were collected and published by friends.

THE grass so little has to do, —
A spear of simple green,
With only butterflies to brood,
And bees to entertain,

And stir all day to pretty tunes
The breezes fetch along,
And hold the sunshine in its lap,
And bow to everything;

And thread the dews all night, like pearls,
And make itself so fine, —
A duchess were too common
For such a noticing.

And even when it dies, to pass
In odors so divine,
As lowly spices gone to sleep,
Or amulets of pine.

And then to dwell in sovereign barns,
And dream the days away, —
The grass so little has to do,
I wish I were the hay!

[1] From *Poems* by Emily Dickinson, copyright, 1890, by Roberts Brothers.

THE BROOK [1]

JOHN B. TABB

John B. Tabb (1845–1909) was a Catholic priest and the author of many brief, enjoyable lyrics. See also :
Halleck's *History of American Literature*, pp. 318–320, 338.

It is the mountain to the sea
That makes a messenger of me :
And, lest I loiter on the way
And lose what I am sent to say,
He sets his reverie to song
And bids me sing it all day long.
Farewell ! for here the stream is slow,
And I have many a mile to go.

WRITTEN IN MARCH

WILLIAM WORDSWORTH

William Wordsworth (1770–1850) is England's greatest nature poet. Nature seemed to him to possess a conscious soul and to enter into the joys and sorrows of man. He thought that every flower enjoyed the air it breathed.   He was born in the wonderful Lake District in north-western England, where he wrote most of his poetry and passed almost all his life. See also :
Halleck's *New English Literature*, pp. 5, 386–398, 443, 445.

The cock is crowing,
The stream is flowing,
The small birds twitter,
The lake doth glitter,
The green field sleeps in the sun ;
The oldest and youngest

Are at work with the strongest;
The cattle are grazing,
Their heads never raising;
There are forty feeding like one!

Like an army defeated
The snow hath retreated,
And now doth fare ill
On the top of the bare hill;
The plowboy is whooping — anon-anon:
There's joy in the mountains;
There's life in the fountains;
Small clouds are sailing,
Blue sky prevailing;
The rain is over and gone.

SONG FROM *PIPPA PASSES*

ROBERT BROWNING

Robert Browning (1812–1889), the author of stirring lyric and dramatic poems, was born at Camberwell, a suburb of London. He is a poet of great originality and force. He loved to write of the trials and growth of human souls. This song of the little silk weaver, Pippa, is a message which she unconsciously conveys to two sinful souls as she passes their house. See also:

Halleck's *New English Literature*, pp. 540–553, 585.
Chesterton's *Robert Browning*.

THE year's at the spring
And day's at the morn;
Morning's at seven:
The hill-side's dew-pearled;
The lark's on the wing;
The snail's on the thorn:
God's in his Heaven —
All's right with the world!

STUDY HINTS

After reading these lyrics twice *aloud* to yourself, study them so as to be able to read them more intelligently to some of your friends. If you read them well, see if your friends do not say that they would like to hear more as good. Memorize the stanzas that you like best.

When you read Stevenson's poem, remember that not only children but the grown Greeks and Romans personified the winds. Homer and Vergil tell how Ulysses and Æneas suffered from hostile winds. One of the greatest lyrics of the English poet, Shelley (1792–1822), begins:

"O wild west wind, thou breath of Autumn's being."

The Evening Wind is one of the fine lyrics of the American poet Bryant (1794–1878). Stevenson's poem is the simplest of them all and perhaps the most widely read.

After the second reading of *The Grass*, tell in prose what the grass does, then reread the verse and notice how much more enjoyable it is. Is this poem as simple as *The Wind?* Is there any hint of humor in either poem?

What is the central idea in *The Brook?* Who sends the message? How does he make sure that it will not be forgotten? Will this poem increase our pleasure in listening to the music of an actual brook? Is this poem as simple as the two preceding ones?

In reading Wordsworth's *Written in March*, we should remember that the English spring comes early. After the two readings aloud, try to tell what Wordsworth saw and heard. Of all the things mentioned, which appeal to you most? Which of these poems is the easiest to understand?

Note that each line in Browning's *Song from Pippa Passes* is a complete sentence and that the verb in each line is "is" (abbreviated to 's). The existence of such beautiful things proves to the poet that God is in heaven and consequently that "All's right with the world." To Browning these lines were probably as self-evident and as simple as any in the preceding poems. Are they so to you? Which of these five poems do you prefer to-day, even if you change your mind when you feel differently?

SUGGESTIONS FOR ADDITIONAL READINGS

Windy Nights (from *A Child's Garden of Verse*). Robert Louis Stevenson.

Who Robbed the Woods? Emily Dickinson.

The Wind in the Chimney. Bret Harte.
The Evening Wind. William Cullen Bryant.
The Wind of Spring. Madison Cawein.

For the teacher to read to the class:

Ode to the West Wind. Percy Bysshe Shelley.
The Voice of the Grass. Sarah Roberts Boyle.
A Song of Clover. Helen Hunt Jackson.
Before the Rain. Thomas Bailey Aldrich.
A Child said, What is the Grass? (from a *Song of Myself*, Section VI).
Walt Whitman.
The Brook. Alfred Tennyson.
Clear and Cool (from *Water Babies*). Charles Kingsley.
The Fountain. James Russell Lowell.
The Waterfall. Frank Dempster Sherman.
Arethusa. Percy Bysshe Shelley.
March. William Cullen Bryant.
Spring. William Blake.
Spring. Celia Thaxter.
Spring Song. Bliss Carman.
How They Brought the Good News from Ghent to Aix. Robert Browning.
Boot and Saddle. Robert Browning.
Muléykeh. Robert Browning.
The Pied Piper of Hamelin. Robert Browning.

HOW MR. RABBIT WAS TOO SHARP FOR MR. FOX[1]

Joel Chandler Harris

Joel Chandler Harris (1848–1908) was born in Georgia. He lived on a plantation and heard from early childhood the stories told by the negroes. Later in life, realizing that they were a part of the folklore that the negro brought from Africa, he collected these stories. The collection, of which the chief narrator is "Uncle Remus," holds a unique place in American literature, and possesses a perennial interest for old and young. See also:

Halleck's *History of American Literature*, pp. 320–323, 338, 340.

Introduction to *Uncle Remus, His Songs and His Sayings*, by Joel Chandler Harris.

[Brer Fox had made a Tar-Baby on purpose to excite Brer Rabbit's curiosity and trap him. Brer Rabbit had attacked Tar-Baby because he would not answer Brer Rabbit's questions. The result was he was stuck fast to Tar-Baby. The story opens at this point.]

"Uncle Remus," said the little boy one evening, when he had found the old man with little or nothing to do, "did the fox kill and eat the rabbit when he caught him with the Tar-Baby?"

"Law, honey, ain't I tell you 'bout dat?" replied the old darky, chuckling slyly. "I 'clar ter grashus I ought er tole you dat, but old man Nod wuz ridin' on my eyeleds 'twel a leetle mo'n I'd a dis'member'd my own name, en den on to dat, here come yo' mammy hollerin' atter you.

[1] Copyright, 1880, 1908, by D. Appleton and Company. This selection and its illustrations are used in this volume by special arrangement with the publishers.

"W'at I tell you w'en I fus begin? I tole you Brer Rabbit wuz a monstus soon[1] creetur; leas'ways dat's w'at I laid out fer ter tell you. Well, den, honey, don't you go en make no udder calkalashuns, kase in dem days Brer Rabbit en his fambly wuz at de head er de gang w'en enny racket wuz on han', en dar dey stayed. 'Fo you begins fer ter wipe yo' eyes 'bout Brer Rabbit, you wait en see whar'bouts Brer Rabbit gwineter fetch up at. But dat's needer yer ner dar.

"W'en Brer Fox fine Brer Rabbit mixt up wid de Tar-Baby, he feel mighty good, en he roll on de groun' en laff.

Bimeby he up'n say, sezee:

"'Well, I speck I got you dis time, Brer Rabbit,' sezee; 'maybe I ain't, but I speck I is. You been runnin' roun' here sassin' atter me a mighty long time, but I speck you done come ter de enn' er de row. You bin cuttin' up yo' capers en bouncin' 'roun in dis neighborhood ontwel[2] you come ter b'leeve yo'se'f de boss er de whole gang. En den youer allers some'rs whar you got no bizness,' sez Brer Fox, sezee. 'Who ax you fer ter come en strike up a 'quaintance wid dish yer Tar-Baby? En who stuck you up dar whar you is? Nobody in de roun' worril. You des tuck en jam yo'se'f on dat Tar-Baby widout waitin' fer enny invite,' sez Brer Fox, sezee, ' en dar you is, en dar you'll stay twel I fixes up a bresh-pile and fires her up, kase I'm gwineter bobbycue[3] you dis day, sho,' sez Brer Fox, sezee.

---

[1] Quick-witted.   [2] *I.e.* until.   [3] Barbecue, roast-whole.

"Den Brer Rabbit talk mighty 'umble.

"'I don't keer w'at you do wid me, Brer Fox,' sezee, 'so you don't fling me in dat brier patch. Roas' me, Brer Fox,' sezee, 'but don't fling me in dat brier patch,' sezee.

"'Hit's so much trouble fer ter kindle a fier,' sez Brer Fox, sezee, 'dat I speck I'll hatter hang you,' sezee.

"'Hang me des as high as you please, Brer Fox,' sez Brer Rabbit, sezee, 'but do fer de Lord's sake don't fling me in dat brier patch,' sezee.

"'I ain't got no string,' sez Brer Fox, sezee, ''en now I speck I'll hatter drown you,' sezee.

"'Drown me des ez deep ez you please, Brer Fox,' sez Brer Rabbit, sezee, 'but do don't fling me in dat brier patch,' sezee.

"'Dey ain't no water nigh,' sez Brer Fox, sezee, ''en now I speck I'll hatter skin you,' sezee.

"'Skin me, Brer Fox,' sez Brer Rabbit, sezee, 'snatch out my eyeballs, t'ar out my years[1] by de roots, en cut off my legs,' sezee, 'but do please, Brer Fox, don't fling me in dat brier patch,' sezee.

"Co'se Brer Fox wanter hurt Brer Rabbit bad ez he kin, so he cotch 'im by de behime legs en slung 'im right in de middle er de brier patch. Dar wuz a considerbul flutter whar Brer Rabbit struck de bushes, en Brer Fox sorter hang 'roun' fer ter see w'at wuz gwineter happen.

[1] Ears.

Bimeby he hear somebody call 'im, en way up de hill he see Brer Rabbit settin' cross-legged on a chinkapin log koamin' de pitch outen his har wid a chip. Den Brer Fox know dat he bin swop off mighty bad. Brer Rabbit wuz bleedzed[1] fer ter fling back some er his sass, en he holler out :

"'Bred en bawn in a brier patch, Brer Fox — bred en bawn in a brier patch!' en wid dat he skip out des ez lively ez a cricket in de embers."

STUDY HINTS

Note how Brer Fox enjoys worrying Brer Rabbit with planning the various forms of his death. Why are Brer Rabbit's replies to Brer Fox's suggestions very wise? Does Brer Rabbit ever lose sight of his purpose? Would there be any difference in your facial expression and other actions if a wealthy pompous man or a ragged cripple slipped in a mud puddle? How is suspense employed in this story?

SUGGESTIONS FOR ORAL AND WRITTEN ENGLISH
THEME SUBJECTS

Tell orally in your own language at least two of the other stories of Uncle Remus and one or two by some other author, for instance by Kipling. Tell a short story of an animal that has played a clever trick.

After comparing some of Kipling's animal stories, such as those in the *Just So Stories* and the *Jungle Books*, with those by Joel Chandler Harris, write one story of your own. Try writing a part of this in the form of a dialogue. Note in the above selection how the dialogue form is paragraphed and punctuated.

SUGGESTIONS FOR ADDITIONAL READINGS

Nights with Uncle Remus.   Joel Chandler Harris.
Uncle Remus: His Songs and His Sayings.   Joel Chandler Harris.
A Story of the War (from *Uncle Remus: His Songs and His Sayings*). Joel Chandler Harris.
A Story of Seven Devils (in *Amos Kilbright*).   Frank R. Stockton.
Marse Chan (from *In Ole Virginia*).   Thomas Nelson Page.

[1] Obliged.

Meh Lady (from *In Ole Virginia*).   Thomas Nelson Page.
Polly.   Thomas Nelson Page.
Bred in the Bone.   Thomas Nelson Page.
Solomon Crow's Christmas Pockets.   Ruth McEnery Stuart.
Sonny.   Ruth McEnery Stuart.
Moriah's Mournin'.   Ruth McEnery Stuart.
Æsop's *Fables* :

A Wolf in Sheep's Clothing.	*The Crow and the Pitcher.*
The Fox and the Grapes.	*Belling the Cat.*

For the teacher to read to the class :

The Wonderful Tar-Baby Story, The Story of the Deluge and How It Came About, Mr. Fox is Again Victimized, Miss Cow Falls a Victim to Mr. Rabbit (from *Uncle Remus; His Songs and His Sayings*).

Kipling's *Rikki-Tikki-Tavi* (*Jungle Book*, I).

Grahame's *The River Bank* (*The Wind in the Willows*).

CHRISTIAN AND HOPEFUL IN THE DUNGEON[1]

JOHN BUNYAN

John Bunyan (1628–1688), born in a little village of England, was the son of a tinker, and followed his father's trade for several years. When grown, he became a preacher but was arrested for preaching without the sanction of the Episcopal Church, and thrown into prison. During his twelve years of imprisonment, he wrote *Pilgrim's Progress*, the greatest of all allegories.[2] It is the story of Christian's journey through this life. He has many experiences, such as with Faintheart, Mr. Worldly Wiseman, Giant Despair, and others, but finally reaches his destination, the Celestial City. Bunyan knew the *Bible* from end to end, and its influence is clearly seen in the simple, direct language of this story. He was finally allowed to return to his preaching, which he continued with the greatest enthusiasm until his death. See also:

Halleck's *New English Literature*, pp. 228–233.

Macaulay's *Essay on Southey's Edition of the Pilgrim's Progress*.

Macaulay's *Life of Bunyan* in his *Essays*.

Now there was, not far from the place where they lay, a castle, called Doubting Castle, the owner whereof was Giant Despair, and it was in his grounds they now were sleeping. Wherefore he, getting up in the morning early, and walking up and down in his fields, caught Christian and Hopeful asleep in his grounds. Then with a grim and surly voice he bid them awake, and asked them whence they were, and what they did in his grounds. They told him they were pilgrims, and that they had lost their way. Then said the giant, "You have this night trespassed on me by trampling in and lying on my grounds, and therefore you must go along

---

[1] From *The Pilgrim's Progress* (1678).

[2] An allegory is a story told with the purpose of teaching a moral lesson. The characters are usually personified qualities.

with me." So they were forced to go, because he was stronger than they.

Now Giant Despair had a wife, and her name was Diffidence. So when he was gone to bed he told his wife what he had done, to wit, that he had taken a couple of prisoners, and cast them into his dungeon for trespassing on his grounds. Then he asked her also what he had best do further to them. So she asked him what they were, whence they came, and whither they were bound, and he told her. Then she counseled him, that when he arose in the morning he should beat them without mercy. So when he arose, he getteth him a grievous crab-tree cudgel, and goes down into the dungeon to them, and there first falls to rating of them as if they were dogs, although they gave him never a word of distaste. Then he falls upon them, and beats them fearfully, in such sort that they were not able to help themselves, or to turn them upon the floor. This done, he withdraws and leaves them there to condole their misery, and to mourn under their distress: so all that day they spent the time in nothing but sighs and bitter lamentations. The next night, she, talking with her husband further about them, and understanding that they were yet alive, did advise him to counsel them to make away with themselves. So when morning was come, he goes to them in a surly manner, as before, and perceiving them to be very sore with the stripes that he had given them the day before, he told them that since they were never like to come out of that place, their only way would be forthwith to make an end of themselves, either with knife, halter, or poison. "For why," said he, "should you choose to live, seeing it is attended with so much bitterness?" But they desired him to let them go. With that he looked ugly upon them, and rushing to them, had doubtless made an end of them himself, but that he fell into one of his fits (for he sometimes in sunshiny weather fell into fits) and lost for a time the use of his hands; wherefore he withdrew, and left them as before to consider what to do.

Well, towards evening the giant goes down into the dungeon again, to see if his prisoners had taken his counsel. But when he came there he found them alive; and truly, alive was all; for now, what for want of bread and water, and by reason of the wounds they received when he beat them, they could do little but breathe. But I say he found them alive; at which he fell into a grievous rage, and told them that seeing they had disobeyed his counsel, it should be worse with them than if they had never been born.

Now the night being come again, his wife asked the giant concerning the prisoners, and if they had taken his counsel: to which he replied, "They are sturdy rogues; they choose rather to bear all hardships than to make away with themselves." Then said she, "Take them into the castle yard to-morrow, and show them the bones and skulls of those that thou hast already dispatched, and make them believe, ere a week comes to an end, thou wilt tear them in pieces, as thou hast done their fellows before them."

So when the morning was come, the giant goes to them again, and takes them into the castle yard, and shows them as his wife had bidden him. "These," said he, "were pilgrims, as you are, once, and they trespassed on my grounds, as you have done; and when I thought fit I tore them in pieces; and so within ten days I will do you; get you down to your den again." And with that he beat them all the way thither. They lay therefore all day on Saturday in a lamentable case, as before.

Now, a little before it was day, good Christian, as one half amazed, broke out into this passionate speech: "What a fool," quoth he, "am I, thus to lie in a stinking dungeon, when I may as well walk at liberty! I have a key in my bosom, called Promise, that will, I am persuaded, open any lock in Doubting Castle." Then said Hopeful, "That is good news; good brother, pluck it out of thy bosom, and try."

Then Christian pulled it out of his bosom, and began to try at the dungeon door, whose bolt, as he turned the key, gave back, and the door flew open with ease, and Christian and Hopeful both came out. Then he went to the outward door that leads into the castle yard, and with his key opened that door also. After that he went to the iron gate, for that must be opened too; but that lock went desperately hard, yet the key did open it. Then they thrust open the gate to make their escape with speed; but that gate, as it opened, made such a creaking that it waked Giant Despair, who hastily rising to pursue his prisoners, felt his limbs to fail, for his fits took him again, so that he could by no means go after them. Then they went on, and came to the King's highway, and so were safe, because they were out of his jurisdiction.

STUDY HINTS

Study the spelling and meaning of these words:

doubt	disobey	fly, flew, flown
dungeon	prisoners	lose, lost, lost
grievous	desperately	choose, chose, chosen
counsel	lie, lay, lain	trespassed

This story is told in so simple and direct a way that it can be readily understood without questions.

SUGGESTIONS FOR ORAL AND WRITTEN ENGLISH
THEME SUBJECTS

In which of the stories you have read so far, is there much conversation? In *Zenobia's Infidelity* does the boy talk to the doctor naturally? Does he say what is necessary for his purpose, and no more? In *How Mr. Rabbit Was Too Sharp for Mr. Fox*, how much of the story is in conversation? Does it add to the interest? When writing dialogue, *i.e.* a conversation between two, for a play, do not write "he said," or similar terms, as you would in the case of novels or short stories. Each time there is a change of speaker, write the speaker's name on the left on a new line and follow it with a colon, then begin the speech as you would begin a sentence. Try to have your speakers express themselves naturally. Perhaps you can give a conversation you have overheard in some public place.

Write in the form of dialogues the indicated conversations between the giant and the pilgrims, and the giant and his wife. Write their names under the heading *Characters*. Take each episode after you have written the dialogue and write the place, the time, and a heading for the episode, as, for example,

Act I., Doubting Castle, — Early Morning.
Giant Despair's Discovery of the Pilgrims.

Can you make a complete outline of four acts? Try to do the same in *Hop O' My Thumb*, or *Jack the Giant Killer*, or any similar fairy tale.

SUGGESTIONS FOR ADDITIONAL READINGS

From *The Pilgrim's Progress:*
　　The Slough of Despond.　　　*At the House Beautiful.*
　　Mr. Great Heart.　　　　　*The Celestial City.*
The Great Stone Face (in *The Snow Image*).　Nathaniel Hawthorne.
Dr. Heidegger's Experiment (in *Twice-Told Tales*).　Nathaniel Hawthorne.
The Man Without a Country.　Edward Everett Hale.
The Dawn of To-morrow.　Frances Hodgson Burnett.

SKIPPER IRESON'S RIDE[1]

JOHN GREENLEAF WHITTIER

The Quaker poet, John Greenleaf Whittier (1807–1892), was born in Haverhill, Massachusetts. He received only two years of academic training. He edited and contributed to newspapers for over twenty years, and published during that time many volumes of poems. His *Snow Bound* is a perfect picture of a New England country home. See also:

Halleck's *History of American Literature*, pp. 234–244, 284.
Carpenter's *John Greenleaf Whittier*.
Perry's *John Greenleaf Whittier*.
Pickard's *Life and Letters of John Greenleaf Whittier;* and *Whittier-Land*.

1. OF all the rides, since the birth of time,
   Told in story or sung in rime —
   On Apuleius's Golden Ass,[2]
   Or one-eyed Calendar's horse of brass,[3]
   Witch astride of a human hack,
   Islam's prophet[4] on Al-Borak[5] —
   The strangest ride that ever was sped
   Was Ireson's, out from Marblehead !
      Old Floyd Ireson, for his hard heart,
      Tarred and feathered and carried in a cart
      By the women of Marblehead !

---

[1] This poem is used by permission of, and by arrangement with, Houghton Mifflin Company, authorized publishers of Whittier's works.
[2] *The Golden Ass*, the most celebrated book of Apuleius, a Roman philosopher of the second century A.D.
[3] A story from *Arabian Nights Entertainments*.   [4] Mohammed.
[5] A wondrous animal on which Mohammed rode from Mecca to Jerusalem.

2. Body of turkey, head of owl,
    Wings a-droop like a rained-on fowl,
    Feathered and ruffled in every part,
    Skipper Ireson stood in the cart.
    Scores of women, old and young,
    Strong of muscle, and glib of tongue,
    Pushed and pulled up the rocky lane,
    Shouting and singing the shrill refrain:
        "Here's Flud Oirson, fur his horrd horrt,
        Torr'd an' futherr'd an' corr'd in a corrt
            By the women o' Morble'ead!"

3. Wrinkled scolds with hands on hips,
    Girls in bloom of cheek and lips,
    Wild-eyed, free-limbed, such as chase
    Bacchus [1] round some antique vase,
    Brief of skirt, with ankles bare,
    Loose of kerchief and loose of hair,
    With conch-shells blowing and fish-horns' twang,
    Over and over the Mænads [2] sang:
        "Here's Flud Oirson, fur his horrd horrt,
        Torr'd an' futherr'd an' corr'd in a corrt
            By the women o' Morble'ead!"

4. Small pity for him! — he sailed away
    From a leaking ship in Chaleur Bay [3] —
    Sailed away from a sinking wreck,
    With his own townspeople on her deck!
    "Lay by! lay by!" they called to him;
    Back he answered, "Sink or swim!
    Brag of your catch of fish again!"
    And off he sailed through the fog and rain!

---

[1] The god of wine.
[2] Priestesses of Bacchus who became frenzied when they danced in his train.
[3] An inlet in the Gulf of St. Lawrence.

Old Floyd Ireson, for his hard heart,
Tarred and feathered and carried in a cart
By the women of Marblehead!

5. Fathoms deep in dark Chaleur
That wreck shall lie for evermore.
Mother and sister, wife and maid,
Looked from the rocks of Marblehead
Over the moaning and rainy sea —
Looked for the coming that might not be!
What did the winds and the sea birds say
Of the cruel captain who sailed away? —
Old Floyd Ireson, for his hard heart,
Tarred and feathered and carried in a cart
By the women of Marblehead!

6. Through the street, on either side,
Up flew windows, doors swung wide,
Sharp-tongued spinsters, old wives gray,
Treble lent the fish-horn's bray.
Sea-worn grandsires, cripple-bound,
Hulks of old sailors run aground,
Shook head and fist and hat and cane,
And cracked with curses the hoarse refrain:
"Here's Flud Oirson, fur his horrd horrt,
Torr'd an' futherr'd an' corr'd in a corrt
By the women o' Morble'ead!"

7. Sweetly along the Salem road
Bloom of orchard and lilac showed.
Little the wicked skipper knew
Of the fields so green and the sky so blue.
Riding there in his sorry trim,
Like an Indian idol glum and grim,

Scarcely he seemed the sound to hear
Of voices shouting far and near:
   "Here's Flud Oirson, fur his horrd horrt,
   Torr'd an' futherr'd an' corr'd in a corrt
   By the women o' Morble'ead!"

8. "Hear me, neighbors!" at last he cried —
"What to me is this noisy ride?
What is the shame that clothes the skin
To the nameless horror that lives within?
Waking or sleeping, I see a wreck,
And hear a cry from a reeling deck!
Hate me and curse me — I only dread
The hand of God and the face of the dead!"
   Said old Floyd Ireson, for his hard heart,
   Tarred and feathered and carried in a cart
   By the women of Marblehead!

9. Then the wife of the skipper lost at sea
Said, *"God has touched him! — why should we?"*
Said an old wife mourning her only son,
"Cut the rogue's tether, and let him run!"
So with soft relentings and rude excuse,
Half scorn, half pity, they cut him loose,
And gave him a cloak to hide him in,
And left him alone with his shame and sin.
   Poor Floyd Ireson, for his hard heart,
   Tarred and feathered and carried in a cart
   By the women of Marblehead!

STUDY HINTS

Study the spelling and meaning of these words:

refrain	rime	treble
loose	horror	scorn
glum	relenting	feathered
nameless	neighbors	lilac

At what season of the year did this event occur? What difference in emotion is expressed in stanzas 3 and 5? Find a picture of an antique vase in a history of Greece or Rome, or look at a piece of old Wedgwood pottery. You will then understand stanza 3 better. What makes the skipper seem so glum? Was he moved by his disgrace? Why? Who were the first to suggest that he be set free? Would you have set him free? Can you find any reason for the changes in the refrain?

SUGGESTIONS FOR ADDITIONAL READINGS

Mabel Martin.   John Greenleaf Whittier.
The Barefoot Boy.   John Greenleaf Whittier.
Maud Muller.   John Greenleaf Whittier.
The Inchcape Rock.   Robert Southey.
The Wreck of the Hesperus.   Henry Wadsworth Longfellow.
Alec Yeaton's Son.   Thomas Bailey Aldrich.
Goody Blake and Harry Gill.   William Wordsworth.

THE TWO MATCHES [1]

ROBERT LOUIS STEVENSON

Robert Louis Stevenson (1850–1894) was born in Edinburgh, Scotland. From early boyhood he was so interested in learning to write that he carried two books in his pocket, one to read, the other for writing. This strong love for writing forced him to drop all other forms of work and to adopt the profession of letters. After seeking health in many places he settled in Samoa, where his talent won from the natives the name Tusitala, "teller of tales." The road to his home was constructed by the natives, who, to show their love for him, named it, "The Road of the Loving Heart." He died in Samoa and lies buried on the top of a mountain in the village of Apia. No one who reads his books, *Treasure Island*, for example, would think that the author had to struggle against illness every day for fourteen years. His writings are full of courage and joyousness. See also:

Halleck's *New English Literature*, pp. 516–523, 583.
Balfour's *The Life of Robert Louis Stevenson*.

ONE day there was a traveler in the woods in California, in the dry season, when the trades were blowing strong. He had ridden a long way, and he was tired and hungry, and dismounted from his horse to smoke a pipe. But when he felt in his pocket, he found but two matches. He struck the first, and it would not light.

"Here is a pretty state of things," said the traveler. "Dying for a smoke; only one match left; and that certain to miss fire! Was there ever a creature so unfortunate? And yet," thought the traveler, "suppose I light this match, and smoke my pipe, and shake out the dottle here in the grass — the grass might catch on fire, for it is dry like tinder; and while I snatch out the flames in front, they might evade

[1] From *Fables* (1887).

and run behind me, and seize upon yon bush of poison oak; before I could reach it, that would have blazed up; over the bush I see a pine tree hung with moss; that too would fly in fire upon the instant to its topmost bough; and the flame of that long torch — how would the trade wind take and brandish that through the inflammable forest! I hear this dell roar in a moment with the joint voice of wind and fire, I see myself gallop for my soul, and the flying conflagration chase and outflank me through the hills; I see this pleasant forest burn for days, and the cattle roasted, and the springs dried up, and the farmer ruined, and his children cast upon the world. What a world hangs upon this moment!"

With that he struck the match, and it missed fire.

"Thank God," said the traveler, and put his pipe in his pocket.

STUDY HINTS

Study the spelling and meaning of these words:

traveler	evade	ride, rode, ridden
unfortunate	inflammable	seize
tinder	conflagration	run, ran, run

What is the situation at the opening of this story? Could a single match have started all the trouble that the traveler feared? What was certain to result if he did not try to strike the match? Was he too much exercised over the matter?

SUGGESTIONS FOR ORAL AND WRITTEN ENGLISH
THEME SUBJECTS

The Two Matches is a fable. Look up "fable" in a dictionary and see if you can understand why this is one. Read one of Æsop's fables, and tell it to the class. Explain the difference between a fable and other short stories. Write a fable on a subject of your own selection, or on one of these:

> No Cloud Without a Silver Lining.
> All is Not Gold That Glisters.
> Nothing Venture, Nothing Have.
> A Stitch in Time Saves Nine.

What is Forestry?
The Duties of a Forester.
How Forestry May Control Floods.
The Best Way to Make a Camp
    Fire.

Some Forestry Laws in my State.
Tree Surgery.
Our National Forests.
How to Make a Fire Without a
    Match.

SUGGESTIONS FOR ADDITIONAL READINGS

Kidnapped.   Robert Louis Stevenson.
The Master of Ballantrae.   Robert Louis Stevenson.
Sire De Maletroit's Door.   Robert Louis Stevenson.
Æsop's *Fables:*
The Dog in the Manger.
The Horse, Hunter, and Stag.
The Shepherd Boy.
The Wind and the Sun.

The Lion in Love.
*The Town Mouse and the Country
    Mouse.*
The Goose with the Golden Eggs.

THE BALLAD OF THE OYSTERMAN [1]

OLIVER WENDELL HOLMES

Oliver Wendell Holmes (1809–1894) was born in Cambridge, Massachusetts, in the same year as Abraham Lincoln. He belonged to the group of writers known as the New England Group, which included Emerson, Thoreau, Hawthorne, Longfellow, Whittier, and Lowell. He wrote novels, essays, and poems, all of which show a delightful vein of humor. In his poetry the humor is particularly rollicking, as is plainly shown in the selection given below. See also:

Halleck's *History of American Literature*, pp. 258–265, 284.
Morse's *Life and Letters of Oliver Wendell Holmes*.

IT was a tall young oysterman lived by the riverside,
His shop was just upon the bank, his boat was on the tide;
The daughter of a fisherman, that was so straight and slim,
Lived over on the other bank, right opposite to him.

It was the pensive oysterman that saw a lovely maid,
Upon a moonlight evening, a-sitting in the shade;
He saw her wave a handkerchief, as much as if to say,
"I'm wide awake, young oysterman, and all the folks away."

Then up rose the oysterman, and to himself said he,
"I guess I'll leave the skiff at home, for fear that folks should see;
I read it in the story book, that, for to kiss his dear,
Leander swam the Hellespont [2] — and I will swim this here."

---

[1] This poem is used by permission of, and by arrangement with, Houghton Mifflin Company, authorized publishers of Holmes's works.

[2] Leander loved Hero, and visited her every night by swimming across the Hellespont. He was drowned in a storm, and Hero, in her grief, flung herself into the water.

And he has leaped into the waves, and crossed the shining
    stream,
And he has clambered up the bank, all in the moonlight gleam ;
Oh, there are kisses sweet as dew, and words as soft as rain —
But they have heard her father's steps, and in he leaps again !

Out spoke the ancient fisherman : "Oh, what was that, my
    daughter ? "
" 'Twas nothing but a pebble, sir, I threw into the water."
"And what is that, pray tell me, love, that paddles off so
    fast ? "
"It's nothing but a porpoise, sir, that's been a-swimming
    past."

Out spoke the ancient fisherman : "Now bring me my har-
    poon !
I'll get into my fishing boat, and fix the fellow soon."
Down fell the pretty innocent, as falls a snow-white lamb ;
Her hair drooped round her pallid cheeks, like seaweed on a
    clam.

Alas for those two loving ones ! she waked not from her
    swound,
And he was taken with the cramp, and in the waves was
    drowned ;
But Fate has metamorphosed [1] them, in pity of their woe,
And now they keep an oyster shop for mermaids down below.

SUGGESTIONS FOR ADDITIONAL READINGS

The Deacon's Masterpiece.   Oliver Wendell Holmes.
The Diverting History of John Gilpin.   William Cowper.
The Walrus and the Carpenter.   Lewis Carroll.
The Courtin'.   James Russell Lowell.

For the teacher to read to the class :
The Chambered Nautilus and *The Boys*, by Holmes.

[1] Changed.

THREE SEA PICTURES AND A MORAL

SAMUEL TAYLOR COLERIDGE

Samuel Taylor Coleridge (1772–1834) was born in Devonshire, England. He was a daydreamer from early childhood. For many years Coleridge lived in the Lake Country and he is known as one of the Lake Poets. The *Ancient Mariner*, from which these selections are taken, was composed while the poet was on a walking tour with his friends, Wordsworth and his sister Dorothy. It is his poetical masterpiece. See also:

Halleck's *New English Literature*, pp. 398–406.
Herford's *The Age of Wordsworth* (Coleridge).
Traill's *Coleridge*.
Caine's *Life of Coleridge*.

I

The Antarctic Ocean and the Albatross

AND now there came both mist and snow,
And it grew wondrous cold:
And ice, mast-high, came floating by,
As green as emerald.

And through the drifts the snowy clifts
Did send a dismal sheen:
Nor shapes of men nor beasts we ken —
The ice was all between.

The ice was here, the ice was there,
The ice was all around:
It cracked and growled, and roared and howled,
Like voices in a swound!

At length did cross an Albatross,[1]
Thorough [2] the fog it came;
As if it had been a Christian soul,
We hailed it in God's name.

It ate the food it ne'er had eat,
And round and round it flew.
The ice did split with a thunder-fit;
The helmsman steered us through!

And a good south wind sprung up behind;
The Albatross did follow,
And every day, for food or play,
Came to the mariner's hollo!

In mist or cloud, on mast or shroud,
It perched for vespers nine;
While all the night, through fog-smoke white,
Glimmered the white moonshine.

"God save thee, ancient Mariner!
From the fiends that plague thee thus! —
Why look'st thou so?" — "With my crossbow
I shot the Albatross."

[1] A large sea bird.   [2] Through.

II

Daytime on the Tropical Ocean

All in a hot and copper sky,
The bloody sun, at noon,
Right up above the mast did stand,
No bigger than the moon.

Day after day, day after day,
We stuck, nor breath nor motion;
As idle as a painted ship
Upon a painted ocean.

Water, water, everywhere,
And all the boards did shrink;
Water, water, everywhere
Nor any drop to drink.

III

Nighttime on the Tropical Ocean

The moving moon went up the sky,
And nowhere did abide:
Softly she was going up,
And a star or two beside —

Her beams bemocked the sultry main,
Like April hoarfrost spread;
But where the ship's huge shadow lay,
The charmèd water burnt alway
A still and awful red.

Beyond the shadow of the ship,
I watched the water snakes;
They moved in tracks of shining white,
And when they reared, the elfish light
Fell off in hoary flakes.

Within the shadow of the ship
I watched their rich attire;
Blue, glossy green, and velvet black,
They coiled and swam; and every track
Was a flash of golden fire.

O happy living things ! no tongue
Their beauty might declare:
A spring of love gushed from my heart,
And I blessed them unaware:
Sure my kind saint took pity on me,
And I blessed them unaware.

The selfsame moment I could pray;
And from my neck so free
The Albatross fell off, and sank
Like lead into the sea.

IV

The Moral

O Wedding-Guest ! this soul hath been
Alone on a wide wide sea:
So lonely, 'twas, that God himself
Scarce seemèd there to be.

O sweeter than the marriage feast,
'Tis sweeter far to me,
To walk together to the kirk,[1]
With a goodly company ! —

To walk together to the kirk,
And all together pray,
While each to his great Father bends,
Old men, and babes, and loving friends
And youths and maidens gay !

[1] Church.

Farewell, farewell ! but this I tell
To thee, thou Wedding-Guest !
He prayeth well, who loveth well
Both man and bird and beast.

He prayeth best, who loveth best
All things both great and small ;
For the dear God who loveth us,
He made and loveth all.

STUDY HINTS

Try to see each picture vividly as it is painted.   Contrast the three.

I. Why did the sailors welcome the albatross so joyfully?   Judging from his hearer's question, how do you think the Ancient Mariner looked when he spoke of killing the bird?   What circumstances made his deed seem more heinous?

II. Contrast the stillness of this with the preceding scene.   What effect does the repetition of such phrases as "day after day" produce on you?

III. Is this scene as full of action as I?   Is it as quiet as II?   What is the difference in each case?

The albatross had been hung around the Mariner's neck by the other sailors as a punishment.   At what point does his punishment end ?   Can you give a reason for this?   Memorize at least the last eight lines.

SUGGESTIONS FOR ADDITIONAL READINGS

Two Years Before the Mast.   R. H. Dana, Jr.

For the teacher to read to the class:

Selections from Coleridge's *Christabel*, and *Kubla Khan.*

A DESCENT INTO THE MAELSTROM

EDGAR ALLAN POE

Edgar Allan Poe (1809–1849) was born in Boston. Being left an orphan at the age of three, he was adopted by a wealthy Virginian. In early manhood he offended his foster father, who finally disowned Poe. His life, a singularly unhappy one, was one long struggle with poverty. He perfected the short story and wrote very unusual poetry as well as prose. *The Raven* is his best-known poem. With the exception of Hawthorne, America has produced no genius equal to Poe. See also:

Halleck's *History of American Literature*, pp. 293–306, 338.
Woodberry's *The Life of Edgar Allan Poe, Personal and Literary*.
Canby's *The Short Story in English*, Chapter XI (Poe).

WE had now reached the summit of the loftiest crag. For some minutes the old man seemed too much exhausted to speak.

"Not long ago," said he at length, "and I could have guided you on this route as well as the youngest of my sons; but, about three years past, there happened to me an event such as never happened before to mortal man — or at least such as no man ever survived to tell of — and the six hours of deadly terror which I then endured have broken me up body and soul. You suppose me a *very* old man — but I am not. It took less than a single day to change these hairs from a jetty black to white, to weaken my limbs, and to unstring my nerves, so that I tremble at the least exertion, and am frightened at a shadow. Do you know I can scarcely look over this little cliff without getting giddy?"

The "little cliff," upon whose edge he had so carelessly thrown himself down to rest that the weightier portion of his body hung over it, while he was only kept from falling by the tenure of his elbow on its extreme and slippery edge — this "little cliff" arose, a sheer unobstructed precipice of black shining rock, some fifteen or sixteen hundred feet from the world of crags beneath us. Nothing would have tempted me to within half a dozen yards of its brink. In truth so deeply was I excited by the perilous position of my companion, that I fell at full length upon the ground, clung to the shrubs around me, and dared not even glance upward at the sky — while I struggled in vain to divest myself of the idea that the very foundations of the mountain were in danger from the fury of the winds. It was long before I could reason myself into sufficient courage to sit up and look out into the distance.

"You must get over these fancies," said the guide, "for I have brought you here that you might have the best possible view of the scene of that event I mentioned — and to tell you the whole story with the spot just under your eye.

"We are now," he continued, in that particularizing manner which distinguished him — "we are now close upon the Norwegian coast — in the sixty-eighth degree of latitude — in the great province of Nordland — and in the dreary district of Lofoden.[1] The mountain upon whose top we sit is Helseggen, the Cloudy. Now raise yourself up a little higher — hold on to the grass if you feel giddy — so — and look out, beyond the belt of vapor beneath us, into the sea."

I looked dizzily, and beheld a wide expanse of ocean, whose waters wore so inky a hue as to bring at once to my mind the Nubian geographer's account of the *Mare Tenebrarum*.[2] A panorama more deplorably desolate no human imagination can conceive. To the right and left, as far as the eye could reach, there lay outstretched, like ramparts of the world, lines of horridly black and beetling cliff, whose character of gloom

[1] Islands west of Norway.   [2] " Sea of Darkness," — the Atlantic.

was but the more forcibly illustrated by the surf which reared high up against it its white and ghastly crest, howling and shrieking forever. Just opposite the promontory upon whose apex we were placed, and at a distance of some five or six miles out at sea, there was visible a small, bleak-looking island; or, more properly, its position was discernible through the wilderness of surge in which it was enveloped. About two miles nearer the land arose another of smaller size, hideously craggy and barren, and encompassed at various intervals by a cluster of dark rocks.

The appearance of the ocean, in the space between the more distant island and the shore, had something very unusual about it. Although, at the time, so strong a gale was blowing landward that a brig in the remote offing [1] lay to under a double-reefed trysail, and constantly plunged her whole hull out of sight, still there was here nothing like a regular swell, but only a short, quick, angry cross dashing of water in every direction — as well in the teeth of the wind as otherwise. Of foam there was little except in the immediate vicinity of the rocks.

"The island in the distance," resumed the old man, "is called by the Norwegians Vurrgh. The one midway is Moskoe. That a mile to the northward is Ambaaren. Yonder are Iflesen, Hoeyholm, Kieldholm, Suarven, and Buckholm. Farther off — between Moskoe and Vurrgh — are Otterholm, Flimen, Sandflesen, and Skarholm. These are the true names of the places — but why it has been thought necessary to name them at all is more than either you or I can understand. Do you hear anything? Do you see any change in the water?"

We had now been about ten minutes upon the top of Helseggen, to which we had ascended from the interior of Lofoden, so that we had caught no glimpse of the sea until it had

[1] Deep water off the shore.

burst upon us from the summit. As the old man spoke, I
became aware of a loud and gradually increasing sound, like
the moaning of a vast herd of buffaloes upon an American
prairie; and at the same moment I perceived that what seamen term the *chopping* character of the ocean beneath us, was
rapidly changing into a current which set to the eastward.
Even while I gazed, this current acquired a monstrous velocity. Each moment added to its speed — to its headlong
impetuosity. In five minutes the whole sea, as far as Vurrgh,
was lashed into ungovernable fury; but it was between
Moskoe and the coast that the main uproar held its sway.
Here the vast bed of the waters, seamed and scarred into a
thousand conflicting channels, burst suddenly into frenzied
convulsion — heaving, boiling, hissing, — gyrating in gigantic
and innumerable vortices, and all whirling and plunging on
to the eastward with a rapidity which water never elsewhere
assumes, except in precipitous descents.

In a few minutes more, there came over the scene another
radical alteration. The general surface grew somewhat more
smooth, and the whirlpools, one by one, disappeared, while
prodigious streaks of foam became apparent where none had
been seen before. These streaks, at length, spreading out to
a great distance, and entering into combination, took unto
themselves the gyratory motion of the subsided vortices, and
seemed to form the germ of another more vast. Suddenly —
very suddenly — this assumed a distinct and definite existence, in a circle of more than a mile in diameter. The edge
of the whirl was represented by a broad belt of gleaming
spray; but no particle of this slipped into the mouth of the
terrific funnel, whose interior, as far as the eye could fathom
it, was a smooth, shining, and jet-black wall of water, inclined
to the horizon at an angle of some forty-five degrees, speeding
dizzily round and round with a swaying and sweltering motion, and sending forth to the winds an appalling voice, half

shriek, half roar, such as not even the mighty cataract of Niagara ever lifts up in its agony to heaven.

The mountain trembled to its very base, and the rock rocked. I threw myself upon my face, and clung to the scant herbage in an excess of nervous agitation.

"This," said I at length, to the old man — " this *can* be nothing else than the great whirlpool of the Maelstrom." [1]

"So it is sometimes termed," said he. "We Norwegians call it the Moskoe-strom, from the island of Moskoe in the midway." . . .

"You have had a good look at the whirl now," said the old man, "and if you will creep round this crag, so as to get in its lee, and deaden the roar of the water, I will tell you a story that will convince you I ought to know something of the Moskoe-strom."

I placed myself as desired, and he proceeded.

"Myself and my two brothers once owned a schooner-rigged smack of about seventy tons burden, with which we were in the habit of fishing among the islands beyond Moskoe, nearly to Vurrgh. In all violent eddies at sea there is good fishing, at proper opportunities, if one has only the courage to attempt it; but among the whole of the Lofoden coastmen we three were the only ones who made a regular business of going out to the islands, as I tell you. The usual grounds are a great way lower down to the southward. There fish can be got at all hours, without much risk, and therefore these places are preferred. The choice spots over here among the rocks, however, not only yield the finest variety, but in far greater abundance; so that we often got in a single day what the more timid of the craft could not scrape together in a week. In fact, we made it a matter of desperate specu-lation — the risk of life standing instead of labor, and courage answering for capital.

[1] Literally " grinding stream ."

"We kept the smack in a cove about five miles higher up the coast than this; and it was our practice, in fine weather, to take advantage of the fifteen minutes' slack to push across the main channel of the Moskoe-strom, far above the pool, and then drop down upon anchorage somewhere near Otterholm, or Sandflesen, where the eddies are not so violent as elsewhere. Here we used to remain until nearly time for slack water again, when we weighed and made for home. We never set out upon this expedition without a steady side wind for going and coming — one that we felt sure would not fail us before our return — and we seldom made a miscalculation upon this point. Twice, during six years, we were forced to stay all night at anchor on account of a dead calm, which is a rare thing indeed just about here; and once we had to remain on the grounds nearly a week, starving to death, owing to a gale which blew up shortly after our arrival, and made the channel too boisterous to be thought of. Upon this occasion we should have been driven out to sea in spite of everything (for the whirlpools threw us round and round so violently, that, at length, we fouled our anchor and dragged it) if it had not been that we drifted into one of the innumerable cross currents — here to-day and gone to-morrow — which drove us under the lee of Flimen, where, by good luck, we brought up.

"I could not tell you the twentieth part of the difficulties we encountered 'on the ground' — it is a bad spot to be in, even in good weather — but we made shift always to run the gantlet of the Moskoe-strom itself without accident; although at times my heart has been in my mouth when we happened to be a minute or so behind or before the slack. The wind sometimes was not as strong as we thought it at starting, and then we made rather less way than we could wish, while the current rendered the smack unmanageable. My eldest brother had a son eighteen years old, and I had

two stout boys of my own. These would have been of great
assistance at such times, in using the sweeps, as well as afterward in fishing — but, somehow, although we ran the risk
ourselves, we had not the heart to let the young ones get into
the danger — for, after all said and done, it *was* a horrible
danger, and that is the truth.

"It is now within a few days of three years since what I am
going to tell you occurred. It was on the tenth of July, 18—,
a day which the people of this part of the world will never
forget — for it was one in which blew the most terrible hurricane that ever came out of the heavens. And yet all the
morning, and indeed until late in the afternoon, there was a
gentle and steady breeze from the southwest, while the sun
shone brightly, so that the oldest seamen among us could not
have foreseen what was to follow.

"The three of us — my two brothers and myself — had
crossed over to the islands about two o'clock P.M., and soon
nearly loaded the smack with fine fish, which, we all remarked,
were more plenty that day than we had ever known them.   It
was just seven, *by my watch*, when we weighed and started for
home, so as to make the worst of the Strom at slack water,
which we knew would be at eight.

"We set out with a fresh wind on our starboard quarter,
and for some time spanked along at a great rate, never dreaming of danger, for indeed we saw not the slightest reason to
apprehend it.   All at once we were taken aback by a breeze
from over Helseggen.   This was most unusual — something
that had never happened to us before — and I began to feel a
little uneasy, without exactly knowing why.   We put the
boat on the wind, but could make no headway at all for the
eddies, and I was upon the point of proposing to return to
the anchorage, when, looking astern, we saw the whole horizon covered with a singular copper-colored cloud that rose
with the most amazing velocity.

"In the meantime the breeze that had headed us off fell away, and we were dead becalmed, drifting about in every direction. This state of things, however, did not last long enough to give us time to think about it. In less than a minute the storm was upon us — in less than two the sky was entirely overcast — and what with this and the driving spray, it became suddenly so dark that we could not see each other in the smack.

"Such a hurricane as then blew it is folly to attempt describing. The oldest seaman in Norway never experienced anything like it. We had let our sails go by the run before it cleverly took us; but, at the first puff, both our masts went by the board as if they had been sawed off — the mainmast taking with it my youngest brother, who had lashed himself to it for safety.

"Our boat was the lightest feather of a thing that ever sat upon water. It had a complete flush [1] deck, with only a small hatch near the bow, and this hatch it had always been our custom to batten [2] down when about to cross the Strom, by way of precaution against the chopping seas. But for this circumstance we should have foundered at once — for we lay entirely buried for some moments. How my elder brother escaped destruction I cannot say, for I never had an opportunity of ascertaining. For my part, as soon as I had let the foresail run, I threw myself flat on deck, with my feet against the narrow gunwale of the bow, and with my hands grasping a ringbolt near the foot of the foremast. It was mere instinct that prompted me to do this — which was undoubtedly the very best thing I could have done — for I was too much flurried to think.

"For some moments we were completely deluged, as I say, and all this time I held my breath, and clung to the bolt. When I could stand it no longer I raised myself upon my

[1] That is, a continuous deck from stem to stern.   [2] Fasten.

knees, still keeping hold with my hands, and thus got my head clear.   Presently our little boat gave herself a shake, just as a dog does in coming out of the water, and thus rid herself, in some measure, of the seas.   I was now trying to get the better of the stupor that had come over me, and to collect my senses so as to see what was to be done, when I felt some-body grasp my arm.   It was my elder brother, and my heart leaped for joy, for I had made sure that he was overboard — but the next moment all this joy was turned into horror — for he put his mouth close to my ear, and screamed out the word '*Moskoe-strom!*'

"No one will ever know what my feelings were at that moment.   I shook from head to foot as if I had had the most violent fit of the ague.   I knew what he meant by that one word well enough — I knew what he wished to make me understand.   With the wind that now drove us on, we were bound for the whirl of the Strom, and nothing could save us !

"You perceive that in crossing the Strom *channel*, we always went a long way up above the whirl, even in the calmest weather, and then had to wait and watch carefully for the slack — but now we were driving right upon the pool it-self, and in such a hurricane as this !   'To be sure,' I thought, 'we shall get there just about the slack — there is some little hope in that ' — but in the next moment I cursed myself for being so great a fool as to dream of hope at all.   I knew very well that we were doomed, had we been ten times a ninety-gun ship.

"By this time the first fury of the tempest had spent itself, or perhaps we did not feel it so much as we scudded before it ; but at all events the seas, which at first had been kept down by the wind, and lay flat and frothing, now got up into absolute mountains.   A singular change, too, had come over the heavens.   Around in every direction it was still as black as pitch, but nearly overhead there burst out, all at once, a

circular rift of clear sky — as clear as I ever saw — and of a
deep bright blue — and through it there blazed forth the
full moon with a luster that I never before knew her to wear.
She lit up everything about us with the greatest distinctness
— but, oh God, what a scene it was to light up!

"I now made one or two attempts to speak to my brother
— but, in some manner which I could not understand, the
din had so increased that I could not make him hear a single
word, although I screamed at the top of my voice, in his ear.
Presently he shook his head, looking as pale as death, and
held up one of his fingers, as if to say *listen !*

"At first I could not make out what he meant — but soon
a hideous thought flashed upon me. I dragged my watch
from its fob. It was not going. I glanced at its face by the
moonlight, and then burst into tears as I flung it far away
into the ocean. *It had run down at seven o'clock ! We were
behind the time of the slack, and the whirl of the Strom was in full
fury !*

"When a boat is well built, properly trimmed, and not
deep laden, the waves in a strong gale, when she is going large,
seem always to slip from beneath her — which appears very
strange to a landsman — and this is what is called *riding*, in
sea phrase.

"Well, so far we had ridden the swells very cleverly; but
presently a gigantic sea happened to take us right under the
counter, and bore us with it as it rose — up — up — as if
into the sky. I would not have believed that any wave
could rise so high. And then down we came with a sweep, a
slide, and a plunge, that made me feel sick and dizzy, as if
I was falling from some lofty mountain top in a dream. But
while we were up I had thrown a quick glance around — and
that one glance was all sufficient. I saw our exact position
in an instant. The Moskoe-strom whirlpool was about a
quarter of a mile dead ahead — but no more like the everyday

Moskoe-strom, than the whirl as you now see it is like a mill race.   If I had known where we were, and what we had to expect, I should not have recognized the place at all.   As it was, I involuntarily closed my eyes in horror. The lids clenched themselves together as if in a spasm.

"It could not have been more than two minutes afterwards until we suddenly felt the waves subside, and were enveloped in foam.   The boat made a sharp half turn to larboard, and then shot off in its new direction like a thunder bolt.   At the same moment the roaring noise of the water was completely drowned in a kind of shrill shriek — such a sound as you might imagine given out by the water pipes of many thousand steam vessels, letting off their steam all together. We were now in the belt of surf that always surrounds the whirl; and I thought, of course, that another moment would plunge us into the abyss — down which we could only see indistinctly on account of the amazing velocity with which we were borne along.   The boat did not seem to sink into the water at all, but to skim like an air bubble upon the surface of the surge.   Her starboard side was next the whirl, and on the larboard arose the world of ocean we had left.   It stood like a huge writhing wall between us and the horizon.

"It may appear strange, but now, when we were in the very jaws of the gulf, I felt more composed than when we were only approaching it.   Having made up my mind to hope no more, I got rid of a great deal of that terror which unmanned me at first.   I suppose it was despair that strung my nerves.

"It may look like boasting — but what I tell you is truth — I began to reflect how magnificent a thing it was to die in such a manner, and how foolish it was in me to think of so paltry a consideration as my own individual life, in view of so wonderful a manifestation of God's power.   I do believe that I blushed with shame when this idea crossed my mind.   After a little while I became possessed with the keenest curiosity about the whirl itself.   I positively felt a *wish* to explore its depths, even at the sacrifice I was going to make; and my principal grief was that I should never be able to tell my old companions on shore about the mysteries I should see. These, no doubt, were singular fancies to occupy a man's mind in such extremity — and I have often thought, since, that the revolutions of the boat around the pool might have rendered me a little light-headed.

"There was another circumstance which tended to restore my self-possession; and this was the cessation of the wind, which could not reach us in our present situation — for, as you saw yourself, the belt of surf is considerably lower than the general bed of the ocean, and this latter now towered above us, a high, black, mountainous ridge. If you have never been at sea in a heavy gale, you can form no idea of the confusion of mind occasioned by the wind and spray together. They blind, deafen, and strangle you, and take away all power of action or reflection. But we were now, in a great measure, rid of these annoyances — just as death-condemned felons in prison are allowed petty indulgences, forbidden them while their doom is yet uncertain.

"How often we made the circuit of the belt it is impossible to say. We careered round and round for perhaps an hour, flying rather than floating, getting gradually more and more into the middle of the surge, and then nearer and nearer to its horrible inner edge. All this time I had never let go of the ringbolt. My brother was at the stern, holding on to a small empty water cask which had been securely lashed under the coop of the counter, and was the only thing on deck that had not been swept overboard when the gale first took us. As we approached the brink of the pit he let go his hold upon this, and made for the ring, from which, in the agony of his terror, he endeavored to force my hands, as it was not large enough to afford us both a secure grasp.   I never felt deeper grief than when I saw him attempt this act — although I knew he was a madman when he did it — a raving maniac through sheer fright. I did not care, however, to contest the point with him. I knew it could make no difference whether either of us held on at all; so I let him have the bolt, and went astern to the cask. This there was no great difficulty in doing; for the smack flew round steadily enough, and upon an even keel — only swaying to and fro, with the immense sweeps and swelters of the whirl. Scarcely had I secured myself in my new position, when we gave a wild lurch to starboard, and rushed headlong into the abyss. I muttered a hurried prayer to God, and thought all was over.

"As I felt the sickening sweep of the descent, I had instinctively tightened my hold upon the barrel, and closed my eyes. For some seconds I dared not open them — while I expected instant destruction, and wondered that I was not already in my death struggles with the water. But moment after moment elapsed. I still lived. The sense of falling had ceased; and the motion of the vessel seemed much as it had been before, while in the belt of foam, with the exception that she now lay more along. I took courage and looked once again upon the scene.

"Never shall I forget the sensations of awe, horror, and admiration with which I gazed about me. The boat appeared to be hanging, as if by magic, midway down, upon the interior surface of a funnel vast in circumference, prodigious in depth, and whose perfectly smooth sides might have been mistaken for ebony, but for the bewildering rapidity with which they spun around, and for the gleaming and ghastly radiance they shot forth, as the rays of the full moon, from that circular rift amid the clouds, which I have already described, streamed in a flood of golden glory along the black walls, and far away down into the inmost recesses of the abyss.

"At first I was too much confused to observe anything accurately. The general burst of terrific grandeur was all that I beheld. When I recovered myself a little, however, my gaze fell instinctively downward. In this direction I was able to obtain an unobstructed view, from the manner in which the smack hung on the inclined surface of the pool. She was quite upon an even keel — that is to say, her deck lay in a plane parallel with that of the water — but this latter sloped at an angle of more than forty-five degrees, so that we seemed to be lying upon our beam ends. I could not help observing, nevertheless, that I had scarcely more difficulty in maintaining my hold and footing in this situation, than if we had been upon a dead level; and this, I suppose, was owing to the speed at which we revolved.

"The rays of the moon seemed to search the very bottom of the profound gulf; but still I could make out nothing distinctly, on account of a thick mist in which everything there was enveloped, and over which there hung a magnificent rainbow, like that narrow and tottering bridge which Mussulmans say is the only pathway between Time and Eternity. This mist, or spray, was no doubt occasioned by the clashing of the great walls of the funnel, as they all met together at the bottom — but the yell that went up to the heavens from out of that mist, I dare not attempt to describe.

"Our first slide into the abyss itself, from the belt of foam above, had carried us to a great distance down the slope; but our farther descent was by no means proportionate. Round and round we swept — not with any uniform movement but in dizzying swings and jerks, that sent us sometimes only a few hundred yards — sometimes nearly the complete circuit of the whirl. Our progress downward, at each revolution, was slow, but very perceptible.

"Looking about me upon the wide waste of liquid ebony on which we were thus borne, I perceived that our boat was

not the only object in the embrace of the whirl.   Both above
and below us were visible fragments of vessels, large masses
of building timber and trunks of trees, with many smaller
articles, such as pieces of house furniture, broken boxes,
barrels, and staves.   I have already described the unnatural
curiosity which had taken the place of my original terrors.
It appeared to grow upon me as I drew nearer and nearer to
my dreadful doom.   I now began to watch, with a strange
interest, the numerous things that floated in our company.
I *must* have been delirious — for I even sought *amusement*
in speculating upon the relative velocities of their several
descents toward the foam below.   'This fir tree,' I found
myself at one time saying, 'will certainly be the next thing
that takes the awful plunge and disappears,' — and then I
was disappointed to find that the wreck of a Dutch merchant ship overtook it and went down before.   At length,
after making several guesses of this nature, and being de-
ceived in all — this fact — the fact of my invariable miscalculation, set me upon a train of reflection that made my
limbs again tremble, and my heart beat heavily once more.

"It was not a new terror that thus affected me, but the
dawn of a more exciting *hope*.   This hope arose partly from
memory, and partly from present observation.   I called to
mind the great variety of buoyant matter that strewed the
coast of Lofoden, having been absorbed and then thrown
forth by the Moskoe-strom.   By far the greater number of
the articles were shattered in the most extraordinary way —
so chafed and roughened as to have the appearance of being
stuck full of splinters — but then I distinctly recollected that
there were *some* of them which were not disfigured at all.
Now I could not account for this difference except by supposing that the roughened fragments were the only ones
which had been. *completely absorbed* — that the others had
entered the whirl at so late a period of the tide, or, from some

reason, had descended so slowly after entering, that they did not reach the bottom before the turn of the flood came, or of the ebb, as the case might be. I conceived it possible, in either instance, that they might thus be whirled up again to the level of the ocean, without undergoing the fate of those which had been drawn in more early or absorbed more rapidly. I made, also, three important observations. The first was, that as a general rule, the larger the bodies were, the more rapid their descent; the second, that, between two masses of equal extent, the one spherical, and the other *of any other shape*, the superiority in speed of descent was with the sphere; the third, that, between two masses of equal size, the one cylindrical, and the other of any other shape, the cylinder was absorbed the more slowly.

"There was one startling circumstance which went a great way in enforcing these observations, and rendering me anxious to turn them to account, and this was that, at every revolution, we passed something like a barrel, or else the yard or the mast of a vessel, while many of these things, which had been on our level when I first opened my eyes upon the wonders of the whirlpool, were now high up above us, and seemed to have moved but little from their original station.

"I no longer hesitated what to do. I resolved to lash myself securely to the water cask upon which I now held, to cut it loose from the counter, and to throw myself with it into the water. I attracted my brother's attention by signs, pointed to the floating barrels that came near us, and did everything in my power to make him understand what I was about to do. I thought at length that he comprehended my design — but, whether this was the case or not, he shook his head despairingly, and refused to move from his station by the ringbolt. It was impossible to reach him; the emergency admitted of no delay; and so, with a bitter

struggle, I resigned him to his fate, fastened myself to the
cask by means of the lashings which secured it to the counter,
and precipitated myself with it into the sea, without another
moment's hesitation.

"The result was precisely what I had hoped it might be.
As it is myself who now tell you this tale — as you see that
I *did* escape — and as you are already in possession of the
mode in which this escape was effected, and must therefore
anticipate all that I have farther to say — I will bring my
story quickly to conclusion. It might have been an hour, or
thereabout, after my quitting the smack, when, having
descended to a vast distance beneath me, it made three or
four wild gyrations in rapid succession, and, bearing my loved
brother with it, plunged headlong, at once and forever, into
the chaos of foam below. The barrel to which I was attached
sank very little farther than half the distance between the
bottom of the gulf and the spot at which I leaped overboard,
before a great change took place in the character of the whirlpool. The slope of the sides of the vast funnel became
momently less and less steep. The gyrations of the whirl
grew, gradually, less and less violent. By degrees, the froth
and the rainbow disappeared, and the bottom of the gulf
seemed slowly to uprise. The sky was clear, the winds had
gone down, and the full moon was setting radiantly in the
west, when I found myself on the surface of the ocean, in
full view of the shores of Lofoden, and above the spot where
the pool of the Moskoe-strom *had been*. It was the hour of
the slack, but the sea still heaved in mountainous waves
from the effects of the hurricane. I was borne violently into
the channel of the Strom, and in a few minutes was hurried
down the coast into the 'grounds' of the fishermen. A boat
picked me up — exhausted from fatigue — and (now that
the danger was removed) speechless from the memory of its
horror. Those who drew me on board were my old mates

and daily companions, but they knew me no more than they would have known a traveler from the spirit land. My hair, which had been raven-black the day before, was as white as you see it now. They say too that the whole expression of my countenance had changed. I told them my story — they did not believe it. I now tell it to you — and I can scarcely expect you to put more faith in it than did the merry fishermen of Lofoden."

STUDY HINTS

Study the spelling and meaning of these words:

summit	route	involuntarily
precipice	instinct	hurricane
ghastly	innumerable	velocity
panorama	precipitate	disappear

How does Poe prepare us for a tale of horror in the first paragraph? What does his description of the "little cliff" show us concerning the old fisherman? Try to see the view from the crag as the speaker saw it. What change took place in the water as they gazed down upon it? Read this magnificent description carefully. Can you find instances of the old man's courage? How did he make his escape? How much time was consumed in this experience? What one feeling is brought out in this story?

SUGGESTIONS FOR ORAL AND WRITTEN ENGLISH
THEME SUBJECTS

While the dramatic method of portraying character is used to some extent in this story, the main purpose of the writer is to arouse in the reader one feeling, that of horror. Recall one moment of terror that you have experienced. Describe your feeling, bearing in mind your climax. When you have written this, look it over carefully and mark out any expression that would weaken the general impression you wish to create. Write after this revision a brief introduction in the form of a conversation to explain whatever is necessary to an understanding of the situation. In order to make others *feel* your experience, you must first "live it" again, then tell it while you are in the mood. Determine that you will make your best friend feel as you did under one of the situations suggested here.

Keeping a Steady Head.	A Wind Storm.
Learning to Swim.	He Could Not Swim!
An Experience with a Sail Boat.	The Ice Broke.
A Terrifying Experience.	Fire!

A Ghost Story.

SUGGESTIONS FOR ADDITIONAL READINGS

The Masque of the Red Death (in *Prose Tales*).   Edgar Allan Poe.
The Pit and the Pendulum.   Edgar Allan Poe.
Hop Frog.   Edgar Allan Poe.
The Fall of the House of Usher.   Edgar Allan Poe.
Ethan Brand (in *The Snow Image*).   Nathaniel Hawthorne.
The Story of the Young Man with the Cream Tarts (in the *New Arabian Nights*).   Robert Louis Stevenson.
No Haid Pawn (*In Ole Virginia*).   Thomas Nelson Page.
The Lazy Tour of Two Idle Apprentices.   Charles Dickens.
King Solomon of Kentucky (in *Flute and Violin*).   James Lane Allen.

A GROUP OF BIRD POEMS

THE SKYLARK

PERCY BYSSHE SHELLEY

Percy Bysshe Shelley (1792–1822) was born in England three years before John Keats. Shelley is one of the great English lyric poets. Although his verse is often ethereal, airy, intangible, he loves to identify himself with the animating spirit of nature, the spirit which he finds so manifest in the skylark, night, and the west wind. No one surpasses him in this field. He was drowned in the Bay of Spezzia, Italy, the year after Keats died, and buried in the Protestant Cemetery in Rome, not far from Keats. See also:

Halleck's *New English Literature*, pp. 416–425, 446, 447.

Dowden's *Life of Shelley*.

Sharp's *Life of Shelley*.

WHAT objects are the fountains
Of thy happy strain?
What fields, or waves, or mountains?
What shapes of sky or plain?
What love of thine own kind? What ignorance of pain?

. . . .

Waking or asleep,
Thou of death must deem
Things more true and deep
Than we mortals dream,
Or how could thy notes flow in such a crystal stream?

We look before and after,
And pine for what is not:

Our sincerest laughter
With some pain is fraught;
Our sweetest songs are those that tell of saddest thought.

Yet if we could scorn
Hate, and pride, and fear;
If we were things born
Not to shed a tear,
I know not how thy joy we ever should come near.

Better than all measures
Of delightful sound,
Better than all treasures
That in books are found,
Thy skill to poet were, thou scorner of the ground!

Teach me half the gladness
That thy brain must know,
Such harmonious madness
From my lips would flow,
The world should listen then, as I am listening now.

THE FIRST MOCKING BIRD IN SPRING [1]

Paul Hamilton Hayne

Paul Hamilton Hayne (1830–1886) was born in Charleston, South Carolina. He was educated for the profession of law, but devoted all his spare time to writing. In the Civil War, he lost both fortune and health. He spent his last years in a rude hut in the woods of Georgia, where he wrote many of his best poems. His poetry is musical, and shows an intimate love of nature. See also:

Halleck's *History of American Literature*, pp. 311, 312, 337.

Pickett's *Literary Hearthstones of Dixie*.

Edward Mims in *Library of Southern Literature*.

[1] Used by special arrangement with Lothrop, Lee, and Shepard Company, publishers of Hayne's *Poetical Works*.

THE wren and the field lark listen
   To the gush from their laureate's throat;
And the bluebird stops on the oak to catch
   Each rounded and perfect note.
The sparrow, his pert head reared aloft,
Has ceased to chirp in the grassy croft,
And is bending the curves of his tiny ear
In the *pose* of a critic wise, to hear.
A blackbird, perched on a glistening gum,
Seems lost in a rapture, deep and dumb;
And as eagerly still in his trancèd hush,
'Mid the copse beneath, is a clear-eyed thrush.
No longer the dove by the thorn-tree root
Moans sad and soft as a far-off flute.
All Nature is hearkening, charmed and mute.

TAMPA ROBINS [1]

SIDNEY LANIER

Sidney Lanier (1842–1881) was born of an old, cultured family in Macon, Georgia. He served four years in the Confederate army, was imprisoned, and suffered many hardships. After six years of struggle with ill health and hard study, he was appointed lecturer on English literature at Johns Hopkins University. He died two years later. In some of his poetry he has never been surpassed by any American poet. See also:

Halleck's *History of American Literature*, pp. 313–317, 338.
Edward Mims's *Sidney Lanier*.
Burt's *The Lanier Book*.
Ward's *Memorial of Sidney Lanier*, in *Poems* by Sidney Lanier, edited by his wife.

   THE robin laughed in the orange tree:
   "Ho, windy North, a fig for thee:

[1] From *Poems* by Sidney Lanier, copyright, 1884, 1891, by Charles Scribner's Sons. Used by special arrangement with the publishers.

While breasts are red and wings are bold
And green trees wave us globes of gold,
   Time's scythe shall reap but bliss for me
   — Sunlight, song, and the orange tree.

" Burn, golden globes in leafy sky,
My orange planets : crimson I
Will shine and shoot among the spheres
(Blithe meteor that no mortal fears)
   And thrid the heavenly orange tree
   With orbits bright of minstrelsy.

" If that I hate wild winter's spite —
The gibbet trees, the world in white,
The sky but gray wind over a grave —
Why should I ache, the season's slave?
   I'll sing from the top of the orange tree
   Gramercy, winter's tyranny.

" I'll south with the sun, and keep my clime ;
My wing is king of the summer time ;
My breast to the sun his torch shall hold ;
And I'll call down through the green and gold
   Time, take thy scythe, reap bliss for me,
   Bestir thee under the orange tree."

THE WHIPPOORWILL [1]

MADISON J. CAWEIN

Madison J. Cawein (1865–1914), the poet, was born in Louisville, Kentucky. From early boyhood he wrote verse. Even his graduation speech at the high school was a poem, which awakened much interest. Probably no American poet of his day received more European recog-

nition.   He published several volumes of poems, all of which show rare
imaginative power and an exquisite appreciation of nature.   See also:

Halleck's *History of American Literature*, pp. 332–334, 338.
Trent's *Southern Writers*, pp. 332–378.
Townsend's *Kentucky in American Letters*, Vol. II, pp. 187–198.
Review of Reviews, *Recent Verse*, Vol. 47, pp. 370–373 (March, 1913).

> ABOVE lone woodland ways that led
> To dells the stealthy twilights tread
> The west was hot geranium red;
>   And still, and still,
> Along old lanes the locusts sow
> With clustered pearls the Maytimes know,
> Deep in the crimson afterglow,
> We heard the homeward cattle low,
> And then the far-off, far-off woe
>   Of "whippoorwill!" of "whippoorwill!"

> Beneath the idle beechen boughs
> We heard the far bells of the cows
> Come slowly jangling toward the house;
>   And still, and still,
> Beyond the light that would not die
> Out of the scarlet-haunted sky;
> Beyond the evening-star's white eye
> Of glittering chalcedony,
> Drained out of dusk the plaintive cry
>   Of "whippoorwill," of "whippoorwill."

> And in the city oft, when swims
> The pale moon o'er the smoke that dims
> Its disk, I dream of wildwood limbs;
>   And still, and still,
> I seem to hear, where shadows grope
> 'Mid ferns and flowers that dewdrops rope, —

Lost in faint deeps of heliotrope
Above the clover-sweetened slope, —
Retreat, despairing, past all hope,
    The whippoorwill, the whippoorwill.

THE FIRST BLUEBIRD [1]

JAMES WHITCOMB RILEY

James Whitcomb Riley (1853–   ) was born in the little town of Greenfield, Indiana. *The Raggedy Man,* and *Little Orphant Annie,* which are among his most familiar poems, illustrate his perfect sympathy with children, and explain their love for him. His poems on nature and rural life, such as *When the Frost is on the Punkin* and *The First Bluebird,* are great favorites. It has been truly said that "he lives in the understanding and affection of the millions." See also:

Halleck's *History of American Literature,* pp. 352–354, 366.

Bookman, 35 : 637–645; 38 : 163–168.

McCoy's *The Boy who was Born in our Town* in *The World's Work,* 25 : 565–567.

Good Housekeeping, 55 : 456–460; *Literary Digest,* 47 : 782.

JEST rain and snow! and rain again!
    And dribble! drip! and blow!
Then snow! and thaw! and slush! and then —
    Some more rain and snow!

This morning I was 'most afeard
    To *wake* up — when, I jing!
I seen the sun shine out and heerd
    The first bluebird of Spring! —
Mother she'd raised the winder some; —
    And in acrost the orchurd come,
      Soft as a angel's wing,
A breezy, treesy, beesy hum,
    Too sweet fer anything!

The winter's shroud was rent a-part —
The sun bust forth in glee, —
And when *that bluebird* sung, my hart
Hopped out o' bed with me !

STUDY HINTS

There are twenty-one stanzas in Shelley's *The Skylark*. Would you not like to read the other fifteen? What does the poet think may be the cause of the skylark's song? Why does he think the bird must know the true and deep realities of death? Does the third stanza express almost universal truths of human nature? How does Shelley compare his own skill with that of the skylark? Is the world now listening to him?

In Hayne's poem why is the mocking bird called the "laureate"? Name the birds that have stopped to listen. What is the different position of each? Does it require careful observation to write verse like this? Visualize in distinct images the eight birds mentioned and describe the appearance of each. Does the poet convey to you the beauty of the mocking bird's song by direct description? What method does he employ?

How is the character of the robin shown in Lanier's poem? In what does the robin find bliss? How many examples of personification are there in this poem? Think carefully over the second line of the last stanza. Reread the poem aloud and see how spirited you can make it. Statistical investigation of children's geographical knowledge shows that they usually agree in considering the same two states the most interesting. Which states do you think these are? Why? Compare the background of *Tampa Robins* with that of *The First Bluebird*.

In Cawein's *The Whippoorwill*, explain why the word "stealthy" is very happily used in this connection. Would any one but a natural poet have thought of such expressions as "stealthy twilights," "hot geranium red," "scarlet-haunted sky"? What is the time of year of this poem? The time of day? If you were an artist, could you embody the first stanza in a picture? How does the second stanza tell you that there is no air stirring? Why is "drained out of dusk" very appropriate for such a "plaintive cry"? Mention the chief natural objects that lend fascination to this poem. Would you be more apt to discover this fascination in nature after reading this poem aloud several times?

Note that Riley's *The First Bluebird* is written in the dialect of the Indiana farmer. Have you ever known a March day, such as the first four lines realistically describe? How does the poet make you feel the fascination of the bluebird's song? In what way does he make the song more effective by its background?

The first is an English bird; the others may be heard in many parts of our own country. Can you name the birds in your own locality? How many bird notes can you whistle?

Of the five poems in this group, which gives you the most pleasure? Which do you think is the greatest? Read them all to some of your friends and learn their opinions. Perhaps some very good-natured friend or company may allow you at some special time to read aloud all of this and the preceding groups, and they may express their preferences. Of the fifteen poems in the three groups in this volume note that all but two are complete and that you are to read *all* of these two if you like them.

SUGGESTIONS FOR ADDITIONAL READINGS

The Skylark. James Hogg.
The Redbreast. William Wordsworth.
The Green Linnet. William Wordsworth.
The Rain-Crow. Madison Cawein.
The Owlet. Madison Cawein.
In the Shadow of the Beeches. Madison Cawein.
There are Fairies. Madison Cawein.
The Shadow Garden. Madison Cawein.
One Day and Another. Madison Cawein.
A Twilight Moth. Madison Cawein.
To a Wind Flower. Madison Cawein.
In Solitary Places. Madison Cawein.
The Spirit of the Forest Spring. Madison Cawein.
A Sudden Shower. James Whitcomb Riley.
A Song. James Whitcomb Riley.
A Life Lesson. James Whitcomb Riley.
The Old Swimmin' Hole. James Whitcomb Riley.
The Boy Lives on Our Farm. James Whitcomb Riley.
Our Hired Girl. James Whitcomb Riley.
The Old Man and Jim. James Whitcomb Riley.
The Name of Old Glory. James Whitcomb Riley.
Our New Neighbors at Ponkapog. Thomas Bailey Aldrich.

CAPTAIN PHIPS'S SEARCH FOR SUNKEN TREASURE [1]

COTTON MATHER

Cotton Mather (1663–1728) was born of Puritan ancestry in New England. He was graduated from Harvard in his sixteenth year. Like his father he was a minister and a writer, publishing in all three hundred and eighty-two works. He was prominent in the persecution of Salem witches. Benjamin Franklin said of his *Essays To Do Good*, "If I have been a useful citizen, the public owes the advantage of it to that book." His greatest work is his *Magnalia*, which he defines as an " Ecclesiastical History of New England." See also :

Halleck's *History of American Literature*, pp. 46–50, 63.
Wendell's *Cotton Mather, the Puritan Priest.*

[Captain William Phips (1651–1695) was born in what is now Bristol, Maine, and died in London. At eighteen years of age he learned to read and write. In 1692 he organized a commission of magistrates to try so-called witches justly and protect them as much as possible. He was governor of Massachusetts, and was knighted by the king of England for his honesty and success in finding treasure. No doubt Cotton Mather heard this account from Captain Phips himself, who was a member of Cotton Mather's church.]

HE was of an inclination cutting rather like a hatchet than like a razor ; he would propose very considerable matters to himself, and then so cut through them that no difficulties could put by the edge of his resolutions. Being thus of the true temper for doing of great things, he betakes himself to the sea, the right scene for such things ; and upon advice of

[1] From *Magnalia*, 1702.

149

a Spanish wreck about the Bahamas, he took a voyage thither; but with little more success than what just served him a little to furnish him for a voyage to England; whither he went in a vessel, not much unlike that which the Dutchmen stamped on their first coin, with these words about it: *Incertum quo Fata ferant*.[1] Having first informed himself that there was another Spanish wreck, wherein was lost a mighty treasure, hitherto undiscovered, he had a strong impression upon his mind that he must be the discoverer; and he made such representations of his design at Whitehall, that by the year 1683 he became the captain of a king's ship, and arrived at New England commander of the *Algier-Rose*, a frigate of eighteen guns and ninety-five men.

To relate all the dangers through which he passed, both by sea and land, and all the tiresome trials of his patience, as well as of his courage, while year after year the most vexing accidents imaginable delayed the success of his design, it would even tire the patience of the reader; for very great was the experiment that Captain Phips made of the Italian observation, "He that cannot suffer both good and evil, will never come to any great preferment." Wherefore I shall supersede all journal of his voyages to and fro, with reciting one incident of his conduct, that showed him to be a person of no contemptible capacity. While he was captain of the *Algier-Rose*, his men growing weary of their unsuccessful enterprise, made a mutiny, wherein they approached him on the quarter-deck, with drawn swords in their hands, and required him to join with them in running away with the ship, to drive a trade of piracy on the South Seas. Captain Phips, though he had not so much of a weapon as an ox-goad, or a jawbone in his hands, yet, like another Shamgar [2] or Samson, with a most undaunted forti-

---

1 "(It is) uncertain whither the Fates may bear (us)."

2 An Old Testament hero who slew six hundred Philistines with an ox-goad.

tude, he rushed in upon them, and with the blows of his bare hands felled many of them, and quelled all the rest.

But this is not the instance which I intended; that which I intend is, that (as it has been related unto me) one day while his frigate lay careening at a desolate Spanish island, by the side of a rock, from whence they had laid a bridge to the shore, the men, whereof he had about an hundred, went all but about eight or ten to divert themselves, as they pretended, in the woods; where they all entered into an agreement, which they signed in a ring, that about seven o'clock that evening they would seize the captain, and those eight or ten which they knew to be true unto him, and leave them to perish on this island, and so be gone away unto the South Sea to seek their fortune. Will the reader now imagine that Captain Phips, having advice of this plot but about an hour and a half before it was to be put into execution, yet within two hours brought all these rogues down upon their knees to beg for their lives? But so it was! For these knaves considering that they should want a carpenter with them in their villainous expedition, sent a messenger to fetch unto them the carpenter, who was then at work upon the vessel; and unto him they shewed [1] their articles; telling him what he must look for if he did not subscribe among them. The carpenter, being an honest fellow, did with much importunity prevail for [2] one half hour's time to consider of the matter; and returning to work upon the vessel, with a spy by them set upon him, he feigned himself taken with a fit of the cholick, for the relief whereof he suddenly ran unto the captain in the great cabin for a dram; where, when he came, his business was only, in brief, to tell the captain of the horrible distress which he was fallen into; but the captain bid him as briefly return to the rogues in the woods, and sign their

---

[1] Note the old-fashioned spelling. Can you find any other illustrations?
[2] *I.e.* obtain.

articles, and leave him to provide for the rest.   The carpenter
was no sooner gone but Captain Phips, calling together the
few friends (it may be seven or eight) that were left him
aboard, whereof the gunner was one, demanded of them,
whether they would stand by him in the extremity which
he informed them was now come upon him; whereto they
replied, "They would stand by him, if he could save them";
and he answered, "By the help of God he did not fear it."

All their provisions
had been carried
ashore to a tent,
made for that pur-
pose there; about
which they had
placed several great
guns to defend it, in
case of any assault
from Spaniards, that
might happen to
come that way.
Wherefore Captain
Phips immediately
ordered those guns
to be silently drawn
and turned; and so
pulling up the bridge, he charged his great guns aboard,
and brought them to bear on every side of the tent.   By
this time the army of rebels comes out of the woods; but
as they drew near to the tent of provisions, they saw such
a change of circumstances, that they cried out, "We are
betrayed!"   And they were soon confirmed in it, when
they heard the captain with a stern fury call to them,
"Stand off, ye wretches, at your peril!"   He quickly saw
them cast into a more than ordinary confusion, when they

saw him ready to fire his great guns upon them, if they offered one step further than he permitted them; and when he had signified unto them his resolve to abandon them unto all the desolation which they had purposed for him, he caused the bridge to be again laid, and his men began to take the provisions aboard. When the wretches beheld what was coming upon them, they fell to very humble entreaties; and at last fell down upon their knees, protesting, 'That they never had anything against him, except only his unwillingness to go away with the king's ship upon the South-Sea design; but upon all other accounts they would chuse rather to live and die with him than with any man in the world. However, since they saw how much he was dissatisfied at it, they would insist upon it no more, and humbly begged his pardon.' And when he had judged that he had kept them on their knees long enough, he having first secured their arms, received them aboard; but he immediately weighed anchor, and arriving at Jamaica, he turned them off.

Now with a small company of other men, he sailed from thence to Hispaniola,[1] where, by the policy of his address, he fished out of a very old Spaniard (or Portuguese) a little advice about the true spot where lay the wreck which he had been hitherto seeking, as unprosperously as the chymists have their aurisick[2] stone; that it was upon a reef of shoals, a few leagues to the northward of Port de la Plata, upon Hispaniola, a port so called, it seems, from the landing of some of the shipwrecked company, with a boat full of plate, saved out of their sinking frigate. . . .

Captain Phips arriving with a ship and a tender at Port de la Plata, made a stout canoe of a stately cotton tree, so large as to carry eight or ten oars, for the making of which

---

[1] Now Haiti in the West Indies near Cuba.
[2] A fabulous stone turning everything to gold.

periaga (as they call it) he did, with the same industry that he did everything else, employ his own hand and adze, and endure no little hardship, lying abroad in the woods many nights together. This periaga, with the tender, being anchored at a place convenient, kept busking to and again, but could only discover a reef of rising shoals thereabouts called "The Boilers," — which, rising to be within two or three foot of the surface of the sea, were yet so steep, that a ship striking on them would immediately sink down, who could say how many fathom, into the ocean? Here they could get no other pay for their long peeping among the boilers, but only such as caused them to think upon returning to their captain with the bad news of their total disappointment. Nevertheless, as they were upon the return, one of the men, looking over the side of the periaga, into the calm water, spied a sea feather, growing, as he judged, out of a rock; whereupon they bade one of their Indians to dive, and fetch this feather, that they might, however, carry home something with them, and make, at least, as fair a triumph as Caligula's.[1] The diver bringing up the feather, brought therewithal a surprising story, that he perceived a number of great guns in the watery world where he had found his feather; the report of which great guns exceedingly astonished the whole company; and at once turned their despondencies for their ill success into assurances that they had now lit upon the true spot of ground which they had been looking for; and they were further confirmed in these assurances, when, upon further diving, the Indian fetched up a sow, as they styled it, or a lump of silver worth perhaps two or three hundred pounds. Upon this they prudently buoyed the place, that they might readily find it again; and they went

[1] A Roman Emperor in the first century. Returning to Rome after a useless campaign, he was granted a triumph by the senate, but too late for a grand entrance into Rome. He therefore entered Rome with no other celebration than that of distributing money to the populace.

back unto their captain, whom for some while they distressed
with nothing but such bad news as they formerly thought
they must have carried him. Nevertheless, they so slipped
in the sow of silver on one side under the table, where they
were now sitting with the captain, and hearing him express
his resolutions to wait still patiently upon the providence of
God under these disappointments, that when he should look
on one side, he might see that odd thing before him. At
last he saw; seeing it, he cried out with some agony, "Why!
what is this? whence comes this?" And then, with changed
countenances, they told him how and where they got it.
"Then," said he, "thanks be to God! we are made"; and
so away they went, all hands to work; wherein they had
this one further piece of remarkable prosperity, that whereas
if they had first fallen upon that part of the Spanish wreck
where the pieces of eight had been stowed in bags among
the ballast, they had seen a more laborious, and less enrich-
ing time of it; now, most happily, they first fell upon that
room in the wreck where the bullion had been stored up;
and they so prospered in this new fishery, that in a little while
they had, without the loss of any man's life, brought up
thirty-two tons of silver; for it was now come to measuring
of silver by tons. Besides which, one Adderly, of Province,
who had formerly been very helpful to Captain Phips in the
search of this wreck, did, upon former agreement, meet him
now with a little vessel here; and he, with his few hands,
took up about six tons of silver; whereof, nevertheless, he
made so little use, that in a year or two he died at Bermudas,
and, as I have heard, he ran distracted some while before
he died.

Thus did there once again come into the light of the sun
a treasure which had been half an hundred years groaning
under the waters; and in this time there was grown upon
the plate a crust like limestone, to the thickness of several

inches; which crust being broken open by iron contrived for that purpose, they knocked out whole bushels of rusty pieces of eight which were grown thereinto. Besides that incredible treasure of plate in various forms, thus fetched up, from seven or eight fathom under water, there were vast riches of gold, and pearls, and jewels, which they also lit upon; and, indeed, for a more comprehensive invoice, I must but summarily say, "All that a Spanish frigate uses to be enriched withal." Thus did they continue fishing till, their provisions failing them, 'twas time to be gone.

Captain Phips now coming up to London in the year 1687, with near three hundred thousand pounds sterling [1] aboard him, did acquit himself with such an exemplary honesty, that partly by his fulfilling his assurances to the seamen, and partly by his exact and punctual care to have his employers defrauded of nothing that might conscientiously belong unto them, he had less than sixteen thousand pounds left unto himself; as an acknowledgment of which honesty in him, the Duke of Albemarle made unto his wife, whom he never saw, a present of a golden cup, near a thousand pound in value. . . . The king, in consideration of the service done by him in bringing such a treasure into the nation, conferred upon him the honor of knighthood; and if we now reckon him a knight of the golden fleece,[2] the style might pretend unto some circumstances that would justify it.

STUDY HINTS

Study the spelling and meaning of these words:

imaginable	villain	feign
supersede	expedition	triumph
contemptible	dissatisfied	buoyed
enterprise	ordinary	anchor

[1] Almost $1,500,000.   [2] What Greek hero went in search of the Golden Fleece?

What qualities has Captain Phips to a very high degree? How do you know? What quality do you find in the second incident that always makes for success? Does Captain Phips seem a real or a "story-book" hero? Why? Which is more interesting to you, the character of the hero, or the plot of the story? Or is the one made interesting because of the other?

SUGGESTIONS FOR ORAL AND WRITTEN ENGLISH
THEME SUBJECTS

What methods of portraying character are employed by the author? (See suggestions on *Wee Willie Winkie*, p. 89.) Write a story on "The Hunt for Buried Treasure" in which the plot is the important feature. Write a story on the same topic in which the character of the leader is delineated by means of the plot. Describe to a friend the character of Captain Phips. Can you compare him with some one both of you know?

The Story (as told by one of the conspirators).

The Story (as told by the carpenter).

What the Diver Found.

Learning to Dive.

Raising the *Maine*.

An Unexpected Discovery.

Pirate Tales that I Like.

An Incident from Jules Verne's *Twenty Thousand Leagues under the Sea*.

SUGGESTIONS FOR ADDITIONAL READINGS

The Goldbug. Edgar Allan Poe.
Treasure Island. Robert Louis Stevenson.
To Have and to Hold. Mary Johnston.
Stolen Treasure. Howard Pyle.
The Pirate. Sir Walter Scott.
Buccaneers and Pirates of our Coast. Frank R. Stockton.
Ocean Life in the Old Sailing-Ship Days. J. D. Whidden.
Two Years Before the Mast. R. H. Dana, Jr.

SPEECH ON A RESOLUTION TO PUT VIRGINIA INTO A STATE OF DEFENSE

Patrick Henry

The British government had taxed the colonies without representation besides heaping many other indignities upon them. The whole country was finally aroused to a state of the highest excitement. The Virginia convention assembled on March 28, 1775, to decide whether Virginia should be put into a state of defense. When a resolution to do this was offered, Patrick Henry (1736–1799), a young Virginia lawyer, one of a group of eloquent orators of that time, arose and delivered this famous speech. After reading it, you will understand how he created the wildest enthusiasm on this occasion. In old St. John's Church in Richmond, Virginia, a brass tablet marks the spot where he stood when delivering this speech. See also:

Morgan's *The True Patrick Henry.*
Wirt's *Life of Patrick Henry.*

MR. PRESIDENT, it is natural for man to indulge in the illusions of hope. We are apt to shut our eyes against a painful truth, and to listen to the song of that siren [1] till she transforms us into beasts. Is this the part of wise men engaged in the great and arduous struggle for liberty? Are we disposed to be of the number of those who having eyes see not, and having ears hear not, the things which so nearly concern their temporal salvation? For my part, whatever anguish of spirit it may cost, I am willing to know the whole truth; to know the worst, and to provide for it.

I have but one lamp by which my feet are guided and that is the lamp of experience. I know of no way of judging

[1] Circe, the enchantress who turned Ulysses' men into swine and other loathsome beasts.

of the future but by the past. And, judging by the past, I wish to know what there has been in the conduct of the British Ministry for the last ten years to justify those hopes with which gentlemen have been pleased to solace themselves and the House. Is it that insidious smile with which our petition has been lately received? Trust it not, sir; it will prove a snare to

ST. JOHN'S CHURCH

your feet. Suffer not yourselves to be betrayed with a kiss. Ask yourselves how this gracious reception of our petition comports with those warlike preparations which cover our waters and darken our land. Are fleets and armies necessary to a work of love and reconciliation? Have we shown ourselves so unwilling to be reconciled that force must be called in to win back our love?

Let us not deceive ourselves, sir. These are the implements of war and subjugation, the last argument to which kings resort. I ask, sir, what means this martial array, if its purposes be not to force us to submission? Can gentlemen assign any other possible motive for it? Has Great Britain any enemy in this quarter of the world to call for all this accumulation of navies and armies? No, sir, she has none. They are meant for us. They can be meant for no other. They are sent over to bind and rivet upon us those chains which the British Ministry have been so long forging.

And what have we to oppose them? Shall we try argument? Sir, we have been trying that for the last ten years. Have we anything new to offer upon the subject? Nothing. We have held the subject up in every light of which it is capable; but it has been all in vain. Shall we resort to entreaty and supplication? What terms shall we find that have not been already exhausted? Let us not, I beseech you, sir, deceive ourselves longer. Sir, we have done everything that could have been done to avert the storm that is now coming on. We have petitioned, we have remonstrated, we have supplicated, we have prostrated ourselves before the throne, and have implored its interposition to arrest the tyrannical hands of the Ministry and Parliament. Our petitions have been slighted, our remonstrances have produced additional violence and insult, our supplications have been disregarded, and we have been spurned with contempt from the foot of the throne. In vain, after these things, may we indulge the fond hope of peace and reconciliation. There is no longer any room for hope. If we wish to be free, if we mean to preserve inviolate these inestimable privileges for which we have been so long contending, if we mean not basely to abandon the noble struggle in which we have been so long engaged, and which we have pledged ourselves never to abandon until the glorious object of our contest shall be obtained, we must fight! I repeat, sir, we must fight! An appeal to arms and to the God of hosts is all that is left us.

They tell us, sir, that we are weak; unable to cope with so formidable an adversary. But when shall we be stronger? Will it be the next week, or the next year? Will it be when we are totally disarmed, and when a British guard shall be stationed in every house? Shall we gather strength by irresolution and inaction? Shall we acquire the means of effectual resistance by lying supinely on our backs, and hugging the delusive phantom of hope, until our enemies shall have bound us hand and foot? Sir, we are not weak if we make a proper use of those means which the God of Nature hath placed in our power.

Three millions of people armed in the holy cause of liberty, and in such a country as that which we possess, are invincible by any force which our enemy can send against us. Besides, sir, we shall not fight our battles alone. There is a just God who presides over the destinies of nations, and who will raise up friends to fight our battles for us. The battle, sir, is not to the strong alone; it is to the vigilant, the active, the brave. Besides, sir, we have no election.[1] If we were base enough to desire it, it is now too late to retire from the contest. There is no retreat but in submission and slavery! Our chains are forged. Their clanking may be heard on the plains of Boston! The war is inevitable, and let it come! I repeat, sir, let it come!

It is vain, sir, to extenuate the matter. Gentlemen may cry, Peace, peace! but there is no peace. The war is actually begun! The next gale that sweeps from the North will bring to our ears the clash of resounding arms! Our brethren are already in the field! Why stand we here idle? What is it that gentlemen wish? What would they have? Is life so dear, or peace so sweet, as to be purchased at the price of chains and slavery? Forbid it, Almighty God! I know not what course others may take, but as for me, give me liberty or give me death!

STUDY HINTS

Study the spelling and meaning of these words:

insidious	rivet	irresolution
revere	entreaty	vigilant
reconciliation	contempt	extenuate
martial	exhausted	inevitable

[1] Choice.

What is the question before the House? What does the speaker say of the condition of affairs in the colonies? What figure is the "lamp of experience"? How had the colonies acted towards the mother country for ten years? Where does Patrick Henry state his opponents' arguments? Notice his reasons for expecting success in the contest. What part of the speech do you think would be most inspiring to his hearers? When was the Declaration of Independence proclaimed? Have any sentences in that as much vigor as some in this speech?

SUGGESTIONS FOR ORAL AND WRITTEN ENGLISH
THEME SUBJECTS

Tell what interested you most in a public speech you have heard. Write a short speech nominating for class president a classmate. Think carefully over all the qualities your friend has which will make him a good leader. Arrange the points so that the best will come last. If you know of any qualities that others may object to, try to think of something that will counterbalance them. Make a spirited speech, full of enthusiasm, so that you will persuade others to agree with you. If you want to go somewhere on "school night," think what arguments you can use to persuade your mother to let you go. Perhaps you have prepared your lessons, or you have a first-hour study period. Arrange your points in the order of the weight you think they will have with your mother, or with your father. Write a speech opposing the nomination of some one who in spite of his good qualities lacks one that makes for success in that particular position. Write a defense of some one — without mentioning the name — that you dislike. You have not prepared your lesson; state your reasons clearly and forcibly, using Patrick Henry's method of repetition, and of reserving his best points for the last. You want a camera, or a new golf stick, or a new hat which your parents think unnecessary; state your arguments in the most effective order.

State, in a way to conciliate, if possible, your opponents, your reasons for preferring a certain style of school pin, or school motto.

Debate: The Editor of a School Paper Must Have High Class Standing.

The United States Should Have a Standing Army.

Girls and Boys Should Have Equal Allowances.

A Good Speaker Wields as Much Power as a Writer.

SUGGESTIONS FOR ADDITIONAL READINGS

The Virginians.   William Makepeace Thackeray.
Hero Tales from American History.   Roosevelt and Lodge.
George Washington.   Woodrow Wilson.
The Youth of Washington.   S. Weir Mitchell.
The Gettysburg Address.   Abraham Lincoln.
The First Bunker Hill Oration.   Daniel Webster.
The New South.   Henry Grady.
The Boys of '76.   Charles Coffin.
Daughters of the Revolution.   Charles Coffin.

THE SKELETON IN ARMOR [1]

HENRY WADSWORTH LONGFELLOW

Henry Wadsworth Longfellow (1807–1882) was born in Portland, Maine. He is the most popular poet of America, and he is the only American poet whose bust has been placed in the famous Poets' Corner of Westminster Abbey. He was a classmate and intimate friend of Nathaniel Hawthorne. Longfellow's poems are noteworthy because they preserve certain phases of American life not given by any one else. Examples of this are *Evangeline*, which deals with an incident of the French and Indian War; *Paul Revere's Ride*, and *The Courtship of Miles Standish*, which portray colonial life; and *The Song of Hiawatha*, which has preserved many Indian myths. He will probably be remembered longest for *The Song of Hiawatha*, though many of his lyrics are familiar to every child in America. *The Skeleton in Armor* refers to the early visits of the Norsemen to America. See also:

Halleck's *History of American Literature*, pp. 222–233, 283, 284.
Samuel Longfellow's *Life of Henry Wadsworth Longfellow*.
Higginson's *Henry Wadsworth Longfellow*.
Robertson's *Life of Henry Wadsworth Longfellow*.
Carpenter's *Henry Wadsworth Longfellow*.

[The period of this poem is the same as that of *Hereward the Wake, i.e.* eleventh century. Two facts suggested this ballad to the poet: the mystery as to the origin of the old Round Tower at Newport, and the unearthing of a skeleton near Fall River, clad in broken and corroded armor.]

"SPEAK! speak! thou fearful guest!
  Who, with thy hollow breast

[1] This poem from Longfellow is used by permission of, and by arrangement with Houghton Mifflin Company, authorized publishers of his works.

Still in rude armor drest,
  Comest to daunt me!
Wrapt not in Eastern balms,[1]
But with thy fleshless palms
Stretched, as if asking alms,
  Why dost thou haunt me?"

Then, from those cavernous eyes
Pale flashes seemed to rise,
As when the Northern skies
  Gleam in December;
And, like the water's flow
Under December's snow,
Came a dull voice of woe
  From the heart's chamber.

"I was a Viking [2] old!
My deeds, though manifold,
No skald [3] in song has told,
  No saga[4] taught thee!
Take heed, that in thy verse
Thou dost the tale rehearse,
Else dread a dead man's curse;
  For this I sought thee.

"Far in the Northern land,
By the wild Baltic's strand,
I, with my childish hand,
  Tamed the gerfalcon; [5]
And, with my skates fast-bound,
Skimmed the half-frozen sound,
That the poor whimpering hound,
  Trembled to walk on.

[1] That is, not after the fashion of an Egyptian mummy.   [2] A Scandinavian pirate.
[3] A Scandinavian poet who celebrated the deeds of heroes, accompanying himself on
the harp.
  [4] A Scandinavian legend.   [5] A particularly fierce species of falcon.

"Oft to his frozen lair
Tracked I the grizzly bear,
While from my path the hare
  Fled like a shadow;
Oft through the forest dark
Followed the werewolf's [1] bark,
Until the soaring lark
  Sang from the meadow.

"But when I older grew,
Joining a corsair's crew,
O'er the dark sea I flew
  With the marauders.
Wild was the life we led;
Many the souls that sped,
Many the hearts that bled,
  By our stern orders.

"Many a wassail-bout
Wore the long winter out;
Often our midnight shout
  Set the cocks crowing,
As we the Berserk's [2] tale
Measured in cups of ale,
Draining the oaken pail,
  Filled to o'erflowing.

"Once as I told in glee
Tales of the stormy sea,
Soft eyes did gaze on me,
  Burning yet tender;
And as the white stars shine
On the dark Norway pine,
On that dark heart of mine
  Fell their soft splendor.

---

[1] A fabulous creature of wolf form, man intelligence.   [2] See p. 53, note.

"I wooed the blue-eyed maid,
Yielding, yet half afraid,
And in the forest's shade
   Our vows were plighted.
Under its loosened vest
Fluttered her little breast,
Like birds within their nest
   By the hawk frighted.

"Bright in her father's hall
Shields gleamed upon the wall,
Loud sang the minstrels all,
   Chanting his glory;
When of old Hildebrand
I asked his daughter's hand,
Mute did the minstrels stand
   To hear my story.

"While the brown ale he quaffed,
Loud then the champion laughed,
And as the wind gusts waft
   The sea foam brightly,
So the loud laugh of scorn,
Out of those lips unshorn,
From the deep drinking horn
   Blew the foam lightly.

"She was a Prince's child,
I but a Viking wild,
And though she blushed and smiled
   I was discarded!
Should not the dove so white
Follow the sea mew's flight,
Why did they leave that night
   Her nest unguarded?

"Scarce had I put to sea,
Bearing the maid with me,
Fairest of all was she
    Among the Norsemen!
When on the white seastrand,
Waving his armèd hand,
Saw we old Hildebrand,
    With twenty horsemen.

"Then launched they to the blast,
Bent like a reed each mast,
Yet we were gaining fast,
    When the wind failed us;
And with a sudden flaw
Came round the gusty Skaw,[1]
So that our foe we saw
    Laugh as he hailed us,

"And as to catch the gale
Round veered the flapping sail,
Death! was the helmsman's hail,
    Death without quarter!
Midships with iron keel
Struck we her ribs of steel;
Down her black hulk did reel
    Through the black water!

"As with his wings aslant,
Sails the fierce cormorant,
Seeking some rocky haunt,
    With his prey laden,
So toward the open main,
Beating to sea again,
Through the wild hurricane,
    Bore I the maiden.

[1] Cape on northwest coast of Denmark.

"Three weeks we westward bore,
And when the storm was o'er,
Cloud-like we saw the shore
   Stretching to leeward;
There for my lady's bower
Built I the lofty tower,
Which, to this very hour,
   Stands looking seaward.

"There lived we many years;
Time dried the maiden's tears;
She had forgot her fears,
   She was a mother;
Death closed her mild blue eyes,
Under that tower she lies;
Ne'er shall the sun arise
   On such another!

"Still grew my bosom then,
Still as a stagnant fen!
Hateful to me were men,
   The sunlight hateful!
In the vast forest here,
Clad in my warlike gear,
Fell I upon my spear,
   O, death was grateful!

"Thus, seamed with many scars,
Bursting these prison bars,
Up to its native stars
   My soul ascended!
There from the flowing bowl
Deep drinks the warrior's soul,
Skoal! to the Northland! *skoal!*" [1]
   — Thus the tale ended.

[1] In Scandinavia, the customary salutation in drinking a health.

STUDY HINTS

How many fine comparisons (*i.e.* similes) can you find in this poem? Has the poet made you feel the fierce, reckless character of the old Viking? Where does he show that he was capable of very tender feeling? What was his fate? Is this not a stirring ballad? Read it aloud and see if the swing of the verse adds to the effect. Memorize two favorite stanzas, if not the entire poem.

SUGGESTIONS FOR ADDITIONAL READINGS

The Discoverer of the North Cape.   Henry Wadsworth Longfellow.
The Leap of Roushan Beg.   Henry Wadsworth Longfellow.
The Courtship of Miles Standish.   Henry Wadsworth Longfellow.
The Old Clock on the Stairs.   Henry Wadsworth Longfellow.
Rain in Summer.   Henry Wadsworth Longfellow.
The Children's Hour.   Henry Wadsworth Longfellow.
The Arrow and the Song.   Henry Wadsworth Longfellow.
The Day is Done.   Henry Wadsworth Longfellow.
Lord Ullin's Daughter.   Thomas Campbell.
Lochinvar (*Marmion*, Canto V).   Sir Walter Scott.
Allan-a-Dale.   Sir Walter Scott.
A Sea Song.   Allan Cunningham.

For the teacher to read to the class:
Selections from Longfellow's *The Building of the Ship.*

THE PINE–TREE SHILLINGS [1]

NATHANIEL HAWTHORNE

Nathaniel Hawthorne (1804–1864) was born in Salem, Massachusetts. He was from early childhood fond of solitude, and of brooding upon tales of witchcraft and legends of the colonial days. Possibly young people know best his *A Wonder Book, Tanglewood Tales*, and *Twice-Told Tales*. His greatest romances are *The Scarlet Letter, The House of the Seven Gables*, and *The Marble Faun*. Many consider Hawthorne America's greatest prose writer. The moral truth and beauty of his stories stamp him as a writer of lofty ideals. See also:

Halleck's *History of American Literature*, pp. 204–221, 283.
Julian Hawthorne's *Nathaniel Hawthorne and his Wife*.
George Woodberry's *Nathaniel Hawthorne*.
Bridge's *Personal Recollections of Nathaniel Hawthorne*.
Introduction to *The Scarlet Letter*.

CAPTAIN JOHN HULL was the mintmaster of Massachusetts, and coined all the money that was made there. This was a new line of business: for, in the earlier days of the colony, the current coinage consisted of gold and silver money of England, Portugal, and Spain. These coins being scarce, the people were often forced to barter their commodities instead of selling them.

For instance, if a man wanted to buy a coat, he perhaps exchanged a bearskin for it. If he wished for a barrel of molasses, he might purchase it with a pile of pine boards. Musket bullets were used instead of farthings. The Indians had a sort of money, called wampum, which was made of clamshells; and this strange sort of specie was likewise taken

[1] From *Grandfather's Chair* (1841). Used by permission of, and by arrangement with, Houghton Mifflin Company, authorized publishers of Hawthorne's works.

in payment of debts by the English settlers. Bank bills had never been heard of. There was not money enough of any kind, in many parts of the country, to pay the salaries of the ministers; so that they sometimes had to take quintals of fish, bushels of corn, or cords of wood, instead of silver or gold.

As the people grew more numerous, and their trade one with another increased, the want of current money was still more sensibly felt. To supply the demand, the general court passed a law for establishing a coinage of shillings,[1] sixpences, and threepences. Captain John Hull was appointed to manufacture this money, and was to have about one shilling out of every twenty to pay him for the trouble of making them.

Hereupon all the old silver in the colony was handed over to Captain John Hull. The battered silver cans and tankards, I suppose, and silver buckles, and broken spoons, and silver buttons of worn-out coats, and silver hilts of swords that had figured at court, all such curious old articles were doubtless thrown into the melting pot together. But by far the greater part of the silver consisted of bullion from the mines of South America, which the English buccaneers (who were little better than pirates) had taken from the Spaniards, and brought to Massachusetts.

All this old and new silver being melted down and coined, the result was an immense amount of splendid shillings, sixpences, and threepences. Each had the date, 1652, on the one side, and the figure of a pine tree on the other. Hence they were called pine-tree shillings. And for every twenty shillings that he coined, you will remember, Captain John Hull was entitled to put one shilling into his own pocket.

The magistrates soon began to suspect that the mint-

---

[1] About twenty-five cents, twelve cents, six cents, respectively.

master would have the best of the bargain. They offered him a large sum of money if he would but give up that twentieth shilling which he was continually dropping into his own pocket. But Captain Hull declared himself perfectly satisfied with the shilling. And well he might be; for so diligently did he labor that in a few years, his pockets, his moneybags, and his strong box were overflowing with pine-tree shillings. This was probably the case when he came into possession of Grandfather's chair; and, as he had worked so hard at the mint, it was certainly proper that he should have a comfortable chair to rest himself in.

When the mintmaster had grown very rich, a young man, Samuel Sewall by name, came a-courting to his only daughter. His daughter — whose name I do not know, but we will call her Betsey — was a fine, hearty damsel, by no means so slender as some young ladies of our own days. On the contrary, having always fed heartily on pumpkin pies, doughnuts, Indian puddings, and other Puritan dainties, she was as round and plump as a pudding herself. With this round, rosy Miss Betsey did Samuel Sewall fall in love. As he was a young man of good character, industrious in his business, and a member of the church, the mintmaster very readily gave his consent.

"Yes — you may take her," said he in his rough way, "and you'll find her a heavy burden enough!"

On the wedding day, we may suppose that honest John Hull dressed himself in a plum-colored coat, all the buttons of which were made of pine-tree shillings. The buttons of his waistcoat were sixpences; and the knees of his small-clothes were buttoned with silver threepences. Thus attired, he sat with great dignity in Grandfather's chair; and, being a portly old gentleman, he completely filled it from elbow to elbow. On the opposite side of the room, between her bridemaids sat Miss Betsey. She was blushing with all her might, and looked like a full blown peony, or a great red apple.

There, too, was the bridegroom, dressed in a fine purple coat and gold lace waistcoat, with as much other finery as the Puritan laws and customs would allow him to put on. His hair was cropped close to his head, because Governor Endicott had forbidden any man to wear it below the ears. But he was a very personable young man; and so thought the bridemaids and Miss Betsey herself.

The mintmaster also was pleased with his new son-in-law; especially as he had courted Miss Betsey out of pure love, and had said nothing at all about her portion. So, when the marriage ceremony was over, Captain Hull whispered a word to two of his menservants, who immediately went out, and soon returned, lugging in a large pair of scales. They were such a pair as wholesale merchants use for weighing bulky commodities; and quite a bulky commodity was now to be weighed in them.

"Daughter Betsey," said the mintmaster, "get into one side of these scales."

Miss Betsey — or Mrs. Sewall, as we must now call her — did as she was bid, like a dutiful child, without any question of the why and wherefore. But what her father could mean, unless to make her husband pay for her by the pound (in which case she would have been a dear bargain), she had not the least idea.

"And now," said honest John Hull to the servants, "bring that box hither."

The box to which the mintmaster pointed was a huge, square, iron-bound, oaken chest; it was big enough, my children, for all four of you to play at hide and seek in. The servants tugged with might and main, but could not lift this enormous receptacle, and were finally obliged to drag it across the floor. Captain Hull then took a key from his girdle, unlocked the chest, and lifted its ponderous lid. Behold! It was full to the brim of bright pine-tree shillings, fresh from the mint; and Samuel Sewall began to think that his father-in-law had got possession of all the money in the Massachusetts treasury. But it was only the mintmaster's honest share of the coinage.

Then the servants, at Captain Hull's command, heaped double handfuls of shillings into one side of the scales, while Betsey remained in the other. Jingle, jingle, went the shillings, as handful after handful was thrown in, till, plump and ponderous as she was, they fairly weighed the young lady from the floor.

"There, son Sewall!" cried the honest mintmaster, resuming his seat in Grandfather's chair. "Take these shillings for my daughter's portion. Use her kindly, and thank heaven for her. It is not every wife that's worth her weight in silver!"

STUDY HINTS

Study the spelling and meaning of these words:

coinage	magistrate	manufacture
bargain	probably	commodities
salary	opposite	ponderous
current	treasury	bulky

Why were there so many different kinds of money in our country at first? What served as money among the Indians? Can you explain why our first money was made in the form of shillings, sixpences, and threepences, instead of the present forms? Did Captain John Hull make a good bargain with the magistrates? Why? Was he fond of a joke? Why was money invented? Did Robinson Crusoe value the bag of gold that he found when first shipwrecked?

SUGGESTIONS FOR ORAL AND WRITTEN ENGLISH
THEME SUBJECTS

Tell the story of the way in which you made your collection of marbles, or posters, or any other collection popular in your community. Describe some form of bartering you have used. Write an imaginary incident of a community which has been robbed of every cent and cannot procure any money for a month. They must not use the "credit" system.

Tell the story of *Miles Standish's Courtship* as if you were Priscilla's sister, and express your opinion of Miles Standish.

Wampum.

Who Designs our Paper Dollars?

A New England Sunday in Colonial Days.

A Visit to a Mint.

The Lincoln Cent.

My Favorite Story of Colonial Times.

SUGGESTIONS FOR ADDITIONAL READINGS

Tanglewood Tales. Nathaniel Hawthorne.

Feathertop (from *Mosses from an Old Manse*). Nathaniel Hawthorne.

Drowne's Wooden Image (from *Mosses from an Old Manse*). Nathaniel Hawthorne.

The Gray Champion (from *Twice-Told Tales*). Nathaniel Hawthorne.

The Gentle Boy (from *Twice-Told Tales*). Nathaniel Hawthorne.

The Great Stone Face (from *The Snow Image*). Nathaniel Hawthorne.

Mr. Higginbotham's Catastrophe (from *Twice-Told Tales*). Nathaniel Hawthorne.

Dr. Heidegger's Experiment (from *Twice-Told Tales*). Nathaniel Hawthorne.

Lady Eleanore's Mantle (from *Twice-Told Tales*). Nathaniel Hawthorne.

The Minister's Black Veil (from *Twice-Told Tales*). Nathaniel Hawthorne.

The Great Carbuncle (from *Twice-Told Tales*). Nathaniel Hawthorne.

Howe's Masquerade (from *Twice-Told Tales*). Nathaniel Hawthorne.

A New England Girlhood. Lucy Larcom.

In Colonial Times. Mary Wilkins Freeman.

The Diary of Anna Green Winslow. A. M. Earle (Ed.).

WOUTER VAN TWILLER [1]

WASHINGTON IRVING

Washington Irving (1783–1859) was born in New York City. He has been rightly called the "Father of American Literature." During his boyhood, the colonies were occupied with establishing a new form of government, and welding themselves into one nation. They had no time for literature. Irving was the first American writer to win recognition in Europe. He spent much of his youth in prying around the quaint Dutch quarters of New York, and he has preserved in his writings much of the early history of New York, gleaned in this way. He was secretary of the legation at London, and later minister to Spain. He, however, gladly returned to spend his remaining years at beautiful Sunnyside, overlooking the Hudson River. His *Legend of Sleepy Hollow* and *Rip Van Winkle* should be familiar to every boy and girl in America. See also:

Halleck's *History of American Literature*, pp. 112–124, 151.
Warner's *Washington Irving*.
Pierre M. Irving's *The Life and Letters of Washington Irving*.

It was in the year of our Lord 1629 that Mynheer Wouter Van Twiller was appointed governor of the province of Nieuw Nederlandts,[2] under the commission and control of their High Mightinesses the Lords States General of the United Netherlands, and the privileged West India Company.

This renowned old gentleman arrived at New Amsterdam [3] in the merry month of June, the sweetest month in all the year; when dan [4] Apollo [5] seems to dance up the transparent

---

[1] From *Knickerbocker's History of New York*.
[2] That part of the American colonies extending from the Delaware to the Connecticut River.
[3] The capital of the Dutch colony, now New York City.
[4] A quaint term for "master."   [5] The Greek god of the sun.

firmament, — when the robin, the thrush, and a thousand other wanton songsters, make the woods to resound with amorous ditties, and the luxurious little boblincon revels among the clover blossoms of the meadows, — all which happy coincidence persuaded the old dames of New Amsterdam, who were skilled in the art of foretelling events, that this was to be a happy and prosperous administration.

The renowned Wouter (or Walter) Van Twiller was descended from a long line of Dutch burgomasters, who had

successively dozed away their lives, and grown fat upon the bench of magistracy in Rotterdam; and who had comported themselves with such singular wisdom and propriety, that they were never either heard or talked of — which, next to being universally applauded, should be the object of ambition of all magistrates and rulers. There are two opposite ways by which some men make a figure in the world: one, by talking faster than they think, and the other, by holding their tongues and not thinking at all. By the first, many a smatterer acquires the reputation of a man of quick parts; by the other, many a dunderpate, like the owl, the stupidest of birds, comes to be considered the very type of wisdom. This, by the way, is a casual remark, which I would not, for the universe, have it thought I apply to Governor Van Twiller. It is true he was a man shut up within himself, like an oyster, and rarely spoke, except in mono-syllables; but then it was allowed he seldom said a foolish thing. So invincible was his gravity that he was never known to laugh or even to smile through the whole course of a long and prosperous life. Nay, if a joke were uttered in his pres-ence, that set light-minded hearers in a roar, it was observed to throw him into a state of perplexity. Sometimes he would deign to inquire into the matter, and when, after much explanation, the joke was made as plain as a pike-staff, he would continue to smoke his pipe in silence, and at length, knocking out the ashes, would exclaim, "Well! I see nothing in all that to laugh about."

With all his reflective habits, he never made up his mind on a subject. His adherents accounted for this by the astonishing magnitude of his ideas. He conceived every subject on so grand a scale that he had not room in his head to turn it over and examine both sides of it. Certain it is, that, if any matter were propounded to him on which ordi-nary mortals would rashly determine at first glance, he would put on a vague, mysterious look, shake his capacious head, smoke some time in profound silence, and at length observe, that "he had his doubts about the matter"; which gained him the reputation of a man slow of belief and not easily imposed upon. What is more, it gained him a lasting name; for to this habit of the mind has been attributed his surname of Twiller; which is said to be a corruption of the original Twijfler, or, in plain English, Doubter.

The person of this illustrious old gentleman was formed and proportioned, as though it had been molded by the hands of some cunning Dutch statuary, as a model of majesty and lordly grandeur. He was exactly five feet six inches in height, and six feet five inches in circumference. His head was a perfect sphere, and of such stupendous dimensions, that Dame Nature, with all her sex's ingenuity, would have been puzzled to construct a neck capable of supporting it; wherefore she wisely declined the attempt, and settled it firmly on the top of his backbone, just between the shoulders. His body was oblong and particularly capacious at the hips; which was wisely ordered by Providence, seeing that he was a man of sedentary habits, and very averse to the idle labor of walking. His legs were short, but sturdy in proportion to the weight they had to sustain; so that when erect he had not a little the appearance of a beer barrel on skids. His face, that infallible index of the mind, presented a vast expanse, unfurrowed by any of those lines and angles which disfigure the human countenance with what is termed expression. Two small gray eyes twinkled feebly in the midst, like two stars of lesser magnitude in a hazy firmament, and his full-fed cheeks, which seemed to have taken toll of everything that went into his mouth, were curiously mottled and streaked with dusky red, like a spitzenburgh apple.

His habits were as regular as his person. He daily took his four stated meals, appropriating exactly an hour to each; he smoked and doubted eight hours, and he slept the remaining twelve of the four and twenty. Such was the renowned Wouter Van Twiller, — a true philosopher, for his mind was either elevated above, or tranquilly settled below, the cares and perplexities of this world. He had lived in it for years, without feeling the least curiosity to know whether the sun revolved round it, or it round the sun; and he had watched, for at least half a century, the smoke curling from his pipe to the ceiling, without once troubling his head with any of those numerous theories by which a philosopher would have perplexed his brain, in accounting for its rising above the surrounding atmosphere.

STUDY HINTS

Study the spelling and meaning of these words:

transparent	perplexity	infallible
coincidence	capacious	countenance
doze	sedentary	ingenuity

Has Irving followed any plan in this description of Van Twiller? What is his plan? What do you think of Van Twiller's character? Of his habits? What does the expression "Taken toll of everything that went into his mouth" mean? Does the author describe his hero directly or indirectly? Prove your point by two illustrations. What do you consider the most humorous part of the description? How would you describe Irving's humor?

SUGGESTIONS FOR ORAL AND WRITTEN ENGLISH
THEME SUBJECTS

Imitating Irving's method of description, describe, without giving his name, a person familiar to the class. Think what it is that causes you to recognize him even before you are near enough to see his face distinctly. Has he any unusual feature that makes him noticeable? Has he any characteristic gestures or expressions? How do his clothes differ from those of other people? Whatever, in a word, that makes him *different* from others should be shown in your description. Describe a building or a room, bringing out its chief feature. Contrast Ichabod Crane with Wouter Van Twiller. Describe a man to show that he is a clergyman or a doctor.

The Roundest Person I ever Saw.   A Tramp.
Why We Called Him "Skinny."   Somebody's Grandmother.

SUGGESTIONS FOR ADDITIONAL READINGS

The Stout Gentleman (in *Bracebridge Hall*). Washington Irving.
Dolph Heyliger (in *Bracebridge Hall*). Washington Irving.
Legends of the Alhambra. Washington Irving.
The Specter Bridegroom (in *Sketchbook*). Washington Irving.
The Belated Travelers (in *Tales of a Traveler*). Washington Irving.
In Leisler's Times. E. S. Brooks.
Nooks and Corners of Old New York. Charles Hemstreet.

A SECOND GROUP OF NATURE LYRICS

ARIEL'S SONG [1]

WILLIAM SHAKESPEARE

[For biographical sketch see page 221.]

WHERE the bee sucks, there suck I;
In a cowslip's bell I lie:
There I couch when owls do cry.
On the bat's back I do fly
After summer, merrily.
Merrily, merrily shall I live now,
Under the blossom that hangs on the bough.

DAFFODILS

WILLIAM WORDSWORTH

[For biographical sketch see page 93.]

I WANDERED lonely as a cloud
That floats on high o'er vales and hills,
When all at once I saw a crowd,
A host, of golden daffodils;
Beside the lake, beneath the trees,
Fluttering and dancing in the breeze.

Continuous as the stars that shine
And twinkle on the milky way,
They stretched in never-ending line
Along the margin of a bay:

[1] From *The Tempest.*

Ten thousand saw I at a glance,
Tossing their heads in sprightly dance.

The waves beside them danced, but they
Outdid the sparkling waves in glee : —
A poet could not but be gay
In such a jocund company :
I gazed — and gazed — but little thought
What wealth the show to me had brought.

For oft when on my couch I lie
In vacant or in pensive mood,
They flash upon that inward eye
Which is the bliss of solitude,
And then my heart with pleasure fills,
And dances with the daffodils.

ON THE GRASSHOPPER AND CRICKET

John Keats

John Keats (1795–1821) was born in London. For a short time he studied surgery but gave it up to become a poet. His poetical creed was: "A thing of beauty is a joy forever." He especially loved the beautiful things in the world of the senses. Before he died, at the age of twenty-five, he had written more beautiful verse than any other poet of his years. One of Shelley's greatest poems is *Adonais*, an elegy on Keats. See also:

Halleck's *New English Literature*, pp. 426–435, 447.
Colvin's *Keats*.
Rossetti's *Life of Keats*.

The poetry of earth is never dead :
When all the birds are faint with the hot sun,
And hide in cooling trees, a voice will run
From hedge to hedge about the new-mown mead ;
That is the grasshopper's — he takes the lead

In summer luxury, — he has never done
With his delights; for when tired out with fun
He rests at ease beneath some pleasant weed.
The poetry of earth is ceasing never;
On a lone winter evening, when the frost
Has wrought a silence, from the stove there shrills
The cricket's song, in warmth increasing ever,
And seems to one in drowsiness half lost,
The grasshopper's among some grassy hills.

THREE PICTURES FROM *THE PALACE OF ART*

ALFRED TENNYSON

Alfred Tennyson (1809–1892) was born in Somersby, Lincolnshire.
He divides honors with Browning as one of the two greater poets of the
Victorian age.   *In Memoriam*, a poem on the death of his most intimate
friend; the *Idylls of the King*, celebrating the deeds of King Arthur and
the Knights of the Round Table; and some of his short lyrics, are his
most famous poems.   He was a careful student of nature and his poetry
reflects the thought of the Victorian age.   The artistic finish of his
verse is one of its great charms.   He said that he could have transferred
many of his stanzas to canvas if he had been a painter.   See also:

Halleck's *New English Literature*, pp. 553–563, 585.
Alfred, Lord Tennyson, A Memoir, by his son.
Benson's *Alfred Tennyson*.
Lyall's *Tennyson*.

ONE showed an iron coast and angry waves.
    You seemed to hear them climb and fall
And roar rock-thwarted under bellowing caves,
    Beneath the windy wall.

And one, a full-fed river winding slow
    By herds upon an endless plain,
The ragged rims of thunder brooding low,
    With shadow-streaks of rain.

And one, an English home — gray twilight poured
    On dewy pastures, dewy trees,
Softer than sleep — all things in order stored,
    A haunt of ancient Peace.

THE LAKE ISLE OF INNISFREE [1]

WILLIAM BUTLER YEATS

    William Butler Yeats (1865–   ), was born in Dublin, Ireland.
He has done much to revive Irish folklore, besides writing exquisite
lyrics, and plays full of patriotic feeling and of the childlike superstition
of his country.   See also:
    Halleck's *New English Literature*, pp. 597–599, 616, 617, 623.
    Krans's *William Butler Yeats and the Irish Literary Revival*.

I WILL arise and go now, and go to Innisfree,
And a small cabin build there, of clay and wattles made;
Nine bean rows will I have there, a hive for the honey bee,
And live alone in the bee-loud glade.

And I shall have some peace there, for peace comes dropping
    slow,
Dropping from the veils of the morning to where the cricket
    sings;
There midnight's all a glimmer, and noon a purple glow,
And evening full of the linnet's wings.

I will arise and go now, for always night and day
I hear lake water lapping with low sounds by the shore;
While I stand on the roadway, or on the pavements gray,
I hear it in the deep heart's core.

STUDY HINTS

When Prospero heard Ariel's song, he said: "Why, that's my dainty Ariel: I shall miss thee." He was the daintiest of Shakespeare's creations, a spirit that thrilled with joy as he sang of his companionship with the beautiful things in nature. We know that Shakespeare loved Ariel and the things in nature that Ariel enjoyed. Note the airiness of this song. What natural objects are mentioned? Is this song as simple as the average of those in the preceding group of nature lyrics (p. 91)?

Can you find the secret of the magic in Wordsworth's *Daffodils?* Note that he calls them a "jocund company." How does the poet convey to you the joyousness of the flowers? Which do you think would be the most quoted of these four stanzas? How many times may one enjoy the same pleasurable experience? Is this poem easily understood?

Note that the poem of Keats is a sonnet. The sonnet is the most artificial of all verse forms, and contains exactly fourteen lines. England's four greatest writers of sonnets are Shakespeare, Milton, Wordsworth, and Keats. What terms does Keats use to describe summer? Under what circumstances does the cricket sing? How does the poet introduce a compliment to the grasshopper in the cricket's part of the poem?

Tennyson is here describing imaginary pictures in his fanciful *Palace of Art.* Do you think that a great artist could paint three pictures from the suggestions in these three stanzas? Which one of the pictures would you prefer? Have you read any other poem where the pictures are as clear-cut and vivid? Try embodying a picture in four lines of your own verse.

Note the simplicity of the first and third stanzas of *The Lake Isle of Innisfree.* Try to *feel* the beauty of the second stanza, which is quite famous. Does the poem make you wish to visit this isle? Would many people be content with the simple things which satisfy the poet? How many of the objects of sense appeal to the eye? To the ear?

Which of this group of five poems pleases you most? Memorize that one. After reading them at least twice aloud to yourself and studying them as directed above, read them to some of your friends and get their opinions. Which of the two groups of nature poems do you prefer as a whole, this one or the one beginning on page 91? Is there a single

obscure poem in either group? Are the poems simple because their
authors were not deep thinkers? Can a great poet present thoughts
easy to understand?

SUGGESTIONS FOR ADDITIONAL READINGS

To the Daisy. William Wordsworth.
The Solitary Reaper. William Wordsworth.
Three Years She Grew in Sun and Shower. William Wordsworth.
She Dwelt among the Untrodden Ways. William Wordsworth.
To the Daisy (5 stanzas). Robert Burns.
To the Dandelion. James R. Lowell.
To the Fringed Gentian. William Cullen Bryant.
A Rose. Emily Dickinson.
A Tulip. Emily Dickinson.
To the Grasshopper and the Cricket. Leigh Hunt.
The Cricket. Percy Mackaye.
To a Cricket. William C. Bennett.
The Revenge. Alfred Tennyson.
Break, Break, Break. Alfred Tennyson.
Songs from *The Princess.* Alfred Tennyson.
    Sweet and Low.
    The Bugle Song.
    Home They Brought her Warrior, Dead.
Crossing the Bar. Alfred Tennyson.
The Lady of Shalott. Alfred Tennyson.

For the teacher to read to the class:
Tennyson's *Sir Galahad;* Selections from *Lancelot and Elaine* **and**
from *Gareth and Lynette.*

LOVE IS STRONGER THAN HATE [1]

CHARLES DICKENS

Charles Dickens (1812–1870) was born in Portsmouth, England. At the age of eleven, he helped to support his family. His boyhood was spent in a hard struggle with poverty, but from this struggle he learned to sympathize with other poor children. No one has done more to improve the condition of children in every walk of life. His Little Nell, Paul Dombey, Sam Weller, and David Copperfield are characters known to most English-speaking people. One of his most dramatic novels is *A Tale of Two Cities*, which is a thrilling story of the French Revolution. See also:

Halleck's *New English Literature*, pp. 495–503, 582, 583.

Chesterton's *Charles Dickens*.

Foster's *Life of Dickens*.

[The French Revolution occurred in the latter part of the eighteenth century (1789–1795). The peasants of France, after centuries of oppression from the nobility, threw off the yoke, executed their king, Louis XVI, and his queen, Marie Antoinette, and set up a republic. Madame Defarge represents the type of woman who took an active part in the atrocities which gave to the latter part of this period the name of the "Reign of Terror."

Madame Defarge has threatened to bring the Evrémondes to the guillotine. Through the aid of Jerry Cruncher, a faithful adherent, and Miss Pross, who has served Evrémonde's wife with lifelong fidelity, they have just escaped from Paris and have started for London.]

THERE were many women during the French Revolution upon whom the time laid a dreadfully disfiguring hand; but there was not one among them more to be dreaded than that ruthless woman, Madame Defarge, now taking her way

[1] From *A Tale of Two Cities*.

along the streets. She was absolutely without pity. To appeal to her, was made hopeless by her having no sense of pity, even for herself.

Such a heart Madame Defarge carried under her rough robe. Carelessly worn, it was a becoming robe enough, in a certain weird way, and her dark hair looked rich under her coarse red cap. Lying hidden in her bosom was a loaded pistol. Lying hidden at her waist was a sharpened dagger. Thus accoutered, and walking with the confident tread of such a character, and with the supple freedom of a woman who had habitually walked in her girlhood, barefoot and barelegged, on the brown sea sand, Madame Defarge took her way along the streets.

Now, when the journey of the traveling coach, at that very moment waiting for the completion of its load, had been planned out last night, the difficulty of taking Miss Pross in it was a serious consideration. Finally, it was settled that Miss Pross and Jerry, who were at liberty to leave the city, should leave it at three o'clock in the lightest-wheeled conveyance known to that period.

Seeing in this arrangement the hope of rendering real service in that pressing emergency, Miss Pross hailed it with joy. She and Jerry had beheld the coach start, had passed some ten minutes in tortures of suspense, and were now concluding their arrangements to follow the coach, even as Madame Defarge, taking her way through the streets, now drew nearer and nearer to the else-deserted lodging in which they held their consultation.

"Now, what do you think, Mr. Cruncher," said Miss Pross, whose agitation was so great that she could hardly speak, or stand, or move, or live. "What do you think of our not starting from this courtyard? Another carriage having gone from here to-day, it might awaken suspicion."

"My opinion, miss," returned Mr. Cruncher, "is as

you're right. Likewise, wot I'll stand by you, right or wrong."

"I am so distracted with fear and hope for our precious creatures, that I am incapable of forming any plan. Are you capable of forming any plan, my dear, good Mr. Cruncher?"

"Respectin' a future spear o' life, miss," returned Mr. Cruncher, "I hope so. Respectin' any present use o' this here blessed head o' mine, I think not. Would you do me the favor, miss, to take notice o' two promises and wows wot it is my wishes fur to record in this here crisis?"

"Oh, for gracious sake! record them at once, and get them out of the way, like an excellent man."

"First," said Mr. Cruncher, who was all in a tremble, and who spoke with an ashy and solemn visage, "them poor things well out o' this, never no more will I do it, never no more!"

"I am quite sure, Mr. Cruncher," returned Miss Pross, "that you never will do it again, whatever it is, and I beg you not to think it necessary to mention more particularly what it is."

"No, miss," returned Jerry, "it shall not be named to you. Second: them poor things well out o' this, and never no more will I interfere with Mrs. Cruncher's flopping, never no more!"

"Whatever housekeeping arrangement that may be," said Miss Pross, striving to dry her eyes and compose herself, "I have no doubt it is best that Mrs. Cruncher should have it entirely under her own superintendence — O my poor darlings!"

"I go so far as to say, miss, morehover, and let my words be took down and took to Mrs. Cruncher through yourself — that wot my opinions respectin' flopping has undergone a change, and that wot I only hope with all my heart as Mrs. Cruncher may be a flopping at the present time."

"There, there, there! I hope she is, my dear man, and I hope she finds it answering her expectations."

And still Madame Defarge, pursuing her way along the streets, came nearer and nearer.

"If we ever get back to our native land," said Miss Pross, "you may rely upon my telling Mrs. Cruncher as much as I may be able to remember and understand of what you have so impressively said; and at all events you may be sure that I shall bear witness to your being thoroughly in earnest at this dreadful time. Now, pray, let us think! My esteemed Mr. Cruncher, let us think!"

Still, Madame Defarge, pursuing her way along the streets, came nearer and nearer.

"If you were to go before," said Miss Pross, "and stop the vehicle and horses from coming here, and were to wait somewhere for me; wouldn't that be best?"

Mr. Cruncher thought it might be best.

"Where could you wait for me?" asked Miss Pross.

Mr. Cruncher was so bewildered that he could think of no locality but Temple Bar. Alas, Temple Bar was hundreds of miles away, and Madame Defarge was drawing very near indeed.

"By the cathedral door," said Miss Pross. "Would it be much out of the way to take me in, near the great cathedral door between the two towers?"

"No, miss," answered Mr. Cruncher.

"Then, like the best of men," said Miss Pross, "go to the posting-house straight, and make that change."

"I am doubtful about leaving of you, you see. We don't known what may happen."

"Heaven knows, we don't," returned Miss Pross, "but have no fear for me. Take me in at the cathedral, at three o'clock, or as near it as you can, and I am sure it will be better than our going from here. I feel certain of it. There! Bless you, Mr. Cruncher! Think — not of me, but of the lives that may depend on both of us!"

This exordium, and Miss Pross's two hands in quiet agonized entreaty clasping his, decided Mr. Cruncher. With an encouraging nod or two, he immediately went out to alter the arrangements, and left her by herself to follow as she had proposed.

The having originated a precaution which was already in course of execution, was a great relief to Miss Pross. The necessity of composing her appearance so that it should attract no special notice in the streets, was another relief. She looked at her watch, and it was twenty minutes past two. She had no time to lose, but must get ready at once.

Afraid, in her extreme perturbation, of the loneliness of the deserted rooms, and of half-imagined faces peeping from behind every open door in them, Miss Pross got a basin of cold water and began laving her eyes, which were swollen and red. Haunted by her feverish apprehensions, she could not bear to have her sight obscured for a minute at a time by the dripping water, but constantly paused and looked round to see that there was no one watching her. In one of those pauses she recoiled and cried out, for she saw a figure standing in the room.

The basin fell to the ground broken, and the water flowed to the feet of Madame Defarge. By strange, stern ways, and through much staining blood, those feet had come to meet that water.

Madame Defarge looked coldly at her, and said, "The wife of Evrémonde; where is she?"

It flashed upon Miss Pross's mind that the doors were all standing open, and would suggest the flight. Her first act was to shut them. There were four in the room, and she shut them all. She then placed herself before the door of the chamber which Lucie had occupied.

Madame Defarge's dark eyes followed her through this rapid movement, and rested on her when it was finished. Miss Pross had nothing beautiful about her; years had not tamed the wildness, or softened the grimness of her appearance; but, she, too, was a determined woman in her different way, and she measured Madame Defarge with her eyes, every inch.

"You might, from your appearance, be the wife of Lucifer. Nevertheless, you shall not get the better of me. I am an Englishwoman."

"On my way yonder," said Madame Defarge, with a slight movement of her hand towards the fatal spot, "where they reserve my chair and my knitting for me, I am come to make my compliments to her in passing. I wish to see her."

"I know that your intentions are evil," said Miss Pross, "and you may depend upon it, I'll hold my own against them."

Each spoke in her own language; neither understood the other's words; both were very watchful, and intent to deduce from look and manner, what the unintelligible words meant.

"It will do her no good to keep herself concealed from me at this moment," said Madame Defarge. "Good patriots will know what that means. Let me see her. Go tell her that I wish to see her. Do you hear?"

"If those eyes of yours were bed-winches," returned Miss Pross, "and I was an English four-poster, they shouldn't loose a splinter of me. No, you wicked foreign woman; I am your match."

"Woman, imbecile and pig-like! I take no answer from you. I demand to see her. Either tell her that I demand to see her, or stand out of the way of the door and let me go to her!" This, with an angry explanatory wave of her right arm.

"I little thought," said Miss Pross, "that I should ever want to understand your nonsensical language; but I would give all I have, except the clothes I wear, to know whether you suspect the truth, or any part of it."

Neither of them for a single moment released the other's eyes. Madame Defarge had not moved from the spot where she stood when Miss Pross first became aware of her; but she now advanced one step.

"I am a Briton," said Miss Pross. "I am desperate. I don't care an English twopence for myself. I know that the longer I keep you here, the greater hope there is for my Ladybird. I'll not leave a handful of that dark hair upon your head, if you lay a finger on me!"

Thus Miss Pross, with a shake of her head and a flash of her eyes between every sentence, and every rapid sentence a whole breath. Thus Miss Pross, who had never struck a blow in her life.

But her courage was of that emotional nature that it brought the irrepressible tears into her eyes. This was a courage that Madame Defarge so little comprehended as to mistake for weakness. "Ha! ha!" she laughed, "you poor wretch! What are you worth! I address myself to that Doctor." Then she raised her voice and called out, "Citizen Doctor! Wife of Evrémonde! Child of Evrémonde! Any person but this miserable fool, answer the Citizeness Defarge!"

Perhaps the following silence, perhaps some latent disclosure in the expression of Miss Pross's face, perhaps a sudden misgiving apart from either suggestion, whispered to Madame Defarge that they were gone. Three of the doors she opened swiftly, and looked in.

"Those rooms are all in disorder, there has been hurried

packing, there are odds and ends upon the ground.   There is no one in that room behind you!   Let me look."

"Never!" said Miss Pross, who understood the request as perfectly as Madame Defarge understood the answer.

"If they are not in that room, they are gone, and can be pursued and brought back," said Madame Defarge to herself.

"As long as you don't know whether they are in that room or not, you are uncertain what to do," said Miss Pross to herself; "and you shall not know that, if I can prevent your knowing it; and know that, or not know that, you shall not leave here while I can hold you."

"I have been in the streets from the first, nothing has stopped me, I will tear you to pieces, but I will have you from that door," said Madame Defarge.

"We are alone at the top of a high house in a solitary courtyard, we are not likely to be heard, and I pray for bodily strength to keep you here, while every minute you are here is worth a hundred thousand guineas to my darling," said Miss Pross.

Madame Defarge made at the door.   Miss Pross, on the instinct of the moment, seized her round the waist in both her arms, and held her tight.   It was in vain for Madame Defarge to struggle and to strike; Miss Pross, with the vigorous tenacity of love, always so much stronger than hate, clasped her tight, and even lifted her from the floor in the struggle that they had.   The two hands of Madame Defarge buffeted and tore her face; but Miss Pross, with her head down, held her round the waist, and clung to her with more than the hold of a drowning woman.

Soon, Madame Defarge's hands ceased to strike, and felt at her encircled waist.   "It is under my arm," said Miss Pross, in smothered tones, "you shall not draw it.   I am stronger than you, I bless heaven for it.   I'll hold you till one or other of us faints or dies!"

Madame Defarge's hands were at her bosom. Miss Pross looked up, saw what it was, struck at it, struck out a flash and a crash, and stood alone — blinded with smoke.

All this was in a second. As the smoke cleared, leaving an awful stillness, it passed out on the air, like the soul of Madame Defarge whose body lay lifeless on the ground.

STUDY HINTS

Study the spelling and meaning of these words:

disfiguring	solemn	emergency
habitually	ruthless	incapable
conveyance	agitation	compliment
suspense	feverish	recoil

Try to visualize, *i.e.* to see with your imagination, Madame Defarge. To what trait of her character does the writer call attention? Compare your first impression of Miss Pross with that of Madame Defarge. What effect is produced upon you by the words "And still Madame Defarge came nearer and nearer"? How do we know that Miss Pross is very much agitated? What does Miss Pross imply when she says, "I am an Englishwoman"? Does she express the same idea at any other point? Does she act as your first impression led you to expect? As Madame Defarge expected? What made her victorious? Is this story thrilling? Why?

SUGGESTIONS FOR ORAL AND WRITTEN ENGLISH
THEME SUBJECTS

The author begins with telling what kind of person Madame Defarge is, then he *proves* it by an illustration. What method does he use in the case of Miss Pross?

Dramatize the selection as in Suggestions, p. 106. Assign the parts to members of the class and act the scene as the story indicates it should be acted.

Make an outline (*i.e.* a scenario) of the chief points of this story for a moving picture. Act the scene silently.

Arrange the dialogue of this story as explained on page 106. Select what you think can be used as stage directions, and insert in parentheses where you think best. Write a story on this same theme, "Love is Stronger than Hate," in which two schoolboys are the characters. Try to develop your idea principally by the use of dialogue.

Tell the story of Miss Pross's encounter, in the character of Miss Pross herself.

Dramatize *The Pine-Tree Shillings*, p. 171, supplying the necessary dialogue. Can you introduce some Indian character to make it more picturesque?

SUGGESTIONS FOR ADDITIONAL READINGS

The Tale of Two Cities.   Charles Dickens.
A Christmas Carol.   Charles Dickens.
Old Curiosity Shop.   Charles Dickens.
David Copperfield.   Charles Dickens.
Lazarre.   Mary H. Catherwood.
Monsieur Beaucaire.   Booth Tarkington.
A Gentleman of France.   Stanley Weyman.
The Adventures of François.   S. Weir Mitchell.
The Three Musketeers.   Alexander Dumas.
The Boyhood and Youth of Napoleon.   Oscar Browning.

A DAY IN JUNE [1]

JAMES RUSSELL LOWELL

James Russell Lowell (1819–1891), born in the suburbs of Cambridge, Massachusetts, was descended from a cultured New England family. He was sent to Harvard and later had a private tutor at Concord, where he knew Emerson. (See *The Humblebee*, p. 246.) Like Washington Irving, he was minister to Spain. Later he was ambassador to England, in which position he won great popularity. In spite of his duties as editor of two well-known magazines, and as lecturer, succeeding Longfellow at Harvard, he published many poems and much prose. *A Day in June* is taken from *The Vision of Sir Launfal*, one of his most widely known poems. He lies buried in Mt. Auburn Cemetery, Cambridge, Massachusetts, not far from Longfellow's resting place. See also:

Halleck's *History of American Literature*, pp. 245–257, 284.
Scudder's *James Russell Lowell: A Biography.*

AND what is so rare as a day in June?
    Then, if ever, come perfect days;
Then Heaven tries earth if it be in tune,
    And over it softly her warm ear lays:
Whether we look, or whether we listen,   5
We hear life murmur, or see it glisten;
Every clod feels a stir of might,
    An instinct within it that reaches and towers,
And, groping blindly above it for light,
    Climbs to a soul in grass and flowers;   10

[1] Used by permission of, and by arrangement with, Houghton Mifflin Company authorized publishers of Lowell's works.

The flush of life may well be seen
   Thrilling back over hills and valleys;
The cowslip startles in meadows green,
   The buttercup catches the sun in its chalice,
And there's never a leaf nor a blade too mean [1]   15
   To be some happy creature's palace;
The little bird sits at his door in the sun,
   Atilt like a blossom among the leaves,
And lets his illumined being o'errun
   With the deluge of summer it receives;   20
His mate feels the eggs beneath her wings,
And the heart in her dumb breast flutters and
    sings;
He sings to the wide world, and she to her nest, —
In the nice [2] ear of Nature which song is the best?
We are happy now because God wills it;   25
No matter how barren the past may have been,
'Tis enough for us now that the leaves are green;
We sit in the warm shade and feel right well
How the sap creeps up and the blossoms swell;
We may shut our eyes, but we cannot help knowing   30
That skies are clear and grass is growing;
The breeze comes whispering in our ear,
That dandelions are blossoming near,
   That maize has sprouted, that streams are flowing,
That the river is bluer than the sky,   35
That the robin is plastering his house hard by;
And if the breeze kept the good news back,
For other couriers we should not lack;
   We could guess it all by yon heifer's lowing, —
And hark! how clear bold chanticleer,   40
Warmed with the new wine of the year,
   Tells all in his lusty crowing!

---

[1] Humble.   [2] Thoughtful, discriminating.

STUDY HINTS

Can you answer the poet's question on line 24? How many things contribute to make a perfect June day? Can you add anything to the poet's list? What is your favorite month? What would constitute a perfect day in that month? Does any part of this resemble Wordsworth's descriptions of nature?

SUGGESTIONS FOR ADDITIONAL READINGS

The Fountain. James Russell Lowell.
Aladdin. James Russell Lowell.
The Shepherd of King Admetus. James Russell Lowell.
Sunthin' in the Pastoral Line (from *The Biglow Papers, Second Series,* No. VI). James Russell Lowell.
Knee-deep in June. James Whitcomb Riley.
Chanticleer. Celia Thaxter.

THE CHAPARRAL [1] PRINCE [2]

O. HENRY

O. Henry (1867–1910), whose real name was William Sydney Porter, was born in Greensboro, North Carolina. He led a very roving life, at one time being a cowboy in Texas, at another, editor of a magazine. He finally went to New York in 1902, where he became widely known as a writer of short stories. Critics have said that he is the best short-story writer that America has produced, with the exception of Poe and Hawthorne. See also:

Bookman, 38 : 168–177 (October, 1913).
World's Work, 18 : 11724–11726 (June, 1909).

NINE o'clock at last, and the drudging toil of the day was ended. Lena climbed to her room in the third half-story of the Quarrymen's Hotel. Since daylight she had slaved, doing the work of a full-grown woman, scrubbing the floors, washing the heavy ironstone plates and cups, making the beds, and supplying the insatiate demands for wood and water in that turbulent and depressing hostelry.

The din of the day's quarrying was over — the blasting and drilling, the creaking of the great cranes, the shouts of the foremen, the backing and shifting of the flat-cars hauling the heavy blocks of limestone. Down in the hotel office three or four of the laborers were growling and swearing over a belated game of checkers. Heavy odors of stewed meat, hot grease, and cheap coffee hung like a depressing fog about the house.

Lena lit the stump of a candle and sat limply upon her

wooden chair. She was eleven years old, thin and ill-nourished. Her back and limbs were sore and aching. But the ache in her heart made the biggest trouble. The last

straw had been added to the burden upon her small shoulders. They had taken away Grimm.[1] Always at night, however tired she might be, she had turned to Grimm for comfort and hope. Each time had Grimm whispered to her that the prince or the fairy would come and deliver her out of the wicked enchantment. Every night she had taken fresh courage and strength from Grimm.

To whatever tale she read she found an analogy in her own condition. The woodcutter's lost child, the unhappy goose girl, the persecuted stepdaughter, the little maiden imprisoned in the witch's hut — all these were but transparent disguises for Lena, the overworked kitchenmaid in the Quarrymen's Hotel. And always when the extremity was direst came the good fairy or the gallant prince to the rescue.

So, here in the ogre's castle, enslaved by a wicked spell, Lena had leaned upon Grimm and waited, longing for the powers of goodness to prevail. But on the day before Mrs. Maloney had found the book in her room and had carried it away, declaring sharply it would not do for servants to read at night; they lost sleep and did not work briskly the next day. Can one only eleven years old, living away from one's mamma, and never having any time to play, live entirely deprived of Grimm? Just try it once, and you will see what a difficult thing it is.

Lena's home was in Texas, away up among the little

[1] The Grimm Brothers' *Fairy Tales*.

mountains on the Pedernales River, in a little town called
Fredericksburg. They are all German people who live in
Fredericksburg. Of evenings they sit at little tables along
the sidewalk and drink beer and play pinochle [1] and scat.[1]
They are very thrifty people.

Thriftiest among them was Peter Hildesmuller, Lena's
father. And that is why Lena was sent to work in the hotel
at the quarries, thirty miles away. She earned three dollars
every week there, and Peter added her wages to his well-
guarded store. Peter had an ambition to become as rich as
his neighbor, Hugo Heffelbauer, who smoked a meerschaum
pipe three feet long and had wiener schnitzel and hasenpfeffer
for dinner every day in the week. And now Lena was quite
old enough to work and assist in the accumulation of riches.
But conjecture, if you can, what it means to be sentenced at
eleven years of age from a home in the pleasant little Rhine
village to hard labor in the ogre's castle, where you must fly
to serve the ogres, while they devour cattle and sheep,
growling fiercely as they stamp white limestone dust from
their great shoes for you to sweep and scour with your weak,
aching fingers. And then — to have Grimm taken away
from you!

Lena raised the lid of an old empty case that had once
contained canned corn and got out a sheet of paper and a
piece of pencil. She was going to write a letter to her
mamma. Tommy Ryan was going to post it for her at
Ballinger's. Tommy was seventeen, worked in the quarries,
went home to Ballinger's every night, and was now waiting
in the shadows under Lena's window for her to throw the
letter out to him. That was the only way she could send a
letter to Fredericksburg. Mrs. Maloney did not like for
her to write letters.

The stump of candle was burning low, so Lena hastily bit

[1] Simple card games.

the wood from around the lead of her pencil and began.
This is the letter she wrote:

"DEAREST MAMMA: — I want so much to see you. And Gretel and
Claus and Heinrich and little Adolf. I am so tired. I want to see you.
To-day I was slapped by Mrs. Maloney and had no supper. I could not
bring in enough wood, for my hand hurt. She took my book yesterday.
I mean 'Grimms's Fairy Tales,' which Uncle Leo gave me. It did not
hurt any one for me to read the book. I try to work as well as I can,
but there is so much to do. I read only a little bit every night. Dear
mamma, I shall tell you what I am going to do. Unless you send for
me to-morrow to bring me home I shall go to a deep place I know in the
river and drown. It is wicked to drown, I suppose, but I wanted to
see you, and there is no one else. I am very tired, and Tommy is waiting for the letter. You will excuse me, mamma, if I do it.
          "Your respectful and loving daughter,

                                                   "LENA."

Tommy was still waiting faithfully when the letter was
concluded, and when Lena dropped it out she saw him pick
it up and start up the steep hillside. Without undressing,
she blew out the candle and curled herself upon the mattress
on the floor.

At 10:30 o'clock old man Ballinger came out of his house
in his stocking feet and leaned over the gate, smoking his
pipe. He looked down the big road, white in the moonshine,
and rubbed one ankle with the toe of his other foot. It was
time for the Fredericksburg mail to come pattering up the
road.

Old man Ballinger had waited only a few minutes when
he heard the lively hoof beats of Fritz's team of little black
mules, and very soon afterward his covered spring wagon
stood in front of the gate. Fritz's big spectacles flashed in
the moonlight and his tremendous voice shouted a greeting
to the postmaster of Ballinger's. The mail carrier jumped
out and took the bridles from the mules, for he always fed
them oats at Ballinger's.

While the mules were eating from their feed bags, old man Ballinger brought out the mail sack and threw it into the wagon.

Fritz Bergmann was a man of three sentiments — or to be more accurate — four, the pair of mules deserving to be reckoned individually. Those mules were the chief interest and joy of his existence. Next came the Emperor of Germany and Lena Hildesmuller.

"Tell me," said Fritz, when he was ready to start, "contains the sack a letter to Frau Hildesmuller from the little Lena at the quarries? One came in the last mail to say that she is a little sick, already. Her mamma is very anxious to hear again."

"Yes," said old man Ballinger, "thar's a letter for Mrs. Helterskelter, or some sich name. Tommy Ryan brung it over when he come. Her little gal workin' over thar, you say?"

"In the hotel," shouted Fritz, as he gathered up the lines; "eleven years old and not bigger as a frankfurter. The close-fist of a Peter Hildesmuller! — some day shall I with a big club pound that man's dummkopf [1] — all in and out the town. Perhaps in this letter Lena will say that she is yet feeling better. So, her mamma will be glad. *Auf wiedersehen*,[2] Herr Ballinger — your feets will take cold out in the night air."

"So long, Fritzy," said old man Ballinger. "You got a nice cool night for your drive."

Up the road went the little black mules at their steady trot, while Fritz thundered at them occasional words of endearment and cheer.

These fancies occupied the mind of the mail carrier until he reached the big post oak forest, eight miles from Ballinger's. Here his ruminations were scattered by the sudden

[1] German for *blockhead*.   [2] German for *Good-by*. Literally, "Till I see you again."

flash and report of pistols and a whooping as if from a whole tribe of Indians. A band of galloping centaurs [1] closed in around the mail wagon. One of them leaned over the front wheel, covered the driver with his revolver, and ordered him to stop. Others caught at the bridles of Donder and Blitzen.

"Donnerwetter!" [2] shouted Fritz, with all his tremendous voice — "was ist? Release your hands from dose mules. Ve vas der United States mail!"

"Hurry up, Dutch!" drawled a melancholy voice. "Don't you know when you're in a stick-up? Reverse your mules and climb out of the cart."

It is due to the breadth of Hondo Bill's demerit and the largeness of his achievements to state that the holding up of the Fredericksburg mail was not perpetrated by way of an exploit. As the lion while in the pursuit of prey commensurate to his prowess might set a frivolous foot upon a casual rabbit in his path, so Hondo Bill and his gang had swooped sportively upon the pacific transport of Meinherr Fritz.

The real work of their sinister night ride was over. Fritz and his mail bag and his mules came as a gentle relaxation, grateful after the arduous duties of their profession. Twenty miles to the southeast stood a train with a killed engine, hysterical passengers, and a looted express and mail car. That represented the serious occupation of Hondo Bill and his gang. With a fairly rich prize of currency and silver the robbers were making a wide detour to the west through the less populous country, intending to seek safety in Mexico by means of some fordable spot on the Rio Grande. The booty from the train had melted the desperate bushrangers to jovial and happy skylarkers.

---

[1] Mythical creatures half man and half horse. The writer means that they rode so well they seemed a part of the horse.

[2] Thunderation!

Trembling with outraged dignity and no little personal apprehension, Fritz climbed out to the road after replacing his suddenly removed spectacles. The band had dismounted and were singing, capering, and whooping, thus expressing their satisfied delight in the life of a jolly outlaw. Rattle-snake Rogers, who stood at the heads of the mules, jerked a little too vigorously at the rein of the tender-mouthed Don-der, who reared and emitted a loud, protesting snort of pain. Instantly Fritz, with a scream of anger, flew at the bulky Rogers and began to assiduously pommel that surprised free-booter with his fists.

"Villain!" shouted Fritz, "dog, bigstiff! Dot mule he has a soreness by his mouth. I vill knock off your shoulders mit your head — robbermans!"

"Yi-yi!" howled Rattlesnake, roaring with laughter and ducking his head, "somebody git this here sauerkrout off'n me!"

One of the band yanked Fritz back by the coat tail, and the woods rang with Rattlesnake's vociferous comments.

"The . . . little wienerwurst," he yelled, amiably. "He's not so much of a skunk, for a Dutchman. Took up for his animile plum quick, didn't he? I like to see a man like his hoss, even if it is a mule. The dad-blamed little Limburger, he went for me, didn't he! Whoa, now, muley — I ain't a-goin' to hurt your mouth agin any more."

Perhaps the mail would not have been tampered with had not Ben Moody, the lieutenant, possessed certain wisdom that seemed to promise more spoils.

"Say, Cap," he said, addressing Hondo Bill, "there's liable to be good pickings in these mail sacks. I've done some hoss tradin' with these Dutchmen around Fredericks-burg, and I know the style of the varmints. There's big money goes through the mails to that town. Them Dutch risk a thousand dollars sent wrapped in a piece of paper before they'd pay the banks to handle the money."

Hondo Bill, six feet two, gentle of voice and impulsive in action, was dragging the sacks from the rear of the wagon before Moody had finished his speech. A knife shone in his hand, and they heard the ripping sound as it bit through the tough canvas. The outlaws crowded around and began tearing open letters and packages, enlivening their labors by swearing affably at the writers, who seemed to have conspired to confute the prediction of Ben Moody. Not a dollar was found in the Fredericksburg mail.

"You ought to be ashamed of yourself," said Hondo Bill, to the mail carrier in solemn tones, "to be packing around such a lot of old, trashy paper as this. What d'you mean by it, anyhow? Where do you Dutchers keep your money at?"

The Ballinger mail sack opened like a cocoon under Hondo's knife. It contained but a handful of mail. Fritz had been fuming with terror and excitement until this sack was reached. He now remembered Lena's letter. He addressed the leader of the band, asking that that particular missive be spared.

"Much obliged, Dutch," he said to the disturbed carrier. "I guess that's the letter we want. Got spondulicks in it, ain't it? Here she is. Make a light, boys."

Hondo found and tore open the letter to Mrs. Hildesmuller. The others stood about, lighting twisted-up letters one from another. Hondo gazed with mute disapproval at the single sheet of paper covered with the angular German script.

"Whatever is this you've humbugged us with, Dutchy? You call this here a valuable letter? That's a mighty low-down trick to play on your friends what come along to help you distribute your mail."

"That's Chiny writin'," said Sandy Grundy, peering over Hondo's shoulder.

"You're off your kazip," declared another of the gang, an effective youth, covered with silk handkerchiefs and nickel plating. "That's shorthand. I seen 'em do it once in court."

"Ach, no, no, no — dot is German," said Fritz. "It is no more as a little girl writing a letter to her mamma. One poor little girl, sick and vorking hard avay from home. Ach! it is a shame. Good Mr. Robberman, you vill please let me have dot letter?"

"What the devil do you take us for, old Pretzels?" said Hondo with sudden and surprising severity. "You ain't presumin' to insinuate that we gents ain't possessed of sufficient politeness for to take an interest in the miss's health, are you? Now, you go on, and you read that scratchin' out loud and in plain United States language to this here company of educated society."

Hondo twirled his six-shooter by its trigger guard and stood towering above the little German, who at once began to read the letter, translating the simple words into English. The gang of rovers stood in absolute silence, listening intently.

"How old is that kid?" asked Hondo when the letter was done.

"Eleven," said Fritz.

"And where is she at?"

"At dose rock quarries — working. Ach, mein Gott — little Lena, she speak of drowning. I do not know if she vill do it, but if she shall I schwear I vill dot Peter Hildesmuller shoot mit a gun."

"You Dutchers," said Hondo Bill, his voice swelling with fine contempt, "make me plenty tired. Hirin' out your kids to work when they ought to be playin' dolls in the sand.

. . . I reckon we'll fix your clock for a while just to show what we think of your old cheesy nation. Here, boys!"

Hondo Bill parleyed aside briefly with his band, and then they seized Fritz and conveyed him off the road to one side. Here they bound him fast to a tree with a couple of lariats. His team they tied to another tree near by.

"We ain't going to hurt you bad," said Hondo reassuringly. "'Twon't hurt you to be tied up for a while. We will now pass you the time of day, as it is up to us to depart. Ausgespielt — nixcumrous,[1] Dutchy. Don't get any more impatience."

Fritz heard a great squeaking of saddles as the men mounted their horses. Then a loud yell and a great clatter of hoofs as they galloped pell-mell back along the Fredericksburg road.

For more than two hours Fritz sat against his tree, tightly but not painfully bound. Then from the reaction after his exciting adventure he sank into slumber. How long he slept he knew not, but he was at last awakened by a rough shake. Hands were untying his ropes. He was lifted to his feet, dazed, confused in mind, and weary of body. Rubbing his eyes, he looked and saw that he was again in the midst of the same band of terrible bandits. They shoved him up to the seat of his wagon and placed the lines in his hands.

"Hit it out for home, Dutch," said Hondo Bill's voice commandingly. "You've given us lots of trouble and we're pleased to see the back of your neck. Spiel! Zwei bier! Vamoose!"[1]

Hondo reached out and gave Blitzen a smart cut with his quirt. The little mules sprang ahead, glad to be moving again. Fritz urged them along, himself dizzy and muddled over his fearful adventure.

---

[1] Like so many other expressions of the robbers, fragments of real German, and nonsensical and humorous imitations of Fritz's speech.

According to schedule time, he should have reached Fredericksburg at daylight. As it was, he drove down the long street of the town at eleven o'clock A.M. He had to pass Peter Hildesmuller's house on his way to the post-office. He stopped his team at the gate and called. But Frau Hildesmuller was watching for him. Out rushed the whole family of Hildesmullers.

Frau Hildesmuller, fat and flushed, inquired if he had a letter from Lena, and then Fritz raised his voice and told the tale of his adventure. He told the contents of the letter that the robber had made him read, and then Frau Hildesmuller broke into wild weeping. Her little Lena drown herself! Why had they sent her from home? What could be done? Perhaps it would be too late by the time they could send for her now. Peter Hildesmuller dropped his meerschaum on the walk and it shivered into pieces.

"Woman!" he roared at his wife, "why did you let that child go away? It is your fault if she comes home to us no more."

Every one knew that it was Peter Hildesmuller's fault, so they paid no attention to his words.

A moment afterward a strange, faint voice was heard to call: "Mamma!" Frau Hildesmuller at first thought it was Lena's spirit calling, and then she rushed to the rear of Fritz's covered wagon, and, with a loud shriek of joy, caught up Lena herself, covering her pale little face with kisses and smothering her with hugs. Lena's eyes were heavy with the deep slumber of exhaustion, but she smiled and lay close to the one she had longed to see. There among the mail sacks, covered in a nest of strange blankets and comforters, she had lain asleep until awakened by the voices around her.

Fritz stared at her with eyes that bulged behind his spectacles.

"Gott in Himmel!" he shouted. "How did you get in

that wagon? Am I going crazy as well as to be murdered and hanged by robbers this day?"

"You brought her to us, Fritz," cried Herr Hildesmuller. "How can we ever thank you enough?"

"Tell mamma how you came in Fritz's wagon," said Frau Hildesmuller.

"I don't know," said Lena. "But I know how I got away from the hotel. The Prince brought me."

"By the Emperor's crown!" shouted Fritz, "we are all going crazy."

"I always knew he would come," said Lena, sitting down on her bundle of bedclothes on the sidewalk. "Last night he came with his armed knights and captured the ogre's castle. They broke the dishes and kicked down the doors. They pitched Mr. Maloney into a barrel of rain water and threw flour all over Mrs. Maloney. The workmen in the hotel jumped out of the windows and ran into the woods when the knights began firing their guns. They wakened me up and I peeped down the stair. And then the Prince

came up and wrapped me in the bedclothes and carried me out. He was so tall and strong and fine. His face was as rough as a scrubbing brush, and he talked soft and kind and smelled of schnapps. He took me on his horse before him and we rode away among the knights. He held me close and I went to sleep that way, and didn't wake up till I got home."

"Rubbish!" cried Fritz Bergmann. "Fairy tales! How did you come from the quarries to my wagon?"

"The Prince brought me," said Lena, confidently.

And to this day the good people of Fredericksburg haven't been able to make her give any other explanation.

STUDY HINTS

Study the spelling and meaning of these words:

turbulent	endearment	canvas
insatiate	rein	exhaustion
nourished	bridle	confidently
enchantment	explanation	clothes

Is your interest in this story awakened at once? What one comfort did Lena have? How did it help her through the long days? Who was Grimm? Which of his stories do you think Lena had specially in mind? Why does the author talk so much about Grimm at the beginning of the story? What connection has Grimm with the title? How does Lena's letter affect you? What expressions arouse your sympathy? Is the letter childlike? How does Fritz show his love for the child? For the mules? Do the German expressions and the dialect of the outlaws add to the interest? Why was Lena so willing to be carried off by a stranger? Does Lena's father feel any shame for his conduct? Does the story end as you expected? Does it seem impossible? How would you feel if you happened to be a member of the jury to try those robbers?

SUGGESTIONS FOR ORAL AND WRITTEN ENGLISH
THEME SUBJECTS

What fairy tales particularly had Lena been reading? Tell one, making it as interesting as possible. Can you recall any fairy tales

that ended differently from what you expected? An unexpected ending is one of the characteristics of O. Henry's stories. Select an incident
for a climax and try to end the story in a manner that will completely
surprise the reader. Be careful that your ending is not impossible.
Tell your favorite fairy tale. Dramatize it as suggested on page 106 in
a simple form for children.

The Story of the Finding of Lena (by one of the robbers).

The Hold-up (as told by Fritz).   How I Help at Home.

Some Child Labor Laws in my State.   The Best Way to Wash Dishes.

The Advantages of a Lively Im-   Rural Delivery.
  agination.   In the Days of the Stagecoach.

Some Disadvantages of a Lively Im-   Autobiography of a Letter.
  agination.   The Parcel Post.

SUGGESTIONS FOR ADDITIONAL READINGS

The Gifts of the Magi (in *The Four Million*). O. Henry.

The Cop and the Anthem (in *The Four Million*). O. Henry.

Thimble, Thimble (in *Options*). O. Henry.

The Lady or the Tiger. Frank R. Stockton.

Marjory Daw. Thomas B. Aldrich.

Little Citizens. Myra Kelly.

Little Aliens. Myra Kelly.

Emmy Lou. George Madden Martin.

Tillie, A Mennonite Maid. H. R. Martin.

Anne of Avonlea. L. M. Montgomery.

Anne of Green Gables. L. M. Montgomery.

A Christmas Mystery. W. J. Locke.

Van Bibber and the Swan Boats. R. H. Davis.

Van Bibber's Burglar. R. H. Davis.

In Grimm's *Fairy Tales: Cinderella, Beauty and the Beast, Snowdrop,
Tom Thumb, The Seven Ravens, Rumpelstiltskin, The Youth Who Could
Not Shudder, Hansel and Gretel*.

THE OLD HUSBAND AND THE YOUNG WIFE [1]

RICHARD BRINSLEY SHERIDAN

Richard Brinsley Sheridan (1751–1816) was born in Dublin and educated at the famous English school of Harrow. He was successful both as a dramatist and as a statesman. His two plays, *The Rivals* (1775) and *The School for Scandal* (1777), are noted for their realistic portrayal of eighteenth-century life and customs. He died in 1816 and was buried in Westminster Abbey.

From 1642, when the Puritans closed the theaters, until 1890, only three plays were written which are much read or acted to-day. The three are these two by Sheridan, and one by Oliver Goldsmith, *She Stoops to Conquer* (1773). See also:

Halleck's *New English Literature*, pp. 210, 262–264, 337.

Rae's *Life of Richard Brinsley Sheridan*.

Sichel's *Sheridan*.

Sir Peter Teazle. But here comes my helpmate! She appears in great good humor. How happy I should be if I could tease her into loving me, though but a little!

Enter LADY TEAZLE.

Lady Teazle. Lud! Sir Peter, I hope you haven't been quarreling with Maria? It is not using me well to be ill humored when I am not by.

Sir Peter. Ah, Lady Teazle, you might have the power to make me good humored at all times.

Lady Teazle. I am sure I wish I had; for I want you to be in a charming sweet temper at this moment. Do be good humored now, and let me have two hundred pounds, will you?

[1] From *The School for Scandal*.

Sir Peter. Two hundred pounds; what, a'n't I to be in a good humor without paying for it! But speak to me thus, and i' faith there's nothing I could refuse you. You shall have it; but seal me a bond for the repayment.

Lady Teazle. O, no — there — my note of hand will do as well.   [*Offering her hand.*]

Sir Peter. And you shall no longer reproach me with not giving you an independent settlement. I mean shortly to surprise you: but shall we always live thus, hey?

Lady Teazle. If you please. I'm sure I don't care how soon we leave off quarreling, provided you'll own you were tired first.

Sir Peter. Well — then let our future contest be, who shall be most obliging.

Lady Teazle. I assure you, Sir Peter, good nature becomes you. You look now as you did before we were married, when you used to walk with me under the elms, and tell me stories of what a gallant you were in your youth, and chuck me under the chin, you would; and ask me if I thought I could love an old fellow, who would deny me nothing — didn't you?

Sir Peter. Yes, yes, and you were as kind and attentive ——

Lady Teazle. Ay, so I was, and would always take your part, when my acquaintance used to abuse you, and turn you into ridicule.

Sir Peter. Indeed!

Lady Teazle. Ay, and when my cousin Sophy has called you a stiff, peevish old bachelor, and laughed at me for thinking of marrying one who might be my father, I have always defended you, and said, I didn't think you so ugly by any means.

Sir Peter. Thank you. And you prophesied right; and we shall now be the happiest couple ——

Lady Teazle. And never differ again?

Sir Peter. No, never! — though at the same time, indeed, my dear Lady Teazle, you must watch your temper very seriously; for in all our little quarrels, my dear, if you recollect, my love, you always began first.

Lady Teazle. I beg your pardon, my dear Sir Peter; indeed, you always gave the provocation.

Sir Peter. Now see, my angel! take care — contradicting isn't the way to keep friends.

Lady Teazle. Then don't you begin it, my love!

Sir Peter. There, now! you — you are going on.

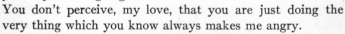

You don't perceive, my love, that you are just doing the very thing which you know always makes me angry.

Lady Teazle. Nay, you know if you will be angry without any reason, my dear ——

Sir Peter. There! now you want to quarrel again.

Lady Teazle. No, I'm sure I don't; but, if you will be so peevish ——

Sir Peter. There now! who begins first?

Lady Teazle. Why, you, to be sure. I said nothing — but there's no bearing your temper.

Sir Peter. No, no, madam; the fault's in your own temper.

Lady Teazle. Ay, you are just what my cousin Sophy said you would be.

Sir Peter. Your cousin Sophy is a forward, impertinent gypsy.

Lady Teazle. You are a great bear, I'm sure, to abuse my relations.

Sir Peter. Now may all the plagues of marriage be doubled on me, if ever I try to be friends with you any more!

Lady Teazle. So much the better.

Sir Peter. No, no, madam: 'tis evident you never cared a pin for me, and I was a madman to marry you — a pert, rural coquette, that had refused half the honest squires in the neighborhood.

Lady Teazle. And I am sure I was a fool to marry you — an old dangling bachelor, who was single at fifty, only because he never could meet with any one who would have him.

Sir Peter. Ay, ay, madam; but you were pleased enough to listen to me: you never had such an offer before.

Lady Teazle. No! didn't I refuse Sir Tivy Terrier, who everybody said would have been a better match? for his estate is just as good as yours, and he has broke his neck since we have been married.

Sir Peter. I have done with you, madam. You are an unfeeling, ungrateful — but there's an end of everything. I believe you capable of everything, that is bad.

Lady Teazle. Take care, Sir Peter! you had better not insinuate any such thing! I'll not be suspected without cause, I promise you.

Sir Peter. Very well, madam! very well! A separate maintenance as soon as you please. Yes, madam, or a divorce! I'll make an example of myself for the benefit of all old bachelors. Let us separate, madam.

Lady Teazle. Agreed! agreed! And now, my dear Sir Peter, we are of a mind once more; we may be the happiest couple, and never differ again, you know; ha! ha! ha! Well, you are going to be in a passion, I see, and I shall only interrupt you — so, bye, bye! [*Exit.*]

Sir Peter. Plagues and tortures! can't I make her angry

either! O, I am the most miserable fellow! But I'll not bear her presuming to keep her temper: no! she may break my heart, but she sha'n't keep her temper. [*Exit.*]

STUDY HINTS

Study the spelling and meaning of these words:

quarreling	interrupt	maintenance
reproach	prophesy	benefit
independent	impertinent	prophesied
recollect	coquette	suspect

This humorous scene between a doting old man and his spoiled young wife must be read aloud to be enjoyed fully. Note how Lady Teazle alternately quarrels with her husband and wheedles him. Each one shows his character unconsciously by what he says. One of the means by which we learn to understand the characters of people around us is by listening to what they say.

SUGGESTIONS FOR ORAL AND WRITTEN ENGLISH
THEME SUBJECTS

Write a conversation that would spring naturally from one of the following situations. For arrangement, turn to page 106. Where the speaker would grow very much interested or excited, indicate in parenthesis just what he should do, and the tone he should employ.

A brother wants to take his sister to a baseball game. She prefers to read.

You wish to attend one school, your chum another.

Two boys discuss a friend who refuses to play on the football team.

Mary urges a friend to subscribe for the school paper.

A girl graduate desires to "put up" her hair on the night of the commencement. Her mother objects.

Two girls plan a picnic.

SUGGESTIONS FOR ADDITIONAL READINGS

The Sleeping Car. W. D. Howells.
The Elevator. W. D. Howells.
The Little Men Play. E. L. Gould.
The Little Women Play. E. L. Gould.

Dramatic Reader, Book V.   Augusta Stevenson.
Patriotic Plays and Pageants.   Constance Mackay.
Short Plays from Dickens.   H. B. Browne.

For the teacher to read to the class:
Selections from *The Piper*, Josephine P. Peabody; *Ulysses*, Stephen Phillips; *The Rivals*, Richard Brinsley Sheridan; *She Stoops to Conquer*, Oliver Goldsmith.

THE STORM AT SEA [1]

William Shakespeare

William Shakespeare (1564–1616) was born in the little town of Stratford-on-Avon, England. Little is known of his life, but people of every civilized nation on the globe read his plays and marvel at his genius. No more beautiful tribute has been paid him than that which some unknown admirer wrote with a pencil upon the mantelpiece in the room where Shakespeare was born. It is:

> "In this poor place his spirit first drew breath
> Who saved the English tongue from fear of death."

See also:

Halleck's *New English Literature*, pp. 174–198, 218.
Lee's *A Life of William Shakespeare*.
Raleigh's *Shakespeare*.
MacCracken, Pierce, and Durham's *An Introduction to Shakespeare*.
Dowden's *Shakespeare, His Mind and Art*.
Brandes's *William Shakespeare*.

Cast of Characters

Alonso, King of Naples.
Sebastian, his brother.
Prospero, the right Duke of Milan.
Antonio, his brother.
Gonzalo, an old counselor of Naples.
Miranda, Prospero's daughter.
Ferdinand, son of the King of Naples.
Ariel, an airy spirit.

[1] From *The Tempest*.

ACT I.

SCENE I : *On a Ship at Sea. A tempestuous noise of thunder and lightning heard.*

Enter a Shipmaster *and a* Boatswain.

Master. Boatswain!

Boatswain. Here, master : what cheer?

Master. Good, speak to the mariners; fall to't yarely,[1] or we run ourselves aground; bestir, bestir! [*Exit.*

Enter Mariners.

Boatswain. Heigh, my hearts; cheerly, cheerly, my hearts; yare, yare! Take in the topsail. Tend to the master's whistle. — Blow till thou burst thy wind[2] if room enough!

Enter ALONSO, SEBASTIAN, ANTONIO, FERDINAND, GONZALO, *and others.*

Alon. Good boatswain, have care. Where's the master? Play the men.

Boatswain. I pray now, keep below.

Ant. Where is the master, boatswain?

Boatswain. Do you not hear him? You mar our labor; keep your cabins : you do assist the storm.

Gon. Nay, good, be patient.

Boatswain. When the sea is. Hence! What care these roarers[3] for the name of king? To cabin : silence : trouble us not.

Gon. Good; yet remember whom thou hast aboard.

Boatswain. None that I more love than myself. You are a counselor; if you can command these elements to silence,

---

[1] Briskly.

[2] In Shakespeare's time the wind was often represented in pictures by the figure of a man blowing with his cheeks puffed.

[3] Waves.

and work the peace of the present, we will not hand a rope more; use your authority: if you cannot, give thanks you have lived so long, and make yourself ready in your cabin for the mischance of the hour, if it so hap. — Cheerly, good hearts. — Out of our way, I say.   [*Exit.*

Gon. I have great comfort from this fellow: methinks he hath no drowning mark upon him; his complexion is perfect gallows. Stand fast, good Fate, to his hanging! make the rope of his destiny our cable, for our own doth little advantage! If he be not born to be hanged, our case is miserable.

.   .   .   .

Enter Mariners, *wet.*

Mariners. All lost! to prayers, to prayers! all lost!
                              [*Exeunt.*

Boatswain. What, must our mouths be cold?

Gon. The king and prince at prayers! let us assist them,
For our case is as theirs.

Seb.   I'm out of patience.

Ant. We are merely cheated of our lives by drunkards. — This   wide-chapped   rascal; — Would   thou   mightst   lie   drowning
The washing of ten tides!

Gon.   He'll be hanged yet,
Though every drop of water swear against it,
And gape at widest to glut [1] him.

[*A confused noise within.* — "Mercy on us! we split, we split!" —"Farewell, my wife and children!"   "Farewell, brother!" — "We split, we split, we split!"]

Ant. Let's all sink with the king.

Seb. Let's take leave of him.

Gon. Now would I give a thousand furlongs of sea for an

[1] To swallow up.

acre of barren ground; long heath, brown furze, any thing.
The wills above be done! but I would fain die a dry death.

SCENE 2: *The Island; before the Cell of* PROSPERO.

Enter PROSPERO *and* MIRANDA.

Mir. If by your art, my dearest father, you have
Put the wild waters in this roar, allay them:
The sky, it seems, would pour down stinking pitch,
But that the sea, mounting to the welkin's [1] cheek,
Dashes the fire out.   O, I have suffered
With those that I saw suffer! a brave vessel,
Who had no doubt some noble creatures in her,
Dashed all to pieces.   O, the cry did knock
Against my very heart!   Poor souls! they perished.
Had I been any god of power, I would
Have sunk the sea within the earth, or ere
It should the good ship so have swallowed, and
The fraughting souls within her.

Pros.   Be collected;
No more amazement: [2] tell your piteous heart,
There's no harm done.

    Mir.   O, woe the day!

    Pros.   No harm.
I have done nothing but in care of thee,
Of thee, my dear one, thee, my daughter, who
Art ignorant of what thou art, nought knowing
Of whence I am; nor that I am more better
Than Prospero, master of a full poor cell,
And thy no greater father.

    Mir.   More to know
Did never meddle with my thoughts.

---

[1] Sky.   [2] Distress of mind.

Pros.   'Tis time
I should inform thee further.   Lend thy hand,
And pluck my magic garment from me. — So;

> [*Lays down his mantle.*

Lie there, my art. — Wipe thou thine eyes; have comfort.
The direful spectacle of the wreck, which touched
The very virtue of compassion in thee,
I have with such provision in mine art
So safely ordered, that there is no soul —
No, not so much perdition as an hair,
Betid to any creature in the vessel
Which thou heard'st cry, which thou saw'st sink.   Sit down;
For thou must now know further.

Mir.   You have often
Begun to tell me what I am, but stopped
And left me to a bootless inquisition;
Concluding, "Stay, not yet." —

Pros.   The hour's now come;
The very minute bids thee ope thine ear;
Obey and be attentive.   Canst thou remember
A time before we came unto this cell?
I do not think thou canst; for then thou wast not
Out three years old.

Mir.   Certainly, sir, I can.

Pros. By what? by any other house, or person?
Of any thing the image tell me that
Hath kept with thy remembrance.

Mir.   'Tis far off,
And rather like a dream than an assurance
That my remembrance warrants.   Had I not
Four or five women once that tended me?

Pros. Thou hadst, and more, Miranda.   But how is it,
That this lives in thy mind?   What seest thou else
In the dark backward and abysm of time?

If thou remember'st aught ere thou camest here,
How thou camest here, thou mayst.

 Mir.   But that I do not.

 Pros. Twelve year since, Miranda, twelve year since,
Thy father was the Duke of Milan, and
A prince of power.

  . . . .

Enter ARIEL.

 Ari. All hail, great master! grave sir, hail! I come
To answer thy best pleasure; be't to fly,
To swim, to dive into the fire, to ride
On the curled clouds; to thy strong bidding task
Ariel and all his quality.

 Pros.   Hast thou, spirit,
Performed to point the tempest that I bade thee?

 Ari.   To every article.
I boarded the king's ship; now on the beak,
Now in the waist, the deck, in every cabin,
I flamed amazement: sometimes, I'ld divide,
And burn in many places; on the topmast,
The yards and bowsprit, would I flame distinctly,
Then meet and join: Jove's lightnings, the precursors
O' the dreadful thunder-claps, more momentary
And sight-outrunning were not: the fire and cracks
Of sulphurous roaring, the most mighty Neptune [1]
Seem to besiege, and make his bold waves tremble,
Yea, his dread trident shake.

 Pros.   My brave spirit!
Who was so firm, so constant, that this coil [2]
Would not infect his reason?

---

[1] The god of the sea, always represented with a trident, *i.e.* a three-pronged scepter.
[2] Disturbance.

Ari.   Not a soul
But felt a fever of the mad, and played
Some tricks of desperation.   All, but mariners,
Plunged in the foaming brine, and quit the vessel,
Then all a-fire with me; the king's son, Ferdinand,
With hair up-staring (then like reeds, not hair),
Was the first man that leaped; cried, "Hell is empty,
And all the devils are here!"
   Pros.   Why, that's my spirit!
But was not this nigh shore?
   Ari.   Close by, my master.
   Pros. But are they, Ariel, safe?
   Ari.   Not a hair perished;
On their sustaining garments not a blemish,
But fresher than before: and, as thou badest me,
In troops I have dispersed them 'bout the isle.
The king's son have I landed by himself;
Whom I left cooling of the air with sighs,
In an odd angle of the isle, and sitting,
His arms in this sad knot.
   Pros.   Of the king's ship,
The mariners, say, how thou hast disposed,
And all the rest o' the fleet?
   Ari.   Safely in harbor
Is the king's ship; in the deep nook, where once
Thou call'dst me up at midnight to fetch dew
From the still-vext Bermoothes,[1] there she's hid:
The mariners all under hatches stowed;
Who, with a charm joined to their suffered labor,
I have left asleep: and for the rest o' the fleet,
Which I dispersed, they all have met again,
And are upon the Mediterranean flote,
Bound sadly home for Naples,

[1] Bermudas.

Supposing that they saw the king's ship wrecked,
And his great person perish.

    Pros.   Ariel, thy charge
Exactly is performed; but there's more work:
What is the time o' the day?

    Ari.   Past the mid season.

    Pros. At least two glasses.[1] The time 'twixt six and
  now
Must by us both be spent most preciously.

    Ari. Is there more toil? Since thou dost give me pains,
Let me remember thee what thou hast promised,
Which is not yet performed me.

    Pros.   How now? moody?
What is't thou canst demand?

    Ari.   My liberty.

    Pros. Before the time be out? No more!

    Ari.   I prithee,
Remember I have done thee worthy service;
Told thee no lies, made thee no mistakings, served
Without or grudge or grumblings: thou didst promise
To bate me a full year.

    Pros.   Dost thou forget
From what a torment I did free thee?

    Ari.   No.

    Pros. Thou dost; and think'st
It much to tread the ooze of the salt deep,
To run upon the sharp wind of the north,
To do me business in the veins o' the earth,
When it is baked with frost.

    Ari.   I do not, sir.

    Pros. Thou liest, malignant thing! Hast thou forgot
The foul witch Sycorax, who, with age and envy,
Was grown into a hoop? hast thou forgot her?

---

[1] Two runnings of the hourglass.

Ari. No, sir.

. . . .

Pros.   Thou, my slave,
As thou report'st thyself, wast then her servant:
And, for thou wast a spirit too delicate
To act her earthy and abhorred commands,
Refusing her grand hests, she did confine thee,
By help of her more potent ministers,
And in her most unmitigable rage,
Into a cloven pine; within which rift
Imprisoned, thou did'st painfully remain
A dozen years; within which space she died,
And left thee there, where thou didst vent thy groans,
As fast as mill wheels strike.   Then was this island
(Save for the son that she did litter here,
A freckled whelp, hag-born) not honored with
A human shape.
     Ari.   Yes; Caliban, her son.
     Pros. Dull thing, I say so; he, that Caliban,
Whom now I keep in service.   Thou best know'st
What torment I did find thee in: thy groans
Did make wolves howl, and penetrate the breasts
Of ever-angry bears; it was a torment
To lay upon the damned, which Sycorax
Could not again undo; it was mine art,
When I arrived, and heard thee, that made gape
The pine, and let thee out.
     Ari.   I thank thee, master.
     Pros. If thou more murmur'st, I will rend an oak,
And peg thee in his knotty entrails till
Thou hast howled away twelve winters.
     Ari.   Pardon, master:
I will be correspondent to command,
And do my spiriting gently.

Pros.   Do so ; and after two days
I will discharge thee.

STUDY HINTS

Notice the active scene on board the ship.   Why does the boatswain
answer the men so curtly?   At what point does he become most exas-
perated with Gonzalo?   Can you blame him?   Does Gonzalo realize the
peril as fully as the boatswain?   How is Miranda affected by the storm?
What had Prospero to do with it?   How does Prospero comfort her?
What proof have you that Ariel is a spirit, not a mortal?   Look for this
also in his exquisite song (p. 182).   Read carefully his description of
the effect he had upon the company on the ship.   What comfort does
he bring to Miranda?   What does he owe to Prospero?   What humor
can you find in this selection?

SUGGESTIONS FOR ADDITIONAL READINGS

As You Like It.   William Shakespeare.
The Merchant of Venice.   William Shakespeare.
Much Ado About Nothing.   William Shakespeare.
A Midsummer Night's Dream.   William Shakespeare.
Master Skylark.   John Bennett.
Judith Shakespeare.   William Black.
Shakespeare the Boy.   William Rolfe.
In the Days of Elizabeth.   Eva March Tappan.

For the teacher to read to the class:
Selections from *Ulysses* and *Nero*, Stephen Phillips.

PLAIN LANGUAGE FROM TRUTHFUL JAMES [1]

Bret Harte

Francis Bret Harte (1839–1902) was born in Albany, New York, but spent the early part of his life in California. As in the case of O. Henry, he lived in many places, and had many experiences which he has perpetuated in excellent short stories. His stories of pioneer life in California are inimitable. *The Heathen Chinee*, which is the popular title for the poem given below, made him famous. The swing of the verse is pleasing, and the humor infectious. Truthful James was a real character living in California and highly respected in his own community. See also:

Halleck's *History of American Literature*, pp. 345–349, 365.
H. C. Merwin's *The Life of Bret Harte*.
Boynton's *Bret Harte*.

Which I wish to remark,
  And my language is plain,
That for ways that are dark
  And for tricks that are vain,
The heathen Chinee is peculiar,
  Which the same I would rise to
    explain.

Ah Sin was his name;
  And I shall not deny,
In regard to the same,
  What that name might imply;

[1] From *Poetical Works*. Used by permission of, and by arrangement with, Houghton Mifflin Company, authorized publishers of Bret Harte's works.

But his smile it was pensive and childlike,
   As I frequent remarked to Bill Nye.

It was August the third,
   And quite soft was the skies;
Which it might be inferred
   That Ah Sin was likewise;
Yet he played it that day upon William
   And me in a way I despise.

Which we had a small game,
   And Ah Sin took a hand.
It was euchre.   The same
   He did not understand;
But he smiled as he sat by the table,
   With the smile that was childlike and bland.

Yet the cards they were stocked
   In a way that I grieve,
And my feelings were shocked
   At the state of Nye's sleeve,
Which was stuffed full of aces and bowers,
   And the same with intent to deceive.

But the hands that were played
   By that heathen Chinee,
And the points that he made,
   Were quite frightful to see, —
Till at last he put down a right bower,
   Which the same Nye had dealt unto me.

Then I looked up at Nye,
   And he gazed upon me;
And he rose with a sigh,
   And said, "Can this be?
We are ruined by Chinese cheap labor," —
   And he went for that heathen Chinee.

In the scene that ensued
    I did not take a hand,
But the floor it was strewed
    Like the leaves on the strand
With the cards that Ah Sin had been hiding,
    In the game "he did not understand."

In his sleeves, which were long,
    He had twenty-four jacks, —
Which was coming it strong,
    Yet I state but the facts;
And we found on his nails, which were taper,
    What is frequent in tapers, — that's wax.

Which is why I remark,
    And my language is plain,
That for ways that are dark
    And for tricks that are vain,
The heathen Chinee is peculiar, —
    Which the same I am free to maintain.

SUGGESTIONS FOR ADDITIONAL READINGS

Chiquita.   Bret Harte.
Tennessee's Partner.   Bret Harte.
How Santa Claus came to Simpson's Bar.   Bret Harte.
The Oregon Trail.   Francis Parkman.
Crossing the Plains.   Joaquin Miller.
The Mountains of California.   John Muir.
Stories of the Great West.   Theodore Roosevelt.
Roughing It.   S. L. Clemens.
Our Little Chinese Cousin.   Isaac Headland.
Boy Life on the Prairie.   Hamlin Garland.
The Led-Horse Claim.   Mary Hallock Foote.
Glimpses of California.   Helen Hunt Jackson.
Romantic California.   E. C. Peixotto.

For the teacher to read to the class:
Grizzly (verse).   Bret Harte.

THE AMBITIOUS GUEST [1]

NATHANIEL HAWTHORNE

[For biographical sketch see page 171.]

ONE September night a family had gathered round their hearth, and piled it high with the driftwood of mountain streams, the dry cones of the pine, and the splintered ruins of great trees that had come crashing down the precipice. Up the chimney roared the fire, and brightened the room with its broad blaze. The faces of the father and mother had a sober gladness; the children laughed; the eldest daughter was the image of Happiness at seventeen; and the aged grandmother, who sat knitting in the warmest place, was the image of Happiness grown old. They had found the "herb, heart's-ease," in the bleakest spot of all New England. This family were situated in the Notch of the White Hills, where the wind was sharp throughout the year, and pitilessly cold in the winter, — giving their cottage all its fresh inclemency before it descended on the valley of the Saco. They dwelt in a cold spot and a dangerous one; for a mountain towered above their heads, so steep, that the stones would often rumble down its sides and startle them at midnight.

The daughter had just uttered some simple jest that filled them all with mirth, when the wind came through the Notch and seemed to pause before their cottage — rattling

[1] Used by permission of, and by arrangement with, Houghton Mifflin Company, authorized publishers of Hawthorne's works.

the door, with a sound of wailing and lamentation, before it passed into the valley. For a moment it saddened them, though there was nothing unusual in the tones. But the family were glad again when they perceived that the latch was lifted by some traveler, whose footsteps had been unheard amid the dreary blast which heralded his approach, and wailed as he was entering, and went moaning away from the door.

Though they dwelt in such a solitude, these people held daily converse with the world. The romantic pass of the Notch is a great artery, through which the lifeblood of internal commerce is continually throbbing between Maine, on one side, and the Green Mountains and the shores of the St. Lawrence, on the other. The stagecoach always drew up before the door of the cottage. The wayfarer, with no companion but his staff, paused here to exchange a word, that the sense of loneliness might not utterly overcome him ere he could pass through the cleft of the mountain, or reach the first house in the valley. And here the teamster, on his way to Portland market, would put up for the night; and, if a bachelor, might sit an hour beyond the usual bedtime, and steal a kiss from the mountain maid at parting. It was one of those primitive taverns where the traveler pays only for food and lodging, but meets with a homely kindness beyond all price. When the footsteps were heard, therefore, between the outer door and the inner one, the whole family rose up, grandmother, children, and all, as if about to welcome some one who belonged to them, and whose fate was linked with theirs.

The door was opened by a young man. His face at first wore the melancholy expression, almost despondency, of one who travels a wild and bleak road, at nightfall and alone, but soon brightened up when he saw the kindly warmth of his reception. He felt his heart spring forward to meet them all, from the old woman, who wiped a chair with her apron, to the little child that held out its arms to him. One glance and smile placed the stranger on a footing of innocent familiarity with the eldest daughter.

"Ah, this fire is the right thing!" cried he; "especially when there is such a pleasant circle round it. I am quite benumbed; for the Notch is just like the pipe of a great pair of bellows; it has blown a terrible blast in my face all the way from Bartlett."

"Then you are going toward Vermont?" said the master of the house, as he helped to take a light knapsack off the young man's shoulders.

"Yes; to Burlington, and far enough beyond," replied he. "I meant to have been at Ethan Crawford's to-night; but a pedestrian lingers along such a road as this. It is no matter; for, when I saw this good fire, and all your cheerful faces, I felt as if you had kindled it on purpose for me, and were waiting my arrival. So I shall sit down among you, and make myself at home."

The frank-hearted stranger had just drawn his chair to the fire when something like a heavy footstep was heard without, rushing down the steep side of the mountain, as with long and rapid strides, and taking such a leap in passing the cottage as to strike the opposite precipice. The family held their breath, because they knew the sound, and their guest held his by instinct.

"The old mountain has thrown a stone at us, for fear we should forget him," said the landlord, recovering himself. "He sometimes nods his head and threatens to come down; but we are old neighbors, and agree together pretty well on the whole. Besides we have a sure place of refuge hard by if he should be coming in good earnest."

Let us now suppose the stranger to have finished his supper of bear's meat; and, by his natural felicity of manner, to have placed himself on a footing of kindness with the whole family, so that they talked as freely together as if he belonged to their mountain brood. He was of a proud, yet gentle spirit — haughty and reserved among the rich and great; but ever ready to stoop his head to the lowly cottage door, and be like a brother or a son at the poor man's fireside. In the household of the Notch he found warmth and simplicity of feeling, the pervading intelligence of New England, and a poetry of native growth, which they had gathered when they little thought of it from the mountain peaks and chasms, and at the very threshold of their romantic and dangerous abode. He had traveled far and alone; his whole life, indeed, had been a solitary path; for, with the lofty caution of his nature, he had kept himself apart from those who might otherwise have been his companions. The family, too, though so kind and hospitable, had that consciousness of unity among themselves, and separation from the world at large, which in every domestic circle, should still keep a holy place where no stranger may intrude. But this evening a prophetic sympathy impelled the refined and educated youth to pour out his heart before the simple mountaineers, and constrained them to answer him with the same free confidence. And thus it should have been. Is not the kindred of a common fate a closer tie than that of birth?

The secret of the young man's character was a high and abstracted ambition. He could have borne to live an undistinguished life, but not to be forgotten in the grave. Yearning desire had been transformed to hope: and hope, long cherished, had become like certainty, that, obscurely as he journeyed now, a glory was to beam on all his pathway, — though not, perhaps, while he was treading it. But when posterity should gaze back into the gloom of what was now the present, they would trace the brightness of his footsteps, brightening as meaner glories faded, and confess that a gifted one had passed from his cradle to his tomb with none to recognize him.

"As yet," cried the stranger — his cheek glowing and his eye flashing with enthusiasm — "as yet, I have done nothing. Were I to vanish from the earth to-morrow, none would know so much of me as you; that a nameless youth came up at nightfall from the valley of Saco, and opened his heart to you in the evening, and passed through the Notch by sunrise, and was seen no more. Not a soul would ask, 'Who was he? Whither did the wanderer go?' But I cannot die till I have achieved my destiny. Then, let death come! I shall have built my monument!"

There was a continual flow of natural emotion, gushing forth amid abstracted reverie, which enabled the family to understand this young man's sentiments, though so foreign from their own. With quick sensibility of the ludicrous, he blushed at the ardor into which he had been betrayed.

"You laugh at me," said he, taking the eldest daughter's hand, and laughing himself. "You think my ambition as nonsensical as if I were to freeze myself to death on the top of Mount Washington, only that people might spy at me from the country round about. And, truly, that would be a noble pedestal for a man's statue!"

"It is better to sit here by this fire," answered the girl, blushing, "and be comfortable and contented, though nobody thinks about us."

"I suppose," said her father, after a fit of musing, "there is something natural in what the young man says; and if my mind had been turned that way, I might have felt just the same. It is strange, wife, how his talk has set my head running on things that are pretty certain never to come to pass."

"Perhaps they may," observed the wife. "Is the man thinking what he will do when he is a widower?"

"No, no!" cried he, repelling the idea with reproachful kindness. "When I think of your death, Esther, I think of mine, too. But I was wishing we had a good farm in Bartlett, or Bethlehem, or Littleton, or some other township round the White Mountains; but not where they could tumble on our heads. I should want to stand well with my neighbors and be called Squire, and sent to General Court for a term or two; for a plain, honest man may do as much good there as a lawyer. And when I should be grown quite an old man, and you an old woman, so as not to be long apart, I might die happy enough in my bed, and leave you all crying around me. A slate gravestone would suit me as well as a marble one — with just my name and age, and a verse of a hymn, and something to let people know that I lived an honest man and died a Christian."

"There now!" exclaimed the stranger; "it is our nature to desire a monument, be it slate or marble, or a pillar of granite, or a glorious memory in the universal heart of man."

"We're in a strange way, to-night," said the wife, with tears in her eyes. "They say it's a sign of something, when folks' minds go a-wandering so. Hark to the children!"

They listened accordingly. The younger children had been put to bed in another room, but with an open door between, so that they could be heard talking busily among themselves. One and all seemed to have caught the infection from the fireside circle, and were outvying each other in wild wishes, and childish projects of what they would do when they came to be men and women. At length a little boy, instead of addressing his brothers and sisters, called out to his mother.

"I'll tell you what I wish, mother," cried he. "I want you and father and grandma'm, and all of us, and the stranger too, to start right away, and go and take a drink out of the basin of the Flume!"

Nobody could help laughing at the child's notion of leaving a warm bed, and dragging them from a cheerful fire, to visit the basin of the Flume, — a brook which tumbles over the precipice, deep within the Notch. The boy had hardly spoken when a wagon rattled along the road, and stopped a moment before the door. It appeared to contain two or three men who were cheering their hearts with the rough chorus of a song, which resounded in broken notes between the cliffs, while the singers hesitated whether to continue their journey or put up here for the night."

"Father," said the girl, "they are calling you by name."

But the good man doubted whether they had really called him, and was unwilling to show himself too solicitous of gain by inviting people to patronize his house. He therefore did not hurry to the door; and the lash being soon applied, the travelers plunged into the Notch, still singing and laughing, though their music and mirth came back drearily from the heart of the mountain.

"There, mother!" cried the boy, again. "They'd have given us a ride to the Flume."

Again they laughed at the child's pertinacious fancy for a night ramble. But it happened that a light cloud passed over the daughter's spirit; she looked gravely into the fire, and drew a breath that was almost a sigh. It forced its way, in spite of a little struggle to repress it. Then starting and blushing, she looked quickly round the circle, as if they had caught a glimpse into her bosom. The stranger asked what she had been thinking of.

"Nothing," answered she, with a downcast smile. "Only I felt lonesome just then."

"Oh, I have always had a gift of feeling what is in other people's hearts," said he, half seriously. "Shall I tell the secrets of yours? For I know what to think when a young girl shivers by a warm hearth, and complains of lonesomeness at her mother's side. Shall I put these feelings into words?"

"They would not be a girl's feelings any longer if they could be put into words," replied the mountain nymph, laughing, but avoiding his eye.

All this was said apart. Perhaps a germ of love was springing in their hearts, so pure that it might blossom in Paradise, since it could not be matured on earth; for women worship such gentle dignity as his; and the proud, contemplative, yet kindly soul is oftenest captivated by simplicity like hers. But while they spoke softly, and he was watching the happy sadness, the lightsome shadows, the shy yearnings of a maiden's nature, the wind through the Notch took a deeper and drearier sound. It seemed, as the fanciful stranger said, like the choral strain of the spirits of the blast, who in old Indian times had their dwelling among these mountains, and made their heights and recesses a sacred region. There was a wail along the road, as if a funeral were passing. To chase away the gloom, the family threw pine branches on their fire, till the dry leaves crackled and the flame arose, discovering once again a scene of peace and humble happiness. The light hovered about them fondly, and caressed them all. There were the little faces of the children, peeping from their bed apart, and here the father's frame of strength, the mother's subdued and careful mien, the high-browed youth, the budding girl, and the good old grandma, still knitting in the warmest place. The aged woman looked up from her task, and, with fingers ever busy, was the next to speak.

"Old folks have their notions," said she, "as well as young ones. You've been wishing and planning; and letting your heads run on one thing and another, till you've set my mind a wandering too. Now what should an old woman wish for, when she can go but a step or two before she comes to her grave? Children, it will haunt me night and day till I tell you."

"What is it, mother?" cried the husband and wife at once.

Then the old woman, with an air of mystery which drew the circle closer round the fire, informed them that she had provided her grave-clothes some years before — a nice linen shroud, a cap with a muslin ruff, and everything of a finer sort than she had worn since her wedding day. But this evening an old superstition had strangely recurred to her. It used to be said, in her younger days, that if anything were amiss with a corpse, if only the ruff were not smooth, or the cap did not set right, the corpse in the coffin and beneath the clods would strive to put up its cold hands and arrange it. The bare thought made her nervous.

"Don't talk so, grandmother!" said the girl, shuddering.

"Now," — continued the old woman, with singular earnestness, yet smiling strangely at her own folly, — "I want one of you, my children — when your mother is dressed and in the coffin — I want one of you to hold a looking-glass over my face. Who knows but I may take a glimpse at myself, and see whether all's right?"

"Old and young, we dream of graves and monuments," murmured the stranger youth. "I wonder how mariners feel when the ship is sinking, and they, unknown and undistinguished, are to be buried together in the ocean — that wide and nameless sepulcher?"

For a moment, the old woman's ghastly conception so engrossed the minds of her hearers that a sound abroad in the night, rising like the roar of a blast, had grown broad, deep, and terrible, before the fated group were conscious of it. The house and all within it trembled; the foundations of the earth seemed to be shaken, as if this awful sound were the peal of the last trump. Young and old exchanged one wild glance, and remained an instant, pale, affrighted, without utterance, or power to move. Then the same shriek burst simultaneously from all their lips.

"The slide! The slide!"

The simplest words must intimate, but not portray, the unutterable horror of the catastrophe. The victims rushed from their cottage, and sought refuge in what they deemed a safer spot — where, in contemplation of such an emergency, a sort of barrier had been reared. Alas! they had quitted their security, and fled right into the pathway of destruction. Down came the whole side of the mountain, in a cataract of ruin. Just before it reached the house, the stream broke into two branches — shivered not a window there, but overwhelmed the whole vicinity, blocked up the road, and annihilated everything in its dreadful course. Long ere the thunder of the great slide had ceased to roar among the mountains, the mortal agony had been endured, and the victims were at peace. Their bodies were never found.

The next morning, the light smoke was seen stealing from the cottage chimney up the mountain side. Within, the fire was yet smoldering on the hearth, and the chairs in a circle round it, as if the inhabitants had but gone forth to view the devastation of the slide, and would shortly return, to thank heaven for their miraculous escape. All had left separate tokens, by which those who had known the family were made to shed a tear for each. Who has not heard their name? The story has been told far and wide, and will forever be a legend of these mountains. Poets have sung their fate.

There were circumstances which led some to suppose that a stranger had been received into the cottage on this awful night, and had shared the catastrophe of all its inmates.

Others denied that there were sufficient grounds for such a
conjecture.   Woe for the high-souled youth, with his dream
of earthly immortality!   His name and person utterly unknown; his history, his way of life, his plans, a mystery
never to be solved, his death and his existence equally a
doubt!   Whose was the agony of that death moment?

[This story is founded upon an actual occurrence as related in J. H.
Spaulding's *Historical Relics of the White Mountains*. "Some time in
June, before the great slide in August, 1826, there came a great storm,
and the old veteran Abel Crawford, coming down the Notch, noticed
the trees slipping down standing upright, and as he was passing Mr.
Willey's he called and informed him of the wonderful fact.   Immediately,
in a less exposed place, Mr. Willey prepared a shelter to which to flee in
case of immediate danger, and in the night of August 28 in that year he
was, with his whole family, awakened by the thundering crash of the
coming avalanche.   Attempting to escape, that family, nine in number,
rushed from the house and were overtaken and buried alive under a
vast pile of rocks, earth, and water.   By a remarkable coincidence the
house remained uninjured, as the slide divided about four rods back
of the house, against a high flat rock, and came down on either side
with overwhelming power."]

STUDY HINTS

Study the spelling and meaning of these words:

coincidence	arrival	catastrophe
perceive	sit, sat, sat	ludicrous
homely	inhabitant	reproachful
familiarity	instinct	glimpse

Does the family seem real to you?   What does Hawthorne mean in
the sentence, "They had found the herb, hearts'-ease, in the bleakest
spot of New England"?   How do the occupants of the cottage impress
the stranger?   What is the topic of their conversation around the fire?
Tell in your own words the ambition of each person.   What contrast do
you find between the interior of the cottage and its setting?   What hints
are given the reader that there will be a catastrophe?   Does the appearance of the cottage afterwards add to your feeling of horror at their fate,
or not?   Is the ending as unexpected as that of *The Chaparral Prince?*

SUGGESTIONS FOR ORAL AND WRITTEN ENGLISH
THEME SUBJECTS

Write for a newspaper in the town where they were known, an account of the fate of the family (their name was Willey). As the public usually reads news hurriedly, put the most important item in the first sentence. Follow with details in the order of their importance, beginning with the most important. How does this method differ from the one you have been following? The newspaper account should answer very near the beginning these questions: Who? When? Where? Why?

Write in a letter to a friend an account of this catastrophe, as if you had *remained in the cottage.*

Imagine that you have had a lucky escape of some kind, and write a telegram to your mother, assuring her of your safety. Follow the telegram with a letter giving fuller details.

Explain your idea of the term, "Home."

Read Robert Burns's *The Cotter's Saturday Night,* and report to the class what is Burns's idea of "home."

Think over an unexpectedly pleasant ending of an adventure that you have had and tell it to the class. Be careful not to hint too strongly that the ending will be pleasant.

SUGGESTIONS FOR ADDITIONAL READINGS

Rappaccini's Daughter (*Mosses from an Old Manse*). Nathaniel Hawthorne.

The White Old Maid (*Twice-Told Tales*). Nathaniel Hawthorne.

The House of the Seven Gables. Nathaniel Hawthorne.

The Cause of the Difficulty (in *Tales of the Home Folks*). Joel Chandler Harris.

Back Home. Irvin Cobb.

The Prophet of the Great Smoky Mountains. Charles Egbert Craddock.

The Mystery of Witch Face Mountain. Charles Egbert Craddock.

Rosy Balm; A Day Off (in *The Country Road*). Alice Brown.

The Burial of the Guns. Thomas Nelson Page.

The Remarkable Wreck of the Thomas Hyde (in *A Chosen Few*). Frank R. Stockton.

Tales of New England. Sarah Orne Jewett.

A Country Doctor. Sarah Orne Jewett.

Country By-Ways. Sarah Orne Jewett.

THE HUMBLEBEE [1]

Ralph Waldo Emerson

Ralph Waldo Emerson (1803–1882) was born in Boston. He was descended from a long line of New England clergymen. As a boy, he was so poor that he and his brother attended school on alternate days because they had only one coat between them. Despite his poverty, he managed to graduate from Harvard. He became a clergyman and preached for a time in Cotton Mather's church. His belief did not wholly accord with that of the church, so he gave up preaching, and spent the rest of his life in writing and lecturing.

His *Essays*, such as the one on *Self-Reliance*, are his most popular works, but he also wrote some exquisite verse. His most enjoyable poetry has some phase of nature for its subject. This was his poetic creed:

> "In the deep heart of man a poet dwells
> Who all the day of life his summer story tells."

See also:
Halleck's *History of American Literature*, pp. 178–193, 283.
Oliver Wendell Holmes's *Ralph Waldo Emerson*.
Woodberry's *Ralph Waldo Emerson*.
Garnett's *Life of Ralph Waldo Emerson*.
Emerson's *Journals*.

> BURLY dozing humblebee!
> Where thou art is clime for me.
> Let them sail for Porto Rique,[2]
> Far-off heats through seas to seek,
> I will follow thee alone,
> Thou animated torrid zone!

[1] This poem is used by permission of, and arrangement with, Houghton Mifflin Company, authorized publishers of Emerson's works.
[2] Porto Rico.

Zig-zag steerer, desert-cheerer,
Let me chase thy waving lines,
Keep me nearer, me thy hearer,
Singing over shrubs and vines.

Insect lover of the sun,
Joy of thy dominion!
Sailor of the atmosphere,
Swimmer through the waves of air,
Voyager of light and noon,
Epicurean of June,[1]
Wait I prithee, till I come
Within earshot of thy hum, —
All without is martyrdom.

When the south wind, in May days,
With a net of shining haze,
Silvers the horizon wall,
And, with softness touching all,
Tints the human countenance
With a color of romance,
And, infusing subtle heats,
Turns the sod to violets,
Thou in sunny solitudes,
Rover of the underwoods,
The green silence dost displace,
With thy mellow breezy bass.

Hot midsummer's petted crone,
Sweet to me thy drowsy tone,
Telling of countless sunny hours,
Long days, and solid banks of flowers,

[1] One who luxuriates in, thoroughly enjoys, June.

Of gulfs of sweetness without bound
In Indian wildernesses found,
Of Syrian peace, immortal leisure,
Firmest cheer and bird-like pleasure.

Aught unsavory or unclean,
Hath my insect never seen,
But violets and bilberry bells,
Maple sap and daffodels,
Grass with green flag half-mast high,
Succory to match the sky,
Columbine with horn of honey,
Scented fern, and agrimony,
Clover, catchfly, adder's-tongue,
And brier-roses dwelt among;
All beside was unknown waste,
All was picture as he passed.

Wiser far than human seer,
Yellow-breeched philosopher !
Seeing only what is fair,
Sipping only what is sweet,
Thou dost mock at fate and care,
Leave the chaff and take the wheat,
When the fierce northwestern blast
Cools sea and land so far and fast,
Thou already slumberest deep.

STUDY HINTS

How many different names does the poet give to the bee? Which do you think suits it best? Explain this allusion and its fitness, "Epicurean of June." What does the last line of the second stanza mean? What does it show? What does he emphasize in order to make May seem attractive? Compare his treatment of May with Lowell's of June (p. 198). Does each poet tend to increase our enjoyment of those months? What, then, is one use of poetry? How does the hum of the bee change from May to midsummer? How many of the flowers and plants mentioned by Emerson have you actually seen? From which have you seen the humblebee "sipping only what is sweet"? Why is he called "wiser far than human seer"? Is it possible for us to determine what we shall see and "sip"? What does Emerson like best in the bee? What does his hum in summer tell the poet? What is your impression of the poet? What words give you this impression? Memorize at least one stanza.

SUGGESTIONS FOR ADDITIONAL READINGS

The Rhodora.   Ralph Waldo Emerson.
Concord Hymn.   Ralph Waldo Emerson.
The Snow Storm.   Ralph Waldo Emerson.
The Mountain and the Squirrel.   Ralph Waldo Emerson.
Forbearance.   Ralph Waldo Emerson.
Solomon and the Bees.   John G. Saxe.
The Taxgatherer (from *Child Verse*).   John B. Tabb.
The Bumblebee.   James Whitcomb Riley.
The Bee.   Emily Dickinson.

AN EPITAPH ON SALATHIEL PAVY

A Child of Queen Elizabeth's Chapel

BEN JONSON

Ben Jonson (1573?–1637) was born in London. He rose from the humble trade of a bricklayer to the position of a popular playwright at the court of James I. He was also the author of some exquisite lyrics, such as, "Drink to me only with thine eyes." He was an intimate friend of Shakespeare. See also:

Halleck's *New English Literature*, pp. 199–205, 219.
Symonds's *Ben Jonson*.

[In Elizabethan days boys acted the female parts in the plays. Ophelia, Portia, Miranda, and Lady Macbeth were all impersonated by boys. The parts of old men were also occasionally played by boys. Salathiel Pavy, the subject of this epitaph, was, as Jonson tells us, a boy who acted such parts.

In the tragedy of *Hamlet*, Shakespeare makes a reference to boy actors (see Halleck's *New English Literature*, p. 166) that shows how popular they had become.]

WEEP with me, all you that read
   This little story;
And know, for whom a tear you shed
   Death's self is sorry.
'Twas a child that so did thrive
   In grace and feature,
As heaven and nature seemed to strive
   Which owned the creature.

Years he numbered scarce thirteen
  When Fates turned cruel,
Yet three filled zodiacs [1] had he been
  The stage's jewel;
And did act, what now we moan,
  Old men so duly,
As, sooth, the Parcæ [2] thought him one, —
  He played so truly.
So, by error to his fate
  They all consented;
But viewing him since, alas, too late
  They have repented;
And have sought to give new birth
  In baths to steep him;
But being so much too good for earth,
  Heaven vows to keep him.

[1] Three years.
[2] The three Greek Fates, Clotho, Lachesis, Atropos, who respectively spun the web of life, measured, and cut it.

TO A WATERFOWL

WILLIAM CULLEN BRYANT

William Cullen Bryant (1794–1878), the first great American poet, was born in Cummington, Massachusetts. He was descended from John and Priscilla Alden, whom Longfellow made famous in the *Courtship of Miles Standish*. When traveling on foot to Plainfield, where he intended practicing law, he saw a bird winging its flight toward the sunset. He was feeling very lonely at the time, but the courage of the bird in its lonely flight gave him new courage. He went on hopefully and at the end of his journey wrote *To a Waterfowl* to commemorate his experience. See also :

Halleck's *History of American Literature*, pp. 135–145, 152.
Godwin's *A Biography of William Cullen Bryant*.
Bradley's *William Cullen Bryant*.

WHITHER, midst falling dew,
While glow the heavens with the last steps of day,
Far, through their rosy depths, dost thou pursue
Thy solitary way?

Vainly the fowler's eye
Might mark thy distant flight to do thee wrong,
As, darkly painted on the crimson sky,
Thy figure floats along.

Seek'st thou the plashy brink
Of weedy lake, or marge of river wide,
Or where the rocking billows rise and sink
On the chafed ocean side?

There is a Power whose care
Teaches thy way along that pathless coast —
The desert and illimitable air —
    Lone wandering, but not lost.

All day thy wings have fanned,
At that far height, the cold, thin atmosphere,
Yet stoop not, weary, to the welcome land,
    Though the dark night is near.

And soon that toil shall end;
Soon shalt thou find a summer home, and rest,
And scream among thy fellows; reeds shall bend,
    Soon, o'er thy sheltered nest.

Thou'rt gone, the abyss of heaven
Hath swallowed up thy form; yet, on my heart
Deeply has sunk the lesson thou hast given,
    And shall not soon depart.

He who, from zone to zone,
Guides through the boundless sky thy certain flight,
In the long way that I must tread alone,
    Will lead my steps aright.

STUDY HINTS

What time of day does the poet describe? What lines show that the bird was a waterfowl? If you were asked to find in this poem a suggestion for a painting, which stanza would you choose? What would you make the central point of interest in the painting? Commit to memory the lesson the poet learned from the bird.

A GROUP OF LETTERS

LETTER TO ST. NICHOLAS [1]

HELEN KELLER

Helen A. Keller was born in Tuscumbia, Alabama, in 1880. At the age of nineteen months, she had an illness which left her deaf, dumb, and blind. When she was six years old, a most talented young girl, Miss Sullivan, became her teacher. Through her aid and her own perseverance, Miss Keller took the degree of B.A. at Radcliffe College in 1904. A few years ago she learned to talk. She has lectured from coast to coast in America, and contributed articles to magazines, besides writing several books. *The World I Live In* and *The Story of My Life* are most interesting accounts of the life and experiences of this woman who has been called the greatest marvel of the twentieth century.

DEAR ST. NICHOLAS, — It gives me very great pleasure to send you my autograph because I want the boys and girls who read St. Nicholas to know how blind children write. I suppose some of them wonder how we keep the lines so straight so I will try to tell them how it is done. We have a grooved board which we put between the pages when we wish to write. The parallel grooves correspond to lines, and when we have pressed the paper into them by means of the blunt end of the pencil, it is very easy to keep the words even. The small letters are all made in the grooves, while the long ones extend above and below them. We guide the pencil with the right hand, and feel carefully with the forefinger of the left hand to see that we shape and space

[1] From *The Story of My Life*, copyright, 1903, by Doubleday, Page and Company. Used by special arrangement with the publishers.

the letters correctly. It is very difficult at first to form them plainly, but if we keep on trying it gradually becomes easier, and after a great deal of practice we can write legible letters to our friends. Then we are very, very happy. Sometime they may visit a school for the blind. If they do, I am sure they will wish to see the pupils write.

Very sincerely your little [1] friend,
HELEN KELLER.

LETTER TO GERTRUDE [2]

LEWIS CARROLL

Lewis Carroll is the pen name of the Reverend Charles Lutwidge Dodgson (1832–1898), who was for many years lecturer on mathematics at Oxford University. He is known most widely as the author of *Alice's Adventures in Wonderland* and *Through the Looking-Glass*. This letter may explain partly why he had so many warm friends among young people.

CHRIST CHURCH, OXFORD, October 13, 1875.

MY DEAR GERTRUDE, — I never give birthday presents, but you see I do sometimes write a birthday letter: so, as I've just arrived here, I am writing this to wish you many and many a happy return of your birthday to-morrow. I will drink your health if only I can remember, and if you don't mind — but perhaps you object?

You see, if I were to sit by you at breakfast, and to drink your tea, you wouldn't like that, would you? You would say, "Boo! hoo! Here's Mr. Dodgson drunk all my tea, and I haven't got any left!" So I am very much afraid, next time Sybil looks for you, she'll find you sitting by the sad sea waves and crying "Boo! hoo! Here's Mr. Dodgson has drunk my health, and I haven't got any left!"

---

[1] She was eleven years old at this time.
[2] Used by courtesy of the Century Company.

And how it will puzzle Mr. Maund, when he is sent for to see you! "My dear madam, I'm sorry to say your little girl has got no health at all! I never saw such a thing in my life!" "You see she would go and make friends with a strange gentleman, and yesterday he drank her health!" "Well, Mrs. Chataway," he will say, "the only way to cure her is to wait till his next birthday, and then for her to drink his health."

And then we shall have changed healths. I wonder how you'll like mine! Oh, Gertrude, I wish you would not talk such nonsense! . . . Your loving friend,

LEWIS CARROLL.

LETTER TO MRS. J. T. FIELDS

CHARLES DICKENS

[For biographical sketch see page 188.]

———

[This letter was written after Dickens's second lecture tour in America. James T. Fields, who was a well-known publisher in Boston, was instrumental in bringing Dickens to America. One of the pleasant results of this tour was that he and Mrs. Fields became warm friends of the great novelist.]

———

GADS HILL, HIGHAM, by ROCHESTER, KENT.
May 25, 1868.

MY DEAR MRS. FIELDS, — As you ask me about the dogs, I begin with them. When I came down first, I came to Gravesend, five miles off. The two Newfoundland dogs, coming to meet me with the usual carriage and the usual driver, and beholding me coming in my usual dress out at he usual door, it struck me that their recollection of my aving been absent for any unusual time was at once can-

celed. They behaved (they are both young dogs) exactly
in their usual manner; coming behind the basket phaëton
as we trotted along, and lifting their heads to have their
ears pulled — a special attention which they receive from
no one else. But when I drove into the stable yard, Linda
(the St. Bernard) was greatly excited; weeping profusely,
and throwing herself on her back, that she might caress my
foot with her great fore paws. Mamie's little dog, too, Mrs.
Bouncer, barked in the greatest agitation on being called
down and asked by Mamie, "Who is this?" and tore round
and round me, like the dog in the Faust outlines. You
must know that all the farmers turned out on the road in
their market chaises to say, "Welcome home, sir!" and that
all the houses along the road were dressed with flags; and
that our servants, to cut the rest, had dressed this house so
that every brick of it was hidden. They had asked Mamie's
permission to "ring the alarm bell" (!) when master drove
up, but Mamie, having some slight idea that that compliment might awaken master's sense of the ludicrous, had
recommended bell abstinence. But on Sunday the village
choir (which includes the bell ringers) made amends. After
some unusually brief pious reflections in the crowns of their
hats, at the end of the sermon, the ringers bolted out, and
rang like mad until I got home. There had been a con-
spiracy among the villagers to take the horse out, if I had
come to our own station, and draw me here. Mamie [1] and
Georgy [1] had got wind of it and warned me.

Divers birds sing here all day, and the nightingales all
night. The place is lovely, and in perfect order. I have
put five mirrors in the Swiss chalet [2] (where I write), and they
reflect and refract in all kinds of ways the leaves that are

[1] His children.
[2] A house where he could write his novels, undisturbed. It was connected with Gads
Hill by an underground passage.

quivering at the windows, and the great fields of waving corn, and the sail-dotted river. My room is up among the branches of the trees, and the birds and the butterflies fly in and out, and the green branches shoot in, at the open windows, and the lights and shadows of the clouds come and go with the rest of the company. The scent of the flowers, and indeed of everything that is growing for miles and miles, is most delicious. . . .

Ever, my dear Mrs. Fields, your most affectionate friend,
CHARLES DICKENS.

LETTER TO GENERAL JOSEPH HOOKER [1]

ABRAHAM LINCOLN

Abraham Lincoln (1809–1865) was born in Hardin County, Kentucky, in a log cabin. He attended school all together one year. His direct, clear language which has become a model of pure English for writers of to-day, was acquired through his own persistent efforts, — through reading and rereading such books as the *Bible*, *The Pilgrim's Progress*, *Robinson Crusoe*, and *Franklin's Autobiography*. By his speeches in a series of debates with Stephen A. Douglas he won a national reputation, and was made president in 1861. Shortly after his second inauguration he was assassinated by a poor half-crazed creature. His best known speech is the *Gettysburg Address*. See also:

Halleck's *History of American Literature*, pp. 343–345.
Schurz's *Abraham Lincoln*.
Nicolay's *Boys' Life of Abraham Lincoln*.
Baldwin's *Abraham Lincoln*.
Tarbell's *Life of Abraham Lincoln*.
Creelman's *Why We Love Lincoln*.

January 26, 1863.

GENERAL:

I have placed you at the head of the army of the Potomac. Of course I have done this upon what appear to me to be sufficient reasons, and yet I think it best for you to know that there are some things in regard to which I am not quite

[1] Used by courtesy of the Century Company.

satisfied with you.   I believe you to be a brave and skillful soldier, which of course I like.   I also believe you do not mix politics with your profession, in which you are right. You have confidence in yourself, which is a valuable if not an indispensable quality.   You are ambitious, which, within reasonable bounds, does good rather than harm ; but I think that during General Burnside's command of the army you have taken counsel of your ambition and thwarted him as much as you could, in which you did a great wrong to the country and to a most meritorious and honorable brother officer.   I have heard, in such a way as to believe it, of your recently saying that both the army and the government needed a dictator.   Of course it was not for this, but in spite of it, that I have given you the command.   Only those generals who gain success can set up dictators.   What I now ask of you is military success, and I will risk the dictatorship. The government will support you to the utmost of its ability, which is neither more nor less than it has done and will do for all commanders.   I much fear that the spirit which you have aided to infuse into the army, of criticizing their commander and withholding confidence from him, will now turn upon you.   I shall assist you as far as I can to put it down. Neither you nor Napoleon, if he were alive again, could get any good out of an army while such a spirit prevails in it ; and now beware of rashness, but with energy and sleepless vigilance go forward and give us victories.

Yours very truly,

A. LINCOLN.

STUDY HINTS

Study the spelling and meaning of these words :

dictator	criticize	rashness
skillful	ability	energy
indispensable	prevail	vigilance
government	confidence	accompany

What did Lincoln think was the duty that an officer owed a superior officer? Does he criticize General Hooker's conduct? Has General Hooker criticized Lincoln's? Does this prevent Lincoln's conferring a great honor upon General Hooker? Does Lincoln show any fine trait at this point? What trait of his own may General Hooker have reason to fear in the soldiers under him? What are some of General Hooker's good traits? Which does Lincoln caution him about? A letter usually shows the writer's character. Does this show Lincoln's? Judging from the letter, what are some of Lincoln's traits?

Three qualities are necessary for all letters; they must be expressed clearly, they must be written neatly, they must be written legibly. In social letter writing, one more valuable quality is — the letter should be interesting. What qualities can you find in this group of letters? All of the writers are famous, yet note what subjects they thought were interesting to write about, and how simply they wrote. How does Lincoln's letter differ from the others?

LETTER HINTS

Explain as if to a blind child your method of writing a letter. Try to be as clear and exact as Helen Keller.

Write a letter explaining every step in the making of some article, closing with an offer to write further details if your friend does not understand your description.

Your friend intends giving a birthday party which you cannot attend. Write a letter expressing your regret that you cannot accept his invitation, and wishing him " many happy returns."

Write a letter full of good wishes to accompany a birthday gift.

You intend giving a birthday party. Write inviting a friend to come, and saying whether it will be a formal or an informal affair.

You have been visiting in another town. On your return home, write to your hostess (*i.e.* the mother of your friend), thanking her for your pleasant visit, and telling some incident of your journey that you think will be interesting.

You have moved to a new home in another city. Write to your friends at the old home, describing the new house, and the new acquaintances that have been friendly.

You have seen a special kind of pocket knife in a shop when visiting a friend. Write to him to buy the knife for you. Describe it. Tell him where it can be bought, how you want it sent. Be sure to state in what form you are sending the money, *i.e.* by stamps, or money order, and that you are adding your friend's street-car fare to the price of the knife.   Close by expressing your regret at giving trouble, and your appreciation of his kindness in attending to the matter.

You want to sell some weekly paper in your town.   Write to the firm that publishes the paper, asking for the right.   State your qualifications as to age, success, if any, in a similar line and your reasons for thinking you will succeed in this undertaking, then *stop* and sign yourself "Very truly yours," followed by your name on the line below.

Write a letter to the principal of your school asking for a recommendation that you can use in applying for a position.

Write thanking him for his letter of recommendation.

A schoolmate is ill.   Write expressing your sympathy, and offering your services.   Close with the school news.

You wish a friend to become a member of the literary society or club to which you belong, but some of the members have objected.   Write to the committee on membership, admitting that your friend has faults, but showing that he has qualities that would make his election beneficial both for him and for the club.

Write an imaginary reply by General Hooker to Lincoln's letter.

SUGGESTIONS FOR ADDITIONAL READINGS

Lincoln, the Great Commoner (verse).   Edwin Markham.
Letters of Robert Louis Stevenson.   Sidney Colvin.
Success in Letter-Writing.   Sherwin Cody.
Letters from Colonial Children.   Eva March Tappan.
The Gentlest Art.   E. V. Lucas.
Life and Letters of Miss Alcott.   E. D. Cheney.
Children's Letters.   Colson and Chittenden.

ANNABEL LEE

Edgar Allan Poe

[For biographical sketch see page 122.]

It was many and many a year ago,
  In a kingdom by the sea,
That a maiden there lived whom you may know
  By the name of Annabel Lee;
And this maiden she lived with no other thought
  Than to love and be loved by me.

I was a child and she was a child,
  In this kingdom by the sea,
But we loved with a love that was more than love,
  I and my Annabel Lee;
With a love that the wingèd seraphs of heaven
  Coveted her and me.

And this was the reason that, long ago,
  In this kingdom by the sea,
A wind blew out of a cloud, chilling
  My beautiful Annabel Lee;
So that her high-born kinsmen came
  And bore her away from me,
To shut her up in a sepulcher
  In this kingdom by the sea.

The angels, not half so happy in heaven,
  Went envying her and me; —

Yes! that was the reason (as all men know,
   In this kingdom by the sea)
That the wind came out of the cloud by night,
   Chilling and killing my Annabel Lee.
But our love it was stronger by far than the love
   Of those who were older than we,
   Of many far wiser than we;
And neither the angels in heaven above,
   Nor the demons down under the sea,
Can ever dissever my soul from the soul
   Of the beautiful Annabel Lee:

For the moon never beams, without bringing me dreams
   Of the beautiful Annabel Lee;
And the stars never rise, but I feel the bright eyes
   Of the beautiful Annabel Lee;
And so, all the nighttide, I lie down by the side
Of my darling — my darling — my life and my bride,
   In her sepulcher there by the sea,
   In her tomb by the sounding sea.

STUDY HINTS

This exquisite poem was written after the death of Poe's idolized wife. They were married when she was only fourteen, and they had six years of rare companionship, despite ill health and hardships of every kind. Why does he think that the seraphs "coveted her and me"? Is there any note of triumph in the poem? Which thought in it do you consider the most beautiful? Give as many reasons as you can to account for the fact that this poem is almost a universal favorite. Read it aloud as musically as you can.

SUGGESTIONS FOR ADDITIONAL READINGS

For the teacher to read to the class:
Vigil Strange I Kept on the Field One Night. Walt Whitman.

THE SEEING HAND [1]

Helen Keller

[For biographical sketch see page 254.]

I HAVE just touched my dog. He was rolling on the
grass, with pleasure in every muscle and limb. I wanted
to catch a picture of him in my fingers, and I touched him
as lightly as I would cobwebs; but lo, his fat body revolved,
stiffened, and solidified into an upright position, and his
tongue gave my hand a lick! He pressed close to me, as if
he were fain to crowd himself into my hand. He loved it
with his tail, with his paw, with his tongue. If he could
speak, I believe he would say with me that paradise is
attained by touch; for in touch is all love and intelligence.

This small incident started me on a chat about hands,
and if my chat is fortunate I have to thank my dog-star. In
any case it is pleasant to have something to talk about that
no one else has monopolized; it is like making a new path
in the trackless woods, blazing the trail where no foot has
pressed before. I am glad to take you by the hand and
lead you along an untrodden way into a world where the
hand is supreme. But at the very outset we encounter a
difficulty. You are so accustomed to light, I fear you will
stumble when I try to guide you through the land of darkness
and silence. The blind are not supposed to be the best of
guides. Still, though I cannot warrant not to lose you, I
promise that you shall not be led into fire or water, or fall
into a deep pit. If you will follow me patiently, you will

[1] From *The World I Live In*. Used by permission of the Century Company.

find that "there's a sound so fine, nothing lives 'twixt it and silence," and that there is more meant in things than meets the eye.

My hand is to me what your hearing and sight together are to you. In large measure we travel the same highways, read the same books, speak the same language, yet our experiences are different. All my comings and goings turn on the hand as on a pivot. It is the hand that binds me to the world of men and women. The hand is my feeler with which I reach through isolation and darkness and seize every pleasure, every activity that my fingers encounter. With the dropping of a little word from another's [1] hand into mine, a slight flutter of the fingers, began the intelligence, the joy, the fullness of my life. Like Job, I feel as if a hand had made me, fashioned me together round about, and molded my very soul.

In all my experiences and thoughts I am conscious of a hand. Whatever moves me, whatever thrills me, is as a hand that touches me in the dark, and that touch is my reality. You might as well say that a sight which makes you glad, or a blow which brings the stinging tears to your eyes, is unreal as to say that those impressions are unreal which I have accumulated by means of touch. The delicate tremble of a butterfly's wings in my hand, the soft petals of violets curling in the cool folds of their leaves or lifting sweetly out of the meadow grass, the clear, firm outline of face and limb, the smooth arch of a horse's neck and the velvety touch of his nose — all these, and a thousand resultant combinations, which take shape in my mind, constitute my world.

Ideas make the world we live in, and impressions furnish ideas. My world is built of touch-sensations, devoid of physical color and sound; but without color and sound it

[1] Miss Sullivan's (now Mrs. Macy), when she began teaching Helen Keller.

breathes and throbs with life. Every object is associated
in my mind with tactual [1] qualities which, combined in
countless ways, give me a sense of power, of beauty, or of
incongruity: for with my hands I can feel the comic as well
as the beautiful in the outward appearance of things. Remember that you, dependent on your sight, do not realize
how many things are tangible. All palpable things are
mobile or rigid, solid or liquid, big or small, warm or cold,
and these qualities are variously modified. The coolness of
a water lily rounding into bloom is different from the coolness of an evening wind in summer, and different again from
the coolness of the rain that soaks into the hearts of growing
things and gives them life and body. The velvet of a rose
is not that of a ripe peach or of a baby's dimpled cheek.
The hardness of the rock is to the hardness of the wood what
a man's deep bass is to a woman's voice when it is low.
What I call beauty I find in certain combinations of all
these qualities, and is largely derived from the flow of curved
and straight lines which is over all things. . . .

When I think of hills, I think of the upward strength I
tread upon. When water is the object of my thought, I
feel the cool shock of the plunge and the quick yielding of
the waves that crisp and curl and ripple about my body.
The pleasing changes of rough and smooth, pliant and rigid,
curved and straight, in the bark and branches of a tree give
the truth to my hand. The immovable rock, with all its
juts and warpèd surface, bends beneath my fingers into all
manner of grooves and hollows. The bulge of a watermelon
and the puffed-up rotundities of squashes that sprout, bud,
and ripen in that strange garden planted somewhere behind
my fingertips are the ludicrous in my tactual memory and
imagination. My fingers are tickled to delight by the soft
ripple of a baby's laugh, and find amusement in the lusty

[1] Relating to touch.

crow of the barnyard autocrat. Once I had a pet rooster that used to perch on my knee and stretch his neck and crow. A bird in my hand was then worth two in the — barnyard.

My fingers cannot, of course, get the impression of a large whole at a glance; but I feel the parts and my mind puts them together. I move around my house, touching object after object in order, before I can form an idea of the entire house. In other people's houses I can touch only what is shown me — the chief objects of interest, carvings on the wall, or a curious architectural feature, exhibited like the family album. Therefore a house with which I am not familiar has for me, at first, no general effect or harmony of detail. It is not a complete conception, but a collection of object-impressions which, as they come to me, are disconnected and isolated. But my mind is full of associations, sensations, theories, and with them it constructs the house. The process reminds me of the building of Solomon's Temple, where was neither saw, nor hammer, nor any tool heard while the stones were being laid one upon another. The silent worker is imagination which decrees reality out of chaos.[1]

STUDY HINTS

Study the spelling and meaning of these words:

incident	isolation	inexhaustible
supreme	seize	rigid
accustom	conscious	lose, lost, lost
pivot	yield	ludicrous

How does Helen Keller's dog show his love for her? Has your dog any senses that are keener than yours? How many senses does Helen Keller's sense of touch replace? Read carefully her illustrations of this. Try to put yourself in her place as you read. Upon what sense do deaf people sometimes learn to depend? It is said that the blind are happier than the deaf. Can you give any reasons for this? Do we take as much

[1] Disorder.

pains to make the deaf happy? Does Helen Keller think she should be pitied? How do we learn to know the world all about us? What passages in this do you think beautiful? Is the title appropriate?

SUGGESTIONS FOR ORAL AND WRITTEN ENGLISH
THEME SUBJECTS

Blindfold yourself and try (a) to find out what some objects are by the sense of touch; (b) to find your way to the door of your room; (c) to see if you can recognize a friend by passing your hand over his face.

Write your experiences. If you know any one who is blind, or deaf, or has lost the use of a limb, watch him for a short while, and see how often he has learned bravely to overcome his disability. Do you know of any people who have succeeded in spite of their handicap? Bring incidents to the class. Express in your own words what Helen Keller says in paragraphs three and four, and in the last paragraph.

SUGGESTIONS FOR ADDITIONAL READINGS

The Story of My Life. Helen Keller.
The World I Live In. Helen Keller.
The Petition of the Left Hand. Benjamin Franklin.
Autobiography. Benjamin Franklin.
Edison: His Life and Inventions. Dyer and Martin.

(THE THREE STRANGERS)

Thomas Hardy

Thomas Hardy (1840–   ) was born in the little town of Bock-
hampton, in the southern part of England. Though educated to be an
architect, he preferred to be a writer. He returned after many years to
his birthplace, to follow his literary pursuits. His well-known *Wessex
Tales*, from which *The Three Strangers* is taken, describes the life of the
country around his birthplace. See also:

Halleck's *New English Literature*, pp. 529–533, 584.
Abercrombie's *Thomas Hardy: A Critical Study*.
Phelps's *Essays on Modern Novelists* (Hardy).

AMONG the few features of agricultural England which
retain an appearance but little modified by the lapse of centuries, may be reckoned the high, grassy, and furzy downs,
coombs, or ewe-leases, as they are indifferently called, that
fill a large area of certain counties in the south and southwest.
If any mark of human occupation is met with hereon it
usually takes the form of the solitary cottage of some
shepherd.

Fifty years ago such a lonely cottage stood on such a
down, and may possibly be standing there now. In spite
of its loneliness, however, the spot, by actual measurement,
was not more than five miles from a county town.

Higher Crowstairs, as the house was called, stood quite
detached and undefended. The only reason for its precise
situation seemed to be the crossing of two footpaths at right
angles hard by, which may have crossed there and thus for
a good five hundred years. Hence the house was exposed
to the elements on all sides. When the shepherd and his

family who tenanted the house were pitied for their sufferings from the exposure, they said that upon the whole they were less inconvenienced by "wuzzes and flames" (hoarses and phlegms) than when they had lived by the stream of a snug neighboring valley.

The night of March 28, 182–, was precisely one of the nights that were wont to call forth these expressions of commiseration. The level rainstorm smote walls, slopes, and hedges like the clothyard shafts of Senlac [1] and Crécy.[1] Such sheep and outdoor animals as had no shelter stood with their buttocks to the winds; while the tails of little birds trying to roost on some scraggy thorn were blown inside out like umbrellas. The gable end of the cottage was stained with wet, and the eavesdropping flapped against the wall. Yet never was commiseration for the shepherd more misplaced, for that cheerful rustic was entertaining a large party in glorification of the christening of his second girl.

The guests had arrived before the rain began to fall, and they were all now assembled in the chief, or living, room of the dwelling. A glance into the apartment at eight o'clock on this eventful evening would have resulted in the opinion that it was as cozy and comfortable a nook as could be wished for in boisterous weather. The calling of its inhabitant was proclaimed by a number of highly polished sheepcrooks without stems that were hung ornamentally over the fireplace, the curl of each shining crook varying from the antiquated type engraved in the patriarchal pictures of old family Bibles to the most approved fashion of the last local sheep fair. The room was lighted by half a dozen candles, having wicks only a trifle smaller than the grease

---

[1] In the battle of Senlac, or Hastings (1066), William the Conqueror defeated Harold, the last of the Saxon kings of England, and established Norman supremacy in England. In the battle of Crécy (1346) Edward the Black Prince, son of Edward III of England, won a victory over the French king against great odds. These battles were fiercely fought by archers whose "shafts fell as thick as rain."

which enveloped them, in candlesticks that were never used but at high days, holy days, and family feasts. The lights were scattered about the room, two of them standing on the chimney piece. This position of candles was in itself significant. Candles on the chimney piece always meant a party.

On the hearth, in front of a back-brand to give substance, blazed a fire of thorns, that crackled "like the laughter of the fool."

Nineteen persons were gathered here. Of these, five women, wearing gowns of various bright hues, sat in chairs along the wall; girls shy and not shy filled the window bench; four men, including Charley Jake, the hedge carpenter, Elijah New, the parish clerk, and John Pitcher, a neighboring dairyman, the shepherd's father-in-law, lolled in the settle; a young man and maid sat beneath the corner cupboard; and an elderly engaged man of fifty or upward moved restlessly about from spots where his betrothed was not, to the spot where she was. Enjoyment was pretty general, and so much the more prevailed in being unhampered by conventional restrictions. Absolute confidence in one another's good opinion begat perfect ease, while the finishing stroke of manner, amounting to a truly princely serenity, was lent to the majority by the absence of any expression or trait denoting that they wished to get on in the world, enlarge their minds, or do any eclipsing thing whatever — which nowadays so generally nips the bloom and *bonhomie* of all except the two extremes of the social scale.

Shepherd Fennel had married well, his wife being a dairyman's daughter from the valley below, who brought fifty guineas in her pocket — and kept them there till they should be required for ministering to the needs of a coming family. This frugal woman had been somewhat exercised as to the character that should be given to the gathering. A sit-still

party had its advantages; but an undisturbed position of
ease in chairs and settles was apt to lead on the men to such
an unconscionable deal of toping that they would sometimes fairly drink the house dry. A dancing party was the
alternative; but this, while avoiding the foregoing objection
on the score of good drink, had a counterbalancing disadvantage in the matter of good victuals, the ravenous
appetites engendered by the exercise causing immense havoc
in the buttery. Shepherdess Fennel fell back upon the
intermediate plan of mingling short dances with short periods
of talk and singing, so as to hinder any ungovernable rage in
either. But this scheme was entirely confined to her own
gentle mind; the shepherd himself was in the mood to exhibit
the most reckless phases of hospitality.

The fiddler was a boy of those parts, about twelve years
of age, who had a wonderful dexterity in jigs and reels,
though his fingers were so small and short as to necessitate a
constant shifting for the high notes, from which he scrambled
back to the first position with sounds not of unmixed purity
of tone. At seven the shrill tweedle-dee of this youngster
had begun, accompanied by a booming ground-bass from
Elijah New, the parish clerk, who had thoughtfully brought
with him his favorite musical instrument, the serpent.[1]
Dancing was instantaneous, Mrs. Fennel privately enjoining
the players on no account to let the dance exceed the length
of a quarter of an hour.

But Elijah and the boy, in the excitement of their position,
quite forgot the injunction. Moreover, Oliver Giles, a man
of seventeen, one of the dancers, who was enamored of his
partner, a fair girl of thirty-three rolling years, had recklessly
handed a new crown-piece to the musicians, as a bribe to
keep going as long as they had muscle and wind. Mrs.
Fennel, seeing the steam begin to generate on the coun-

[1] A species of horn shaped like a serpent.

tenances of her guests, crossed over and touched the fiddler's elbow and put her hand on the serpent's mouth. But they took no notice, and fearing she might lose her character of genial hostess if she were to interfere too markedly, she retired and sat down helpless. And so the dance whizzed on with cumulative fury, the performers moving in their planet-like courses, direct and retrograde, from apogee to perigee, till the hand of the well-kicked clock at the bottom of the room had traveled over the circumference of an hour.

While these cheerful events were in course of enactment within Fennel's pastoral dwelling, an incident having considerable bearing on the party had occurred in the gloomy night without. Mrs. Fennel's concern about the growing fierceness of the dance corresponded in point of time with the ascent of a human figure to the solitary hill of Higher Crowstairs from the direction of the distant town. This personage strode on through the rain without a pause, following the little-worn path which, further on in its course, skirted the shepherd's cottage.

It was nearly the time of the full moon, and on this account, though the sky was lined with a uniform sheet of dripping cloud, ordinary objects out of doors were readily visible. The sad, wan light revealed the lonely pedestrian to be a man of supple frame; his gait suggested that he had somewhat passed the period of perfect and instinctive agility, though not so far as to be otherwise than rapid of motion when occasion required. In point of fact, he might have been about forty years of age. He appeared tall, but a recruiting sergeant, or other person accustomed to the judging of men's heights by the eye, would have discerned that this was chiefly owing to his gauntness, and that he was not more than five feet eight or nine.

Notwithstanding the regularity of his tread there was caution in it, as in that of one who mentally feels his way;

and despite the fact that it was not a black coat nor a dark garment of any sort that he wore, there was something about him which suggested that he naturally belonged to the black-coated tribes of men. His clothes were of fustian, and his boots hobnailed, yet in his progress he showed not the mud-accustomed bearing of hobnailed and fustianed peasantry.

By the time that he had arrived abreast of the shepherd's premises the rain came down, or rather came along, with yet more determined violence. The outskirts of the little settlement partially broke the force of wind and rain, and this induced him to stand still. The most salient of the shepherd's domestic erections was an empty sty at the forward corner of his hedgeless garden, for in these latitudes the principle of masking the homelier features of your establishment by a conventional frontage was unknown. The traveler's eye was attracted to this small building by the pallid shine of the wet slates that covered it. He turned aside, and, finding it empty, stood under the pent-roof for shelter.

While he stood, the boom of the serpent within the adjacent house, and the lesser strains of the fiddler, reached the spot as an accompaniment to the surging hiss of the flying rain on the sod, its louder beating on the cabbage leaves of the garden, on the eight or ten beehives just discernible by the path, and its dripping from the eaves into a row of buckets and pans that had been placed under the walls of the cottage. For at Higher Crowstairs, as at all such elevated domiciles, the grand difficulty of housekeeping was an insufficiency of water; and a casual rainfall was utilized by turning out, as catchers, every utensil that the house contained. . . .

At last the notes of the serpent ceased and the house was silent. This cessation of activity aroused the solitary pedestrian from the reverie into which he had lapsed, and, emerging from the shed, with an apparently new intention, he walked up the path to the house door. Arrived here, his first act was to kneel down on a large stone beside the row of vessels, and to drink a copious draft from one of them. Having quenched his thirst he rose and lifted his hand to knock, but paused with his eye upon the panel. Since the dark surface of the wood revealed absolutely nothing, it was evident that he must be mentally looking through the door, as if he wished to measure thereby all the possibilities that a house of this sort might include, and how they might bear upon the question of his entry.

In his indecision he turned and surveyed the scene around. Not a soul was anywhere visible. The garden path stretched downward from his feet, gleaming like the track of a snail; the roof of the little well (mostly dry), the well-cover, the top rail of the garden gate, were varnished with the same dull liquid glaze; while, far away in the vale, a faint whiteness of more than usual extent showed that the rivers were high in the meads. Beyond all this winked a few bleared lamplights through the beating drops, lights that denoted the situation of the county town from which he had appeared to come. The absence of all notes of life in that direction seemed to clinch his intentions, and he knocked at the door.

Within, a desultory chat had taken the place of movement and musical sound. The hedge carpenter was suggesting a song to the company, which nobody just then was inclined to undertake, so that the knock afforded a not unwelcome diversion.

"Walk in," said the shepherd, promptly.

The latch clicked upward, and out of the night our pedestrian appeared upon the doormat. The shepherd arose, snuffed two of the nearest candles, and turned to look at him.

Their light disclosed that the stranger was dark in complexion and not unprepossessing as to feature. His hat, which for a moment he did not remove, hung low over his eyes, without concealing that they were large, open, and determined, moving with a flash rather than a glance round the room. He seemed pleased with the survey, and, baring his shaggy head, said, in a rich deep voice, "The rain is so heavy, friends, that I ask leave to come in and rest a while."

"To be sure, stranger," said the shepherd. "And faith, you've been lucky in choosing your time, for we are having a bit of a fling for a glad cause."

"And what may be this glad cause?" asked the stranger.

"A birth and christening," said the shepherd.

The stranger hoped his host might not be made unhappy either by too many or too few of such episodes, and being invited by a gesture to a pull at the mug, he readily acquiesced. His manner, which, before entering, had been so dubious, was now altogether that of a careless and candid man.

"Late to be traypsing athwart this coomb — hey?" said the engaged man of fifty.

"Late it is, master, as you say. I'll take a seat in the chimney corner, if you have nothing to urge against it, ma'am, for I am a little moist on the side that was next the rain."

Mrs. Shepherd Fennel assented, and made room for the self-invited comer, who, having got completely inside the chimney corner, stretched out his legs and his arms with the expansiveness of a person quite at home.

"Yes, I am rather thin in the vamp," he said, freely, seeing that the eyes of the shepherd's wife fell upon his boots, "and I am not well fitted, either. I have had some rough times lately, and have been forced to pick up what I can get in the way of wearing, but I must find a suit better fit for working days when I reach home."

"One of hereabouts?" she inquired.

"Not quite that — farther up the country."

"I thought so. And so am I; and by your tongue you come from my neighborhood."

"But you would hardly have heard of me," he said, quickly. "My time would be long before yours, ma'am, you see."

This testimony to the youthfulness of his hostess had the effect of stopping her cross-examination.

"There is only one thing more wanted to make me happy," continued the new-comer, "and that is a little 'baccy, which I am sorry to say I am out of."

"I'll fill your pipe," said the shepherd.

"I must ask you to lend me a pipe likewise."

"A smoker, and no pipe about ye?"

"I have dropped it somewhere on the road."

The shepherd filled and handed him a new clay pipe, saying, as he did so, "Hand me your 'baccy-box — I'll fill that too, now I am about it."

The man went through the movement of searching his pockets.

"Lost that too?" said his entertainer, with some surprise.

"I am afraid so," said the man, with some confusion. "Give it to me in a screw of paper." Lighting his pipe at the candle with a suction that drew the whole flame into the bowl, he resettled himself in the corner, and bent his looks upon the faint steam from his damp legs, as if he wished to say no more.

Meanwhile the general body of guests had been taking little notice of this visitor by reason of an absorbing discussion in which they were engaged with the band, about a tune for the next dance. The matter being settled, they were about to stand up, when an interruption came in the shape of another knock at the door.

At sound of the same the man in the chimney corner took up the poker and began stirring the fire as if doing it thoroughly were the one aim of his existence; and a second time the shepherd said, "Walk in!" In a moment another man stood upon the straw-woven doormat. He, too, was a stranger.

This individual was one of a type radically different from the first. There was more of the commonplace in his manner, and a certain jovial cosmopolitanism sat upon his features. He was several years older than the first arrival, his hair being slightly frosted, his eyebrows bristly, and his whiskers cut back from his cheeks. His face was rather full and flabby, and yet it was not altogether a face without power. A few grog-blossoms marked the neighborhood of his nose. He flung back his long drab greatcoat, revealing that beneath it he wore a suit of cinder-gray shade throughout; large, heavy seals of some metal or other that would take a polish, dangling from his fob, as his only personal ornament. Shaking the water drops from his low-crowned glazed hat, he said, "I must ask for a few minutes' shelter, comrades, or I shall be wetted to my skin before I get to Casterbridge."

"Make yourself at home, master," said the shepherd, perhaps a trifle less heartily than on the first occasion. Not that Fennel had the least tinge of niggardliness in his composition; but the room was far from large, spare chairs were not numerous, and damp companions were not altogether desirable at close quarters for the women and girls in their bright-colored gowns.

However, the second comer, after taking off his greatcoat, and hanging his hat on a nail in one of the ceiling beams as if he had been specially invited to put it there, advanced and sat down at the table. This had been pushed so closely into the chimney corner, to give all available room to the dancers, that its inner edge grazed the elbow of the

man who had ensconced himself by the fire; and thus the
two strangers were brought into close companionship. They
nodded to each other by way of breaking the ice of un-
acquaintance, and the first stranger handed his neighbor the
family mug — a huge vessel of brown ware, having its upper
edge worn away like a threshold by the rub of whole generations of thirsty lips that had gone the way of all flesh, and
bearing the following inscription burned upon its rotund side
in yellow letters:

> THERE IS NO FUN
> UNTILL I CUM.

The other man, nothing loath, raised the mug to his lips,
and drank on, and on, and on — till a curious blueness over-
spread the countenance of the shepherd's wife, who had
regarded with no little surprise the first stranger's free offer
to the second of what did not belong to him to dispense.

"I knew it!" said the toper to the shepherd, with much
satisfaction. "When I walked up your garden before coming
in, and saw the hives all of a row, I said to myself, 'Where
there's bees there's honey, and where there's honey there's
mead.' But mead of such a truly comfortable sort as this I
really didn't expect to meet in my older days." He took
yet another pull at the mug, till it assumed an ominous
elevation.

"Glad you enjoy it!" said the shepherd, warmly.

"It is goodish mead," assented Mrs. Fennel, with an
absence of enthusiasm which seemed to say that it was possible to buy praise for one's cellar at too heavy a price. "It
is trouble enough to make, and really I hardly think we shall
make any more. For honey sells well, and we ourselves can
make shift with a drop o' small mead and metheglin [1] for
common use from the comb-washings."

[1] A drink made of fermented honey.

"Oh, but you'll never have the heart!" reproachfully cried the stranger in cinder-gray, after taking up the mug a third time and setting it down empty. "I love mead when 'tis old like this, as I love to go to church o' Sundays, or to relieve the needy any day of the week."

"Ha, ha, ha!" said the man in the chimney corner, who, in spite of the taciturnity induced by the pipe of tobacco, could not or would not refrain from this slight testimony to his comrade's humor.

Now, the old mead of those days, brewed of the purest first-year or maiden honey — four pounds to the gallon, with its due complement of white of eggs, cinnamon, ginger, cloves, mace, rosemary, yeast, and processes of working, bottling, and cellaring — tasted remarkably strong; but it did not taste so strong as it actually was. Hence, presently the stranger in cinder-gray at the table, moved by its creeping influence, unbuttoned his waistcoat, threw himself back in his chair, spread his legs, and made his presence felt in various ways.

"Well, well, as I say," he resumed, "I am going to Caster-bridge, and to Casterbridge I must go. I should have been almost there by this time; but the rain drove me into your dwelling, and I'm not sorry for it."

"You don't live in Casterbridge?" said the shepherd.

"Not as yet, though I shortly mean to move there."

"Going to set up in trade, perhaps?"

"No, no," said the shepherd's wife. "It is easy to see that the gentleman is rich, and don't want to work at any-thing."

The cinder-gray stranger paused, as if to consider whether he would accept that definition of himself. He presently rejected it by answering, "Rich is not quite the word for me, dame. I do work, and I must work. And even if I only get to Casterbridge by midnight I must begin work there at eight to-morrow morning. Yes, het or wet, blow or snow, famine or sword, my day's work to-morrow must be done."

"Poor man! Then, in spite o' seeming, you be worse off than we," replied the shepherd's wife.

"'Tis the nature of my trade, men and maidens. 'Tis the nature of my trade more than my poverty. . . . But really and truly I must be up and off, or I shan't get a lodging in the town." However, the speaker did not move, and directly added, "There's time for one more draft of friendship before I go, and I'd perform it at once if the mug were not dry."

"Here's a mug o' small," said Mrs. Fennel. "Small, we call it, though to be sure 'tis only the first wash o' the combs."

"No," said the stranger, disdainfully. "I won't spoil your first kindness by partaking o' your second."

"Certainly not," broke in Fennel. "We don't increase and multiply every day, and I'll fill the mug again." He went away to the dark place under the stairs where the barrel stood. The shepherdess followed him.

"Why should you do this?" she said, reproachfully, as soon as they were alone. "He's emptied it once, though it held enough for ten people; and now he's not contented wi' the small, but must needs call for more o' the strong! And a stranger unbeknown to any of us. For my part, I don't like the look o' the man at all."

"But he's in the house, my honey; and 'tis a wet night, and a christening. Daze it, what's a cup of mead more or less? there'll be plenty more next bee-turning."

"Very well — this time, then," she answered, looking wistfully at the barrel. "But what is the man's calling, and where is he one of, that he should come in and join us like this?"

"I don't know. I'll ask him again."

The catastrophe of having the mug drained dry at one pull by the stranger in cinder-gray was effectually guarded against this time by Mrs. Fennel. She poured out his allowance in a small cup, keeping the large one at a discreet distance from him. When he had tossed off his portion the shepherd renewed his inquiry about the stranger's occupation.

The latter did not immediately reply, and the man in the chimney corner, with sudden demonstrativeness, said, "Anybody may know my trade — I'm a wheelwright."

"A very good trade for these parts," said the shepherd.

"And anybody may know mine — if they've the sense to find it out," said the stranger in cinder-gray.

"You may generally tell what a man is by his claws," observed the hedge carpenter, looking at his own hands. "My fingers be as full of thorns as an old pincushion is of pins."

The hands of the man in the chimney corner instinctively sought the shade, and he gazed into the fire as he resumed his pipe. The man at the table took up the hedge carpenter's remark, and added, smartly, "True; but the oddity of my trade is that, instead of setting a mark upon me it sets a mark upon my customers."

No observation being offered by anybody in elucidation of this enigma, the shepherd's wife once more called for a song. The same obstacles presented themselves as at the former time — one had no voice, another had forgotten the first verse. The stranger at the table, whose soul had now risen to a good working temperature, relieved the difficulty by exclaiming that, to start the company, he would sing himself. Thrusting one thumb into the armhole of his waistcoat, he waved the other hand in the air, and, with an extemporizing gaze at the shining sheepcrooks above the mantel piece began:

"Oh, my trade it is the rarest one,
            Simple shepherds all —
    My trade is a sight to see;
For my customers I tie, and take them up on high,
    And waft 'em to a far countree!"

The room was silent when he had finished the verse — with
one exception, that of the man in the chimney corner, who,
at the singer's word, "Chorus!" joined him in a deep bass
voice of musical relish —

    "And waft 'em to a far countree!"

Oliver Giles, John Pitcher the dairyman, the parish clerk, the
engaged man of fifty, the row of young women against the
wall, seemed lost in thought not of the gayest kind. The
shepherd looked meditatively on the ground, the shepherdess
gazed keenly at the singer and with some suspicion; she
was doubting whether this stranger were merely singing an
old song from recollection, or was composing one there and
then for the occasion. All were as perplexed at the obscure
revelation as the guests at Belshazzar's Feast, except the
man in the chimney corner, who quietly said, "Second verse,
stranger," and smoked on.

The singer thoroughly moistened himself from his lips
inward, and went on with the next stanza as requested:

        "My tools are but common ones,
                Simple shepherds all —
        My tools are no sight to see;
    A little hempen string, and a post whereon to swing,
        Are implements enough for me!"

Shepherd Fennel glanced round. There was no longer
any doubt that the stranger was answering his question
rhythmically. The guests one and all started back with
suppressed exclamations. The young woman engaged to
the man of fifty fainted halfway, and would have proceeded,

but finding him wanting in alacrity for catching her, she sat down trembling.

"Oh, he's the ——!" whispered the people in the background, mentioning the name of an ominous public officer. "He's come to do it. 'Tis to be at Casterbridge jail tomorrow — the man for sheep-stealing — the poor clockmaker we heard of, who used to live away at Shottsford and had no work to do — Timothy Sommers, whose family were a-starving, and so he went out of Shottsford by the highroad, and took a sheep in open daylight, defying the farmer and the farmer's wife and the farmer's lad, and every man jack among 'em. He" (and they nodded toward the stranger of the deadly trade) "is come from up the country to do it because there's not enough to do in his own county town, and he's got the place here now our own countyman's dead; he's going to live in the same cottage under the prison wall."

The stranger in cinder-gray took no notice of this whispered string of observations, but again wetted his lips. Seeing that his friend in the chimney corner was the only one who reciprocated his joviality in any way, he held out his cup toward that appreciative comrade, who also held out his own. They clinked together, the eyes of the rest of the room hanging upon the singer's actions. He parted his lips for the third verse, but at that moment another knock was audible upon the door. This time the knock was faint and hesitating.

The company seemed scared; the shepherd looked with consternation toward the entrance, and it was with some effort that he resisted his alarmed wife's deprecatory glance, and uttered for the third time the welcoming words, "Walk in!"

The door was gently opened, and another man stood upon the mat. He, like those who had preceded him, was a stranger. This time it was a short, small personage, of fair complexion, and dressed in a decent suit of dark clothes.

"Can you tell me the way to ——?" he began; when, gazing round the room to observe the nature of the company among whom he had fallen, his eyes lighted on the stranger in cinder-gray. It was just at the instant when the latter, who had thrown his mind into his song with such a will that he scarcely heeded the interruption, silenced all whispers and inquiries by bursting into his third verse:

> "To-morrow is my working day,
> Simple shepherds all —
> To-morrow is a working day for me:
> For the farmer's sheep is slain, and the lad who did it ta'en,
> And on his soul may God ha' merc-y!"

The stranger in the chimney corner, waving cups with the singer so heartily that his mead splashed over on the hearth, repeated in his bass voice as before:

> "And on his soul may God ha' merc-y!"

All this time the third stranger had been standing in the doorway. Finding now that he did not come forward or go on speaking, the guests particularly regarded him. They noticed, to their surprise, that he stood before them the picture of abject terror — his knees trembling, his hand shaking so violently that the door latch by which he supported himself rattled audibly; his white lips were parted, and his eyes fixed on the merry officer of justice in the middle of the room. A moment more and he had turned, closed the door, and fled.

"What a man can it be?" said the shepherd.

The rest, between the awfulness of their late discovery and the odd conduct of this third visitor, looked as if they knew not what to think, and said nothing. Instinctively they withdrew further and further from the grim gentleman in their midst, whom some of them seemed to take for the Prince of Darkness himself, till they formed a remote circle, an empty space of floor being left between them and him —

"... circulus, cujus centrum diabolus." [1]

The room was so silent — though there were more than twenty people in it — that nothing could be heard but the patter of the rain against the window shutters, accompanied by the occasional hiss of a stray drop that fell down the chimney into the fire, and the steady puffing of the man in the corner, who had now resumed his pipe of long clay.

The stillness was unexpectedly broken. The distant sound of a gun reverberated through the air — apparently from the direction of the county town.

"Be jiggered!" cried the stranger who had sung the song, jumping up.

"What does that mean?" asked several.

"A prisoner escaped fom the jail — that's what it means."

All listened. The sound was repeated, and none of them spoke but the man in the chimney corner, who said, quietly, "I've often been told that in this county they fire a gun at such times; but I never heard it till now."

"I wonder if it is *my* man?" murmured the personage in cinder-gray.

[1] Latin for "A little circle whose center is the Evil One."

"Surely it is!" said the shepherd, involuntarily. "And surely we've seen him! That little man who looked in at the door by now, and quivered like a leaf when he seed ye and heard your song."

"His teeth chattered, and the breath went out of his body," said the dairyman.

"And his heart seemed to sink within him like a stone," said Oliver Giles.

"And he bolted as if he'd been shot at," said the hedge carpenter.

"True — his teeth chattered, and his heart seemed to sink; and he bolted as if he'd been shot at," slowly summed up the man in the chimney corner.

"I didn't notice it," remarked the hangman.

"We were all a-wondering what made him run off in such a fright," faltered one of the women against the wall, "and now 'tis explained."

The firing of the alarm gun went on at intervals, low and sullenly, and their suspicions became a certainty. The sinister gentleman in cinder-gray roused himself. "Is there a constable here?" he asked, in thick tones. "If so, let him step forward."

The engaged man of fifty stepped quavering out of the corner, his betrothed beginning to sob on the back of the chair.

"You are a sworn constable?"

"I be, sir."

"Then pursue the criminal at once, with assistance, and bring him back here. He can't have gone far."

"I will, sir, I will — when I've got my staff. I'll go home and get it, and come sharp here, and start in a body."

"Staff! — never mind your staff; the man'll be gone!"

"But I can't do nothing without my staff — can I, William, and John, and Charles Jake? No; for there's the King's royal crown a-painted on en in yaller and gold, and the lion and the unicorn, so as when I raise en up and hit my prisoner, 'tis made a lawful blow thereby. I wouldn't 'tempt to take up a man without my staff — no, not I. If I hadn't the law to gie me courage, why, instead o' my taking up him he might take up me!"

"Now, I'm a King's man myself, and can give you authority enough for this," said the formidable officer in gray. "Now then, all of ye, be ready. Have ye any lanterns?"

"Yes — have ye any lanterns? — I demand it!" said the constable.

"And the rest of you able-bodied —"

"Able-bodied men — yes — the rest of ye!" said the constable.

"Have you some good stout staves and pitchforks —"

"Staves and pitchforks — in the name o' the law! And take 'em in yer hands and go in quest, and do as we in authority tell ye!"

Thus aroused, the men prepared to give chase. The evidence was, indeed, though circumstantial, so convincing, that but little argument was needed to show the shepherd's guests that after what they had seen it would look very much like connivance if they did not instantly pursue the unhappy third stranger, who could not as yet have gone more than a few hundred yards over such uneven country.

A shepherd is always well provided with lanterns; and, lighting these hastily, and with hurdle staves in their hands, they poured out of the door, taking a direction along the crest of the hill, away from the town, the rain having fortunately a little abated.

Disturbed by the noise, or possibly by unpleasant dreams of her baptism, the child who had been christened began to cry heart-brokenly in the room overhead. These notes of grief came down through the chinks of the floor to the ears of the women below, who jumped up one by one, and seemed glad of the excuse to ascend and comfort the baby, for the incidents of the last half hour greatly oppressed them. Thus in the space of two or three minutes the room on the ground floor was deserted quite.

But it was not for long. Hardly had the sound of foot-steps died away when a man returned round the corner of the house from the direction the pursuers had taken. Peep-ing in at the door, and seeing nobody there, he entered leisurely. It was the stranger of the chimney corner, who had gone out with the rest. The motive of his return was shown by his helping himself to a cut piece of skimmer-cake that lay on a ledge beside where he had sat, and which he had apparently forgotten to take with him. He also poured out half a cup more mead from the quantity that remained, ravenously eating and drinking these as he stood. He had not finished when another figure came in just as quietly — his friend in cinder-gray.

"Oh — you here?" said the latter, smiling. "I thought you had gone to help in the capture." And this speaker also revealed the object of his return by looking solicitously round for the fascinating mug of old mead.

"And I thought you had gone," said the other, continuing his skimmer-cake with some effort.

"Well, on second thoughts, I felt there were enough with-out me," said the first, confidentially, "and such a night as it is, too. Besides, 'tis the business o' the government to take care of its criminals — not mine."

"True; so it is. And I felt as you did, that there were enough without me."

"I don't want to break my limbs running over the humps and hollows of this wild country."

"Nor I neither, between you and me."

"These shepherd people are used to it — simple-minded

souls, you know, stirred up to anything in a moment. They'll have him ready for me before the morning, and no trouble to me at all."

"They'll have him, and we shall have saved ourselves all labor in the matter."

"True, true. Well, my way is to Casterbridge; and 'tis as much as my legs will do to take me that far. Going the same way?"

"No, I am sorry to say! I have to get home over there" (he nodded indefinitely to the right), "and I feel as you do, that it is quite enough for my legs to do before bedtime."

The other had by this time finished the mead in the mug, after which, shaking hands heartily at the door, and wishing each other well, they went their several ways.

In the meantime the company of pursuers had reached the end of the hog's-back elevation which dominated this part of the coomb. They had decided on no particular plan of action; and, finding that the man of the baleful trade was no longer in their company, they seemed quite unable to form any such plan now. They descended in all directions down the hill, and straightway several of the party fell into the snare set by Nature for all misguided midnight ramblers over this part of the cretaceous formation. The "lynchets," or flint slopes, which belted the escarpment at intervals of a dozen yards, took the less cautious ones unawares, and losing their footing on the rubbly steep, they slid sharply downward, the lanterns rolling from their hands to the bottom, and there lying on their sides till the horn was scorched through.

When they had again gathered themselves together, the shepherd, as the man who knew the country best, took the lead, and guided them round these treacherous inclines. The lanterns, which seemed rather to dazzle their eyes and warn the fugitive than to assist them in the exploration, were extinguished, due silence was observed; and in this more rational order they plunged into the vale. It was a grassy, briery, moist defile, affording some shelter to any person who had sought it; but the party perambulated it in vain, and ascended on the other side. Here they wandered apart, and after an interval closed together again to report progress. At the second time of closing in they found themselves near a lonely ash, the single tree on this part of the upland, probably sown there by a passing bird some fifty years before. And here, standing a little to one side of the trunk, as motionless as the trunk itself, appeared the man they were in quest of, his outline being well defined against the sky beyond. The band noiselessly drew up and faced him.

"Your money or your life!" said the constable, sternly, to the still figure.

"No, no," whispered John Pitcher. "'Tisn't our side ought to say that. That's the doctrine of vagabonds like him, and we be on the side of the law."

"Well, well," replied the constable, impatiently; "I must say something, mustn't I? and if you had all the weight o' this undertaking upon your mind, perhaps you'd say the wrong thing too! Prisoner at the bar, surrender, in the name of the Father — the Crown, I mane!"

The man under the tree seemed now to notice them for the first time, and giving them no opportunity whatever for exhibiting their courage, he strolled slowly toward them. He was, indeed, the little man, the third stranger; but his trepidation had in a great measure gone.

"Well, travelers," he said, "did I hear ye speak to me?"

"You did; you've got to come and be our prisoner at once," said the constable. "We arrest ye on the charge of not biding in Casterbridge jail in a decent proper manner to be hung to-morrow morning. Neighbors, do your duty, and seize the culpet!"

On hearing the charge, the man seemed enlightened, and, saying not another word, resigned himself with preternatural civility to the search party, who, with their staves in their hands, surrounded him on all sides, and marched him back toward the shepherd's cottage.

It was eleven o'clock by the time they arrived. The light shining from the open door, a sound of men's voices within, proclaimed to them as they approached the house that some new events had arisen in their absence.

On entering they discovered the shepherd's living room to be invaded by two officers from Casterbridge jail, and a well-known magistrate who lived at the nearest country-seat, intelligence of the escape having become generally circulated.

"Gentlemen," said the constable, "I have brought back your man — not without risk and danger; but every one must do his duty! He is inside this circle of able-bodied persons, who have lent me useful aid, considering their ignorance of Crown work. Men, bring forward your prisoner!" And the third stranger was led to the light.

"Who is this?" said one of the officials.

"The man," said the constable.

"Certainly not," said the turnkey; and the first corroborated his statement.

"But how can it be otherwise?" asked the constable. "Or why was he so terrified at sight o' the singing instrument of the law who sat there?" Here he related the strange behavior of the third stranger on entering the house during the hangman's song.

"Can't understand it," said the officer, coolly. "All I know is that it is not the condemned man. He's quite a different character from this one; a gauntish fellow, with dark hair and eyes, rather good-looking, and with a musical bass voice that if you heard it once you'd never mistake as long as you lived."

"Why, souls — 'twas the man in the chimney corner!"

"Hey — what?" said the magistrate, coming forward after inquiring particulars from the shepherd in the background. "Haven't you got the man after all?"

"Well, sir," said the constable, "he's the man we were in search of, that's true; and yet he's not the man we were in search of. For the man we were in search of was not the man we wanted, sir, if you understand my everyday way; for 'twas the man in the chimney corner!"

"A pretty kettle of fish altogether!" said the magistrate. "You had better start for the other man at once."

The prisoner now spoke for the first time. The mention of the man in the chimney corner seemed to have moved him as nothing else could do. "Sir," he said, stepping forward to the magistrate, "take no more trouble about me. The time is come when I may as well speak. I have done nothing; my crime is that the condemned man is my brother. Early this afternoon I left home at Shottsford to tramp it all the way to Casterbridge jail to bid him farewell. I was benighted, and called here to rest and ask the way. When I opened the door I saw before me the very man, my brother, that I thought to see in the condemned cell at Casterbridge. He was in this chimney corner; and jammed close to him, so that he could not have got out if he had tried, was the executioner who'd come to take his life, singing a song about it, and not knowing that it was his victim who was close by, joining in to save appearances. My brother looked a glance of agony at me, and I knew he meant, 'Don't reveal what you see, my life depends on it.' I was so terror-struck that I could hardly stand, and, not knowing what I did, I turned and hurried away."

The narrator's manner and tone had the stamp of truth,

and his story made a great impression on all around. "And do you know where your brother is at the present time?" asked the magistrate.

"I do not. I have never seen him since I closed this door."

"I can testify to that, for we've been between ye ever since," said the constable.

"Where does he think to fly to? — what is his occupation?"

"He's a watch and clock maker, sir."

"'A said 'a was a wheelwright — a wicked rogue," said the constable.

"The wheels of clocks and watches he meant, no doubt," said Shepherd Fennel. "I thought his hands were palish for 's trade."

"Well, it appears to me that nothing can be gained by retaining this poor man in custody," said the magistrate. "Your business lies with the other, unquestionably."

And so the little man was released off-hand; but he looked nothing the less sad on that account, it being beyond the power of magistrate or constable to raze out the written troubles in his brain, for they concerned another whom he regarded with more solicitude than himself. When this was done, and the man had gone his way, the night was found to be so far advanced that it was deemed useless to renew the search before the next morning.

Next day, accordingly, the quest for the clever sheep-stealer became general and keen, to all appearance at least. But the intended punishment was cruelly disproportioned to the transgression, and the sympathy of a great many country folk in that district was strongly on the side of the fugitive. Moreover, his marvelous coolness and daring in hob-and-nobbing with the hangman, under the unprecedented circumstances of the shepherd's party, won their admiration. So that it may be questioned if all those who ostensibly made themselves so busy in exploring woods and fields and lanes were quite so thorough when it came to the private examination of their own lofts and out-houses. Stories were afloat of a mysterious figure being occasionally seen in some old overgrown track-way or other, remote from turnpike roads; but when a search was instituted in any of these suspected quarters nobody was found. Thus the days and weeks passed without tidings.

In brief, the bass-voiced man of the chimney corner was never recaptured. Some said that he went across the sea, others that he did not, but buried himself in the depths of a populous city. At any rate, the gentleman in cinder-gray never did his morning's work at Casterbridge, nor met anywhere at all, for business purposes, the genial comrade with whom he had passed an hour of relaxation in the lonely house on the coomb.

The grass has long been green on the graves of Shepherd Fennel and his frugal wife; the guests who made up the christening party have mainly followed their entertainers to the tomb; the baby in whose honor they all had met is a matron in the sear and yellow leaf. But the arrival of the three strangers at the shepherd's that night, and the details connected therewith, is a story as well known as ever in the country about Higher Crowstairs.

STUDY HINTS

Study the spelling and meaning of these words:

audible	assistance	magistrate
marvelous	connivance	agony
fugitive	exhibiting	busy
narrator	proclaimed	business

The scene of this story is laid in the southern part of England, in Hardy's "Wessex," a name which he gives to Dorsetshire and the adjacent district. How does he describe this part of "agricultural England"?

What is the chief occupation of its inhabitants? Describe the interior of the shepherd's room. How many people were in the party? Describe them and their aims. How does Hardy artistically present the general fact, "It rained hard"? Why are not three such words in regard to the rain all that are necessary? Is there a difference in the conduct of the first stranger before he enters the cottage and after? How did the second stranger reveal his business? Does the fact that he was well dressed and jovial make his trade seem *more* or *less* dreadful? How does he affect the others? Would the third stranger have been so much overcome by the situation at any other time in the evening?

What convinces the shepherd and his friends that the third stranger is the escaped prisoner? What happens to deepen this belief? Why did the first two strangers return to the house? Does the return of the second affect the first in any way? Did you actually know who was the real fugitive when you had read no farther than the disappearance of the third stranger?

As you look back, how many suspicious acts of the guilty person do you recall? From one point of view, this story of the time of George IV (1820–1830) is a chapter in the social history of England. For centuries property holders alone had made the laws, and any offense against property was terrible in their eyes. Death was still the penalty for small thefts. What was the prisoner's offense? Would you have been willing to live on mere bread for a week if that had been a condition of his escape? Do you feel sympathy for him because you like his personality, or resent such punishment, or for both reasons? How many touches of humor do you find during the progress of the story?

SUGGESTIONS FOR ORAL AND WRITTEN ENGLISH
THEME SUBJECTS

You have read stories by three of the best writers of the modern short story, Kipling, O. Henry, and Thomas Hardy, and two of the best earlier short-story writers, Hawthorne and Poe. Which have been strong in character portrayal? Which in plot development? Can you find any trait that is common to Hawthorne, Poe, and Hardy? Reread each story and note where the scene is laid. Do the characters in *Wee Willie Winkie* and *The Chaparral Prince*, for example, speak alike? Does the old stage driver in the latter story differ in speech from the robbers? In *The Ambitious Guest* and *The Three Strangers*, what resemblances and what differences do you find? The comment of one of the shepherds on the hands of the first stranger explains the effect of a man's trade upon him. How does a factory boy differ in appearance from a farmer's boy? Our geographical location determines largely what we do for a living. These two — location and business — combined, affect our appearance, customs, speech, and opinions. When one community differs from another in these respects, we call this difference "local color." A very amusing story on this subject is *A Local Colorist* by Annie Trumbull Slosson. Give examples of local color from other selections that you have read; and also from what you have seen. Narrate an incident showing local color, the class deciding what points illustrate this. Write one side of a telephone conversation in which you show, without naming it, the business of the person at the other end of the line.

Tell a story of some guilty person, in which you throw the hearer off the scent until the conclusion. Some one has taken your umbrella; write your efforts at detective work. Send a telegram describing a man whom you have seen picking a pocket, but who escaped. You have seen two strangers who appear suspicious; tell your reasons for thinking so, as if to a detective. A servant has been wrongly suspected of taking some money. Defend him by showing what he has done under similar circumstances. Explain away what others think looks suspicious, such as his blushing and his silence.

SUGGESTIONS FOR ADDITIONAL READINGS

The Withered Arm (in *Wessex Tales*). Thomas Hardy.

A Double-Barreled Detective Story (in *The Man That Corrupted Hadleyburg*). Samuel L. Clemens.

My Disreputable Friend, Mr. Raegen (in *Gallegher*). Richard Harding Davis.

The Ship of Stars. A. T. Quiller-Couch.

The Drawn Blind (in *A Delectable Duchy*). A. T. Quiller-Couch.

After All (in *Meadow Grass*). Alice Brown.

Joint Owners in Spain. Alice Brown.

The Prince and the Pauper. Samuel L. Clemens.

Tom Sawyer. Samuel L. Clemens.

An Old Mathematician. M. E. W. Freeman.

The Revolt of Mother. M. E. W. Freeman.

The Grasshopper and the Ant. Margaret Deland.

Mrs. Wiggs of the Cabbage Patch. Alice Hegan Rice.

New Chronicles of Rebecca. Kate Douglas Wiggin.

LAUGH AND BE MERRY [1]

John Masefield

John Masefield (1875–   ), born in Shropshire, England, is a realistic poet who often paints life in dull, gray tones. Some of his short lyrics, like *Laugh and be Merry*, are tonic with hope and cheerfulness. See also:

Halleck's *New English Literature*, pp. 601, 602, 623.

John Masefield, Seaman-Author, by Milton Bronner in *Bookman*, 33 : 584–591 (August, 1911).

A Visit to John Masefield, by John Cournos in *The Independent*, Vol. LXXIII, pp. 533–538.

LAUGH and be merry, remember, better the world with a song,
Better the world with a blow in the teeth of a wrong.
Laugh, for the time is brief, a thread the length of a span.
Laugh and be proud to belong to the old proud pageant of
    man.

Laugh and be merry: remember, in olden time,
God made Heaven and Earth for joy He took in a rime,
Made them, and filled them full with the strong red wine of
    His mirth,
The splendid joy of the stars: the joy of the earth.

So we must laugh and drink from the deep blue cup of the
    sky,
Join the jubilant song of the great stars sweeping by,
Laugh, and battle, and work, and drink of the wine outpoured
In the dear green earth, the sign of the joy of the Lord.

[1] From *The Story of a Round House and Other Poems*, copyright, 1912, by The Macmillan Company. Used by special arrangement with the publishers.

Laugh and be merry together, like brothers akin,
Guesting awhile in the rooms of a beautiful inn,
Glad till the dancing stops, and the lilt of the music ends.
Laugh till the game is played; and be you merry. my friends.

STUDY HINTS

" Better, " in lines 1 and 2, means " make better." Line 2, of stanza 2, means that God made Heaven and Earth belong together as two words that rime.

Memorize at least one stanza and recite it in a spirited way, so that those who hear you will feel the splendid vigor of the poetry.

SUGGESTIONS FOR ADDITIONAL READINGS

Sea-Fever. John Masefield.
Roadways. John Masefield.
I Saw A Ship A-Sailing. John Masefield.
Typhoon. Joseph Conrad.

THE LONDON VISITS OF A COUNTRY LORD
IN THE TIME OF CHARLES II[1]

Thomas Babington Macaulay

Thomas Babington Macaulay (1800–1859) was born in Leicestershire, England. As a small boy, he was a great reader and picked up thereby an unusual and large vocabulary. His memory was also remarkable. He studied law and was elected a member of Parliament. While he was valuable to his country in this capacity, he is best known on account of his writings. His *Essays* retain their popularity on both sides of the Atlantic. His style is clearness itself, and frequently so brilliant that his *History of England*, for example, is thought by many to be as interesting as a novel. He is buried in Westminster Abbey. See also:

Halleck's *New English Literature*, pp. 466–472, 581.
Trevelyan's *Life and Letters of Macaulay*.
Minto's *Manual of English Prose Literature*.
Morrison's *Macaulay*.

ONLY very great men were in the habit of dividing the year between town and country. Few esquires came to the capital thrice in their lives. Nor was it yet the practice of all citizens in easy circumstances to breathe the fresh air of the fields and woods during some weeks of every summer. A cockney, in a rural village, was stared at as much as if he had intruded into a Kraal of Hottentots. On the other hand, when the lord of a Lincolnshire or Shropshire manor appeared in Fleet Street, he was as easily distinguished from the resident population as a Turk or a Lascar. His dress, his gait, his accent, the manner in which he stared at the shops, stumbled into the gutters, ran against the porters, and stood under the waterspouts, marked him out as an

[1] From *History of England*, Vol. I, Chapter III.

excellent subject for the operations of swindlers and banterers. Bullies jostled him into the kennel. Hackney-coachmen splashed him from head to foot. Thieves explored with perfect security the huge pockets of his horseman's coat, while he stood entranced by the splendor of the lord mayor's show. Money droppers, sore from the cart's tail, introduced themselves to him, and appeared to him the most honest, friendly gentlemen that he had ever seen. If he asked his way to St. James's, his informants sent him to Mile End. If he went into a shop, he was instantly discerned to be a fit purchaser of everything that nobody else would buy, of second-hand embroidery, copper rings, and watches that would not go. If he rambled into any fashionable coffeehouse, he became a mark for the insolent derision of fops and the grave waggery of templars. Enraged and mortified, he soon returned to his mansion, and there, in the homage of his tenants and the conversation of his boon companions, found consolation for the vexations and humiliations which he had undergone. There he once more

felt himself a great man; and he saw nothing above him except when at the assizes he took his seat on the bench near the judge, or when at the muster of the militia he saluted the lord lieutenant.

The chief cause which made the fusion of the different elements of society so imperfect was the extreme difficulty which our ancestors found in passing from place to place. Of all inventions, the alphabet and the printing press alone excepted, those inventions which abridge distance have done most for the civilization of our species. Every improvement of the means of locomotion benefits mankind morally and intellectually as well as materially, and not only facilitates the interchange of the various productions of nature and art, but tends to remove national and provincial antipathies, and to bind together all the branches of the great human family. In the seventeenth century, the inhabitants of London were, for almost every practical purpose, farther from Reading than they now are from Edinburgh, and farther from Edinburgh than they now are from Vienna.

STUDY HINTS

Study the spelling and meaning of these words:

thief	mortified	antipathy
resident	homage	alphabet
embroidery	humiliation	difficulty
insolent	facilitate	practical

Did the treatment of a man from the country by city rogues differ very greatly from that of to-day? How was the lord recognized as from the country? What inventions of our day "abridge distance"? The second and third sentences of the last paragraph are very thoughtful. See if you can understand them.

SUGGESTIONS FOR ORAL AND WRITTEN ENGLISH
THEME SUBJECTS

Using the same method as in *Wouter Van Twiller*, describe a city gentleman in the country, or a country gentleman in the city. Or, using the method of Patrick Henry's speech, write down your points in the following:

Resolved: That the City Boy is as "Green" in the Country, as the Country Boy is in the City.

How We Knew He Was Country-bred.   How We Knew She Was City-bred.

What the Interurban Has Done for City People.   What the Interurban Has Done for the Farmer.

A Day in The City.

Describe an automobile for some one who has never seen one.

What the Street Railway Does for our Town.

The Way Grandfather Traveled.

A Busy City Corner.

SUGGESTIONS FOR ADDITIONAL READINGS

Lays of Ancient Rome. Thomas Babington Macaulay.

The Battle of Naseby. Thomas Babington Macaulay.

The Story of the Railroad. Cy Warman.

Stories of Inventors. Russell Doubleday.

My Garden Acquaintance. James Russell Lowell.

A Reputed Changeling. Charlotte M. Yonge.

For the teacher to read to the class:

Selections from *Peveril of the Peak*, Sir Walter Scott; *Warren Hastings* and *Life of Samuel Johnson*, Thomas Babington Macaulay.

HOW MANY WAYS [1]

CALE YOUNG RICE

Cale Young Rice (1872–   ) was born in Dixon, Kentucky. He is not only an exquisite lyric poet, but also a rarely gifted writer of poetic dramas. See also:

Townsend's *Kentucky in American Letters*, Vol. II, pp. 284–289.

Cale Young Rice, Poet and Dramatist, Book News Monthly, October, 1909.

How many ways the Infinite has
   To-night, in earth and sky:
A falling star, a rustling leaf,
   The night wind ebbing by.
How many ways the Infinite has:
   A firefly over the lea,
A whippoorwill on the wooded hill,
   And your dear love to me.

How many ways the Infinite has:
   The moon out of the East;
A cloud that waits her shepherding,
   To wander silver-fleeced.
How many ways the Infinite has:
   A home-light in the West,
And joy deep-glowing in your eyes,
   Wherein is all my rest.

[1] From *At the World's Heart* (1914). Used by special arrangement with the author.

STUDY HINTS

From the poems you have read in this book, one thought must have come to you: that everything in the world, from a leaf to a star, is wonderful and brings joy to us if we will only open our eyes to it.

Notice how reverently Cale Young Rice has expressed this thought, and that each stanza begins and ends with the two most wonderful things in the world. What are they? Mention some of the many ways in which the poet says the Infinite expresses Himself. Specify some additional beautiful ways that occur to you.

THE CELESTIAL SURGEON

ROBERT LOUIS STEVENSON

[For biographical sketch see page 112.]

If I have faltered more or less
In my great task of happiness;
If I have moved among my race
And shown no glorious morning face;
If beams from happy human eyes
Have moved me not; if morning skies,
Books, and my food, and summer rain
Knocked on my sullen heart in vain: —
Lord, thy most pointed pleasure take
And stab my spirit broad awake;
Or, Lord, if too obdurate I,
Choose thou, before that spirit die,
A piercing pain, a killing sin,
And to my dead heart run them in!

STUDY HINTS

Does Stevenson consider his task one merely of being happy himself, or also of making others happy? What lines prove your opinion? What are some of the things that he thinks should cause happiness? Would you find it in the same things? It is the idea of this poem, which he held during years of ill health, that has made Stevenson beloved of so many readers.

SUGGESTIONS FOR ADDITIONAL READINGS

Read Stevenson's *A Child's Garden of Verse* and see how many forms of happiness he shows in those poems. Can you find a similar idea in *The Tomb of Tusitala*, by Stevenson? "Tusitala," "teller of tales," was the name given Stevenson by the South Sea Islanders whom he used to entertain with his stories.

THE GAME OF LIFE[1]

THOMAS HENRY HUXLEY

Thomas Henry Huxley (1825–1895), the famous scientist, was born in England in the little village of Ealing near London. He began as early as 1855 lecturing in simple language to workingmen on the laws of nature and man's place in nature. He was a close student of nature throughout his long life. His lectures and publications on this subject in both America and England won for him in 1883 the presidency of the famous Royal Society, which was the highest honor in the gift of the scientific world. His ideal was: to be in work and life absolutely sincere. See also:

Huxley's *Autobiography*.
Huxley's *Collected Essays*, Vol. I.
Thomas Henry Huxley, by Edward Clodd (in *Modern English Writers*).
Life and Letters of Thomas Henry Huxley by Leonard Huxley.

SUPPOSE it were perfectly certain that the life and fortune of every one of us would, one day or other, depend upon his winning or losing a game of chess. Don't you think that we should all consider it to be a primary duty to learn at least the names and the moves of the pieces; to have a notion of a gambit, and a keen eye for all the means of giving and getting out of check? Do you not think that we should look with a disapprobation amounting to scorn, upon the father who allowed his son, or the state which allowed its members, to grow up without knowing a pawn from a knight?

Yet it is very plain and elementary truth, that the life, the fortune, and the happiness of every one of us, and, more or less, of those who are connected with us, do depend upon our knowing something of the rules of a game infinitely

[1] From *A Liberal Education and Where to Find It* (1868).

more difficult and complicated than chess. It is a game which has been played for untold ages, every man and woman of us being one of the two players in a game of his or her own. The chessboard is the world, the pieces are the phenomena of the universe, the rules of the game are what we call the laws of nature. The player on the other side is hidden from us. We know that his play is always fair, just, and patient. But also we know, to our cost, that he never overlooks a mistake, or makes the smallest allowance for ignorance. To the man who plays well, the highest stakes are paid, with that sort of overflowing generosity with which the strong shows delight in strength. And one who plays ill is checkmated — without haste, but without remorse.

My metaphor will remind some of you of the famous picture in which Retzsch has depicted Satan playing at chess with man for his soul. Substitute for that mocking fiend in that picture a calm, strong angel who is playing for love, as we say, and would rather lose than win — and I should accept it as an image of human life.

Well, what I mean by education is learning the rules of this mighty game. In other words, education is the instruction of the intellect in the laws of nature, under which name I include not merely things and their forces, but men and their ways; and the fashioning of the affections and of the will into an earnest and loving desire to move in harmony with those laws. For me, education means neither more nor less than this. Anything which professes to call itself education must be tried by this standard, and if it fails to stand the test, I will not call it education, whatever may be the force of authority, or of numbers, upon the other side.

STUDY HINTS

Give in your own words the substance of what Huxley says in the first paragraph. Do you think he is arguing correctly? Why is the game of chess something like the game of life? Suppose that you do not know the physical laws of digestion, ventilation, temperance, cleanliness; should punishment follow? Will it follow? Suppose that you do not know or obey the moral laws of life, what is the result? Are the Ten Commandments some of the rules of the game of life? Do you know whether Shakespeare and Huxley agree? Did you ever hear of any of Shakespeare's characters endeavoring to "shove past consequence" and do you know whether they succeeded? If you have not yet read Shakespeare, can you point to instances in history? In your own neighborhood? Which is the sweeter and happier and more inspiring, Huxley's idea of the hidden player or Retzsch's? Give Huxley's definition of education. What does he include under the "laws of nature"? Under which of his classifications (intellect, affections, will) would he put the control of one's temper, sympathy with human beings, the power to say "No" to temptation, a Good Samaritan act? What sort of reward does Huxley say comes to the man who plays the game of life well?

SUGGESTIONS FOR ADDITIONAL READINGS

A Natural History for Young People. Theodore Wood.
Starland. Sir Robert I. Ball.
The Fairyland of Science. A. B. Buckley.
The Boy Mineral Collectors. Jay G. Kelley.
Scholars' A. B. C. of Electricity. William H. Meadowcroft.
Things a Boy Should Know About Electricity. Thomas M. St. John
The Boys' Book of Explorations. Tudor Jenks.
The Boys' Book of Modern Marvels. C. J. L. Clarke.
The Land of Little Rain. Mary Austin.
Camp and Trail. Stewart Edward White.
Our Vanishing Wild Life. W. T. Hornaday.
Trail and Camp Fire. Grinnell and Roosevelt.
The Life of the Spider. Henri Fabre.
Nearest the Pole. Robert E. Peary.

A COUNTRY SUNDAY [1]

JOSEPH ADDISON

Joseph Addison (1672–1719) was born in Wiltshire, England. He was trained for the diplomatic service and held many offices of state, including that of chief Secretary of State. He had a singularly winning personality. This sketch was taken from his most famous work, the *Sir Roger de Coverley Papers*, which were published in *The Spectator*, a paper issued six days of the week. This series forms a most entertaining description of an English country gentleman, Sir Roger de Coverley, and the people of Addison's day. Addison was buried in Westminster Abbey, the resting place of many of England's most famous men. See also:

Halleck's *New English Literature,* pp. 285–292, 302.
Macaulay's *Essay on Addison.*
Thackeray's *English Humorists* (Addison).
Courthope's *Addison.*
Johnson's *Lives of the Poets* (Addison).

I AM always very well pleased with a country Sunday, and think if keeping holy the seventh day were only a human institution, it would be the best method that could have been thought of for the polishing and civilizing of mankind. It is certain the country people would soon degenerate into a kind of savages and barbarians, were there not such frequent returns of a stated time in which the whole village meet together with their best faces and in their cleanliest habits to converse with one another upon indifferent subjects, hear their duties explained to them, and join together in adoration of the Supreme Being. Sunday clears away the rust of the whole week, not only as it refreshes in their minds the

[1] From *The Spectator*, No. 112, Monday, July 9, 1711.

notions of religion, but as it puts both the sexes upon appearing in their most agreeable forms and exerting all such qualities as are apt to give them a figure in the eye of the village. A country fellow distinguishes himself as much in the church-yard as a citizen does upon the Change,[1] the whole parish politics being generally discussed in that place either after sermon or before the bell rings.

My friend Sir Roger, being a good churchman, has beautified the inside of his church with several texts of his own choosing. He has likewise given a handsome pulpit cloth, and railed in the Communion table at his own expense. He has often told me that at his coming to his estate he found his parishioners very irregular, and that, in order to make them kneel and join in the responses, he gave every one of them a hassock and a Common Prayer Book, and at the same time employed an itinerant singing master, who goes about the country for that purpose, to instruct them rightly in the tunes of the psalms, upon which they now very much value themselves, and, indeed, outdo most of the country churches that I have ever heard.

As Sir Roger is landlord to the whole congregation, he keeps them in very good order, and will suffer nobody to sleep in it besides himself; for if by chance he has been surprised into a short nap at sermon, upon recovering out of it he stands up and looks about him, and if he sees anybody else nodding, either wakes them himself or sends his servant to them. Several other of the old knight's particularities break out upon these occasions: sometimes he will be lengthening out a verse in the singing psalms half a minute after the rest of the congregation have done with it; sometimes, when he is pleased with the matter of his devotion, he pronounces amen three or four times to the same prayer; and sometimes stands up when everybody else is upon their

---

[1] Exchange.

knees to count the congregation, or see if any of his tenants are missing.

I was yesterday very much surprised to hear my old friend, in the midst of the service, calling out to one John Matthews to mind what he was about, and not disturb the congregation. This John Matthews, it seems, is remarkable for being an idle fellow, and at that time was kicking his heels for his diversion. This authority of the knight, though exerted in that odd manner which accompanies him in all circumstances of life, has a very good effect upon the parishioners, who are not polite enough to see anything ridiculous in his behavior; besides that, the general good sense and worthiness of his character make his friends observe these little singularities as foils that rather set off than blemish his good qualities.

As soon as the sermon is finished, nobody presumes to stir till Sir Roger is gone out of the church. The knight walks down from his seat in the chancel between a double row of his tenants that stand bowing to him on each side; and every now and then inquires how such a one's wife, or mother, or son, or father do whom he does not see at church; which is understood as a secret reprimand to the person that is absent.

The chaplain has often told me that upon a catechizing day, when Sir Roger has been pleased with a boy that answers well, he has ordered a Bible to be given him next day for his encouragement, and sometimes accompanies it with a flitch of bacon to his mother. Sir Roger has likewise added five pounds a year to the clerk's place; and, that he may encourage the young fellows to make themselves perfect in the church service, has promised, upon the death of the present incumbent, who is very old, to bestow it according to merit.

The fair understanding between Sir Roger and his chaplain, and their mutual concurrence in doing good, is the more remarkable because the very next village is famous for the differences and contentions that rise between the parson and the squire, who live in a perpetual state of war. The parson is always preaching at the squire, and the squire, to be revenged on the parson, never comes to church. The squire has made all his tenants atheists and tithe stealers; while the parson instructs them every Sunday in the dignity of his order, and insinuates to them in almost every sermon that he is a better man than his patron. In short, matters are come to such an extremity that the squire has not said his prayers either in public or private this half year, and that the parson threatens him, if he does not mend his manners, to pray for him in the face of the whole congregation.

Feuds of this nature, though too frequent in the country, are very fatal to the ordinary people, who are so used to be dazzled with riches that they pay as much deference to the understanding of a man of an estate as of a man of learning; and are very hardly brought to regard any truth, how important soever it may be, that is preached to them when they know there are several men of five hundred a year who do not believe it.

STUDY HINTS

Study the spelling and meaning of these words:

cleanly	tenants	behavior
surprise	civilize	reprimand
occasion	village	parishioner

Aside from the religious idea of the Sabbath, what reason does Addison give for observing the day? What does he mean by "the rust of the week"? Have you known any one whose conduct at church is like Sir Roger's? Give illustrations of Sir Roger's kindness to the people of his parish. How do you think they feel toward him? The author does not say whether he and the chaplain are friendly. What is your opinion on this point? Compare them with the squire and his chaplain in the next village. What method of showing Sir Roger's character does Addison employ? (See Suggestions, p. 89.) How many instances of humor are there in this selection?

SUGGESTIONS FOR ORAL AND WRITTEN ENGLISH
THEME SUBJECTS

Using Addison's method, write a character sketch of some one in your church who is very generous: it may be either of a man who gives money or of a woman who uses her time and strength in service.

Make your own title and write a theme on one of the following topics:

The Old Gentlemen in the Front Pew.	A Country Church.
Our Church Bazaar.	A Sabbath in Colonial Days.
Winning a Sunday School Prize.	What I Do Sunday Afternoon.
Why I Attend Sunday School.	What is the Sabbath for?

SUGGESTIONS FOR ADDITIONAL READINGS

From *The Spectator:* No. 109, *Sir Roger's Ancestors;* No. 115, *Bodily Exercise;* No. 116, *Sir Roger and the Chase;* No. 130, *Sir Roger and the Gypsies;* No. 132, *The Journey to London.*

From Irving's *Sketch Book: The Country Church; The Stagecoach; Christmas Eve; Christmas Day.*

AUTOBIOGRAPHY

John Ruskin

John Ruskin (1819–1900), art critic, essayist, and social philosopher, was born in London. He was one of the great prose writers who helped to mold the thought of the Victorian age. His greatest works are *Modern Painters* and *The Stones of Venice*. *Sesame and Lilies*, a volume of essays, and *The King of the Golden River*, an altruistic story, are perhaps his most popular books. The following selection from his autobiography, to which he gave the title *Præterita* ("Things Past"), is important because it shows what early reading helped to make him a great prose writer. See also:

Halleck's *New English Literature*, pp. 488–495, 582.
Cook's *The Life of John Ruskin*.
Harrison's *John Ruskin*.

I AM, and my father was before me, a violent Tory of the old school; (Walter Scott's school, that is to say, and Homer's,) [1] I name these two out of the numberless great Tory writers, because they were my own two masters. I had Walter Scott's novels, and the *Iliad* (Pope's translation) for my only reading when I was a child, on week days: on Sundays their effect was tempered by *Robinson Crusoe* and the *Pilgrim's Progress;* my mother having it deeply in her heart to make an evangelical clergyman of me. Fortunately, I had an aunt more evangelical than my mother; and my aunt gave me cold mutton for Sunday's dinner, which — as I much preferred it hot — greatly diminished the influence of the *Pilgrim's Progress*, and the end of the matter was, that I got all the noble imaginative teaching of Defoe and Bunyan, and yet — am not an evangelical clergyman.

[1] A Greek epic poet, author of the *Iliad* and the *Odyssey*.

I had, however, still better teaching than theirs, and that compulsorily, and every day of the week.

Walter Scott and Pope's *Homer* were reading of my own election, but my mother forced me, by steady daily toil, to learn long chapters of the *Bible* by heart; as well as to read it every syllable through, aloud, hard names and all, from *Genesis* to the *Apocalypse*,[1] about once a year: and to that discipline — patient, accurate, and resolute — I owe, not only a knowledge of the book, which I find occasionally serviceable, but much of my general power of taking pains, and the best part of my taste in literature. From Walter Scott's novels I might easily, as I grew older, have fallen to other people's novels; and Pope might, perhaps, have led me to take Johnson's[2] English, or Gibbon's,[3] as types of language; but, once knowing the 32nd of *Deuteronomy*, the 119th *Psalm*, the 15th of *First Corinthians*, the *Sermon on the Mount*, and most of the *Apocalypse*, every syllable by heart, and having always a way of thinking with myself what words meant, it was not possible for me, even in the foolishest times of youth, to write entirely superficial or formal English.

STUDY HINTS

Study the spelling and meaning of these words:

privileges	superficial	serviceable
imagination	evangelical	formal
occasionally	syllable	literature

What instances of humor do you find? What authors does he specially mention? What is his opinion of the value of his early training? Do you think that his opinion is correct? Aside from the subject matter, what else did Ruskin learn in reading the *Bible*? How did he acquire a vocabulary? Which of the books that he read are you suffi-

[1] *The Revelation*, the last book in the *New Testament*.

[2] Samuel Johnson (1709-1784), a noted converser and writer, who loved long words derived from the Latin.

[3] Edward Gibbon (1737-1794), author of *The Decline and Fall of the Roman Empire*, who was also fond of words of Latin origin.

ciently familiar with to give some of their general characteristics? How many of the same books did Abraham Lincoln (p. 258) and Ruskin read early in life?

SUGGESTIONS FOR ORAL AND WRITTEN ENGLISH
THEME SUBJECTS

My Autobiography.

My Early Reading.

Give two reasons for thinking the *Bible* a model for those who speak or write.

(Quote passages to justify your statements.)

The Reading That I now Like and Why I Like It.

Relate orally three Biblical stories.

Debate: Should Sunday Reading Differ from that of Week Days?

SUGGESTIONS FOR ADDITIONAL READINGS

Read from the *Bible*: The Story of Creation; The Story of Abraham; The Story of David; The Story of Samson; The Story of Ruth; Daniel in the Lions' Den; The Description of the New Jerusalem (*Revelation*, xxi, xxii).

Read from Pope's or Bryant's translation of Homer's *Odyssey*: Ulysses (Odysseus) and Calypso (Book v); The Lotus-Eaters and the Cyclops (Book ix); Æolus and Circe (Book x); The Sirens, Scylla and Charybdis (Book xii).

Defoe's *Robinson Crusoe*. (Note the Biblical simplicity of his style.)

Franklin's *Autobiography* (the first twenty-five pages).

Ruskin's *The King of the Golden River* and *Sesame and Lilies, Lecture II*. (The part relating to Shakespeare.)

SATAN

John Milton

John Milton (1608–1674) was born in London, England. He is, next to Shakespeare, the greatest English poet. This description of Satan is taken from the sublimest epic in the English language, *Paradise Lost*. Milton was totally blind at the time he produced this, so that he was obliged to dictate it to his daughters. It was a tremendous task, for the epic embraces twelve books. Milton has exerted great influence upon English poetry and prose. See also:

Halleck's *New English Literature*, pp. 238–252, 255.
Pattison's *Milton*.
Raleigh's *Milton*.
Macaulay's *Essay on Milton*.
Masson's *The Life of John Milton*.

———

[In the poem, Satan led a host of rebellious angels against God and was cast out of heaven. He then set up a kingdom in the "infernal world."]

———

Farewell, happy fields,
Where joy for ever dwells! Hail, horrors! hail,
Infernal world![1] and thou, profoundest hell,
Receive thy new possessor — one who brings
A mind not to be changed by place or time.   5
The mind is its own place, and in itself
Can make a heaven of hell, a hell of heaven. . . .
Here we may reign secure; and in my choice
To reign is worth ambition, though in hell:
Better to reign in hell, than serve in heaven. . . .   10

[1] Lower world.

His spear, to equal which the tallest pine,
Hewn on Norwegian hills to be the mast
Of some great ammiral,[1] were but a wand,
He walk'd with to support uneasy steps
Over the burning marl; not like those steps   15
On heaven's azure: and the torrid clime
Smote on him sore besides, vaulted with fire.
Nathless he so endured, till on the beach
Of that inflamed sea he stood, and called
His legions, angel forms, who lay entranced,   20
Thick as autumnal leaves that strew the brooks
In Vallambrosa, where the Etrurian shades
High over-arched imbower . . .
                    . . . he, above the rest
In shape and gesture proudly eminent,   25
Stood like a tower: his form had yet not lost
All her original brightness, nor appeared
Less than archangel ruined, and the excess
Of glory obscured: as when the sun new risen
Looks through the horizontal misty air,   30
Shorn of his beams; or from behind the moon,
In dim eclipse, disastrous twilight sheds
On half the nations, and with fear of change
Perplexes monarchs.   Darkened so, yet shone
Above them all the archangel.   35

STUDY HINTS

Read this aloud until you can feel Milton's mastery of harmonious rhythm and understand the secret of his influence in English poetry.

Do you agree with the poet in lines 6 and 7 that our happiness in large measure depends upon our way of looking at things? L. 21. "Thick as autumnal leaves," etc. is a very famous expression. Try to picture

[1] The ship with which the admiral leads the fleet. "Ammiral" is the old spelling for admiral.

the scene. Read aloud the lines that show the indomitable pride of Satan. What fine comparisons can you point out? What impression do you get of his great size? After studying this selection carefully, read it aloud again, then try to think what words will best describe the impression it leaves on you.

SUGGESTIONS FOR ADDITIONAL READINGS

Lycidas. John Milton.
On the Morning of Christ's Nativity. John Milton.
Sonnet on His Blindness. John Milton.
The Binding of the Strong. A. E. W. Mason.

For the teacher to read to the class:
Selections from Milton's *L'Allegro, Comus, Il Penseroso,* and Book I of *Paradise Lost.*

M

JEFF

UNCLE SA
U. S.